MICHAEL BOOTH

Michael Booth is the author of five books, including the international bestseller, *The Almost Nearly Perfect People*, winner of the British Guild of Travel Writers award for Book of the Year, and *Sushi and Beyond*, which won the Guild of Food Writers award for the best book on food and travel.

D1340065

ALSO BY MICHAEL BOOTH

Just As Well I'm Leaving
Doing Without Delia
Sushi and Beyond
Eat, Pray, Eat
The Almost Nearly Perfect People

MICHAEL BOOTH

The Meaning of Rice

A Culinary Tour of Japan

VINTAGE

1 3 5 7 9 10 8 6 4 2

Vintage
20 Vauxhall Bridge Road,
London SW1V 2SA

Vintage is part of the Penguin Random House group of companies
whose addresses can be found at global.penguinrandomhouse.com

Penguin
Random House
UK

First published in Vintage in 2018
First published in trade paperback by Jonathan Cape in 2017

penguin.co.uk/vintage

A CIP catalogue record for this book is available from the British Library

ISBN 9781784704230

Printed and bound in Great Britain by Clays Ltd, Elcograf S.p.A.

Penguin Random House is committed to a sustainable future
for our business, our readers and our planet. This book is made
from Forest Stewardship Council® certified paper.

To my family

'The whole of Japan is a pure invention .... There is no such country, there are no such people'.

Oscar Wilde

Contents

CONTENTS

THE MEANING OF RICE

Chapter 1

The Return

A decade ago, in the autumn of 2007, I boarded a plane with my wife and our two sons and flew to Tokyo.

We were living in Paris where I had spent twelve months learning the techniques of classical French cooking at the Cordon Bleu school and then working in Michelin-starred restaurants in the city. I had wanted to learn how to cook without recipes, without the guidance of Jamie, Delia or Nigella, and I did, but along the way I had consumed about as much butter, cream, sugar and pastry as any man's elasticated waistband could accommodate. I was, if not jaded by dishes like *blanquette de veau* and *lièvre à la royale*, then definitely feeling the effects of the calorific overload brought on by an excess of classical French cooking. My stomach was now entering rooms before the rest of me. Bits kept moving after others had stopped.

By way of an antidote, a friend had given me a copy of Shizuo Tsuji's *Japanese Cooking: A Simple Art*, back then one of the few books on traditional Japanese cooking available in English. Its recipes – seasonal, light, healthy, modern and, as the title promised, simple – were a revelation.

Inspired to find out more about what the Japanese ate and how they prepared it, I had booked four open tickets to Tokyo. My family and I ended up spending just over three months travelling the length of the country from Hokkaido in the chilly north to subtropical Okinawa in the south, exploring the dazzling diversity of Japan's food culture, dining with sumo wrestlers, meeting Japan's most famous food TV stars and discovering the secrets of how the centenarians of Okinawa lived well into three digits, among other adventures.

I wrote a book about our journey, *Sushi and Beyond*, but, rather than getting Japan out of my system, the whole experience only made me more eager to return. A new world had opened up of unfamiliar ingredients and strange techniques, a world which was utterly alien, often tantalisingly inaccessible, yet never less than beguiling. From the edible aquarium that was Tsukiji fish market, to Tokyo's smoky yakitori alleyways, I was captivated. From the minimalist kaiseki restaurants where I held my breath between courses for fear of disrupting the flower arrangements, to the ascetic temple food of Mount Koya, I was perplexed yet fascinated.

I knew that on that first visit we had only really scratched the surface of Japan's extraordinarily refined culinary landscape. We had visited fewer than a dozen of its forty-seven prefectures; so much about the Japanese – what they ate, and why – remained a mystery. That chronic sense of missing out had barely diminished over the years despite several return visits on my part to write food and travel stories for newspapers and magazines.

In the decade since our first visit to Japan there had been several major developments on the country's food scene. There were headlines around the world when, in 2007, the first Michelin guide to Tokyo awarded more of its precious stars to the Japanese capital than to Paris. Whatever one's views of the value of Michelin, it seemed that Tokyo was now the world's food capital, and subsequent guides, not just to the capital but to other Japanese cities, have reinforced the country's status as the most starry in the culinary firmament. Then, in 2013, UNESCO granted Japanese cuisine 'Intangible Cultural Heritage' status. This also made headlines globally and, although I suspect it meant more to the Japanese than it did to the rest of the world, as a result still more foreign chefs have visited Japan in the years since and been inspired by Japanese techniques, ingredients and presentation styles. Japan is, for instance, the source of all the snazzy open-kitchen counter restaurants and fixed multi-course menus which have come to define 'high-end' dining in London, New York, Paris, Copenhagen and elsewhere; and the Japanese were doing the local/seasonal thing long before anyone else. Meanwhile, the fooderati – bloggers, social media and conventional food media – had gone crazy for ramen, and were slowly discovering other Japanese fast foods and ingredients. Had this given the Japanese a new pride in their so-called 'B-kyu gurume' (B-class gourmet) foods about which Tsuji and Japan's food elite had always tended to be rather sniffy? At least the Japanese had finally woken up to the branding potential of their food culture in terms of tourism and, as a result, there had been a record growth in foreign visitors in recent years, many of whom I suspect came primarily for its food. The tourist boom is likely to continue with the Olympics, awarded to Tokyo for 2020. How had the Japanese reacted to all this attention? How were its restaurants preparing to welcome the world, I wondered.

On 11 March 2011 an earthquake measuring 9.0 on the Richter scale struck just off the Pacific coast of eastern Japan, destroying entire towns and killing over 18,000 people. It was the most powerful earthquake ever to hit Japan and I suspect many around the world shared my horror as they watched the footage of the destruction of an entire region of the country. Since then, we have also witnessed the stoic resilience of the Japanese people in recovering from 3/11 but, among other things, the earthquake, tsunami and ensuing nuclear disaster devastated what had been an important food-producing region of Japan. What have been the long-term effects of the disaster?

So, ten years since our first visit, it seemed time for my family and I to return to Japan for a new journey, to delve deeper into the country's food culture, to see what we'd missed, and get to know the Japanese a little better.

On landing in Tokyo, we will transfer straight to Okinawa, a three-hour flight south. After some days there we will head north to the first of Japan's four main islands, Kyushu (the other three being Shikoku; the largest island, Honshu; and Hokkaido in the far north-east). Kyushu has been calling to me for years now. On that first trip we saw only Fukuoka in the north-east of the island, but ever since I had been hearing rumours that there were some extraordinary things to eat there. This time I want to drive from Kagoshima in the south up the western coast of Kyushu to, among other places, Nagasaki, which has a unique, internationally influenced cuisine dating back centuries. Crossing Kyushu, heading east, we will hop over to Honshu, the largest of the Japanese islands but, instead of then taking the more travelled Inland Sea coast route via Hiroshima to Osaka, we will travel along the Japan Sea coast through Shimane Prefecture. This is the 'other' Japan, a sparsely inhabited region rarely visited by Westerners; actually, it is rarely visited by the rest of the Japanese. On route from there to Tokyo we will stop in Kyoto to sample a rather fearful delicacy, as well as revisit Osaka, one of the most thrilling food cities in the world, from where I will take a detour to Shikoku.

Nagoya, Gifu, Nagano and Japan's wine region, Yamanashi, are all on our radar too; each of them has a range of weird and wonderful specialities. You could spend a lifetime eating in Tokyo, of course, but we will also see more of the prefectures of Kanto, eastern Honshu, including, of course, Fukushima. Finally, there will be Hokkaido – the 'end of the world' to many Japanese, beyond which lie frozen seas and frosty Russia. On our first trip to Hokkaido we had only seen the main city, Sapporo – lovely, lively and liveable, but really just the gateway to what I knew was one of the great landscapes, and the source of so much stunning produce and seafood.

On that first visit almost ten years ago my sons, Asger, then six, and Emil, four, had been not much more than toddlers. Now teenagers, they have somehow managed to avoid reading *Sushi and Beyond* so their memories are based mostly on photographs and family mythology ('Do you remember that time you pushed a sumo over in the training ring?', 'How we laughed when you projectile-vomited those fermented squid guts', and so on). I was curious to see how their reaction to Japan might differ now they were proper humans, and in particular I had a feeling that Japan might offer a few worthwhile lessons for two boys heading rapidly towards manhood.

There are a few qualities I have observed about the Japanese and their society over the years that I want my children to witness, characteristics that have struck me as impressive but increasingly rare in the West: things like dedication, duty, diligence, discipline, determination (for some reason, they all begin with the letter 'd'). I wouldn't say my children are particularly lacking in any of these but, equally, I reason, it won't hurt to see them in action. So many people in the Japanese food world – chefs and food producers, artisans and farmers – have dedicated their lives to tending and perfecting their small patch of the culinary landscape without much consideration for wealth or adulation. Though it is true that my children will be missing some school to travel for around ten weeks in all (we live in Denmark where they are slightly more relaxed about this, as the Danes are about most things), I am convinced that there will be educational value enough in arranging for them to meet some of these 'shokunin', as such artisans, or craftsmen, are known in Japan, and watching them at work.

The suitcases are waiting in the hall. I have taken out the rubbish, unplugged the TV, checked that the passports are where they should be in my bag five times now. I am just brushing my teeth one last time before we leave for the airport for our flight to Tokyo when my wife walks into the bathroom.

'Have you seen this?' she says, showing me her phone. 'There's been a major volcanic eruption in Kyushu. And North Korea has just launched a long-range missile test over Okinawa.'

And so our journey begins.

OKINAWA

Chapter 2

Sweet Potatoes

The Queen of Okinawa is not happy.

'Japan needs a detox. We have the highest levels of additives in our food in the world,' she says, for some reason dropping a handful of dried chillis into the glowing hearth in front of us. Within a few seconds our eyes are streaming from the smoke. Hers remain unaffected.

She exhales imperiously. 'Our nutritionists in Japan are still telling us to eat margarine, so I don't really trust their advice any more. My children have never eaten instant ramen or micro meals and, now, my guests are like my children. I opened this place to change the eating habits of the Okinawans.' She sets four frothing glasses of a foaming, purple-coloured liquid before us. Emil's nose twitches suspiciously.

The last time we visited Okinawa, a decade ago, it was to uncover the secrets of the Okinawans' longevity. The islands of Japan's southernmost archipelago were becoming famous for having the greatest proportion of centenarians in the world. Gerontologists had been flocking there to find out why so many Okinawans lived beyond a hundred years. The reasons, we discovered, included strong social cohesion and genetics but in particular a diet which was low in fat with lots of seafood, tofu, seaweed and vegetables, along with specific additions like turmeric, jasmine tea and mineral-rich black sugar. Crucially, the Okinawans didn't eat too much of anything. Calorific restriction, embodied by the local saying 'hara hachi bu' (eat until you are 80 per cent full), kept their intake much lower than the Western, or even the mainland Japanese average. But already the indicators for the future health of the islanders had been looking less rosy. The generations following those who had survived World War II were ditching the traditional Okinawan diet in favour of Western foods introduced by the occupying US forces: burgers, fried chicken, Spam, and the famous (and quite horrid) Okinawan taco rice. Today, the Okinawans are the biggest per capita consumers of KFC in Japan with a bucket of the Colonel's chicken a common gift at parties, birthdays and – forget silver tankards – christenings. The younger generation of Okinawans are consuming considerably more calories than their parents, and exhibiting troubling levels of obesity, heart disease and diabetes as a result. In fact, as I was now learning, the Okinawans are the unhealthiest people in all Japan, and have lost their longevity crown to the prefecture of Nagano.

'The most dramatic impact of the Western diet on the Japanese people has been felt here in Okinawa,' the Queen of Okinawa continues. 'That's because this is where the US military first came, and they have had this big base here ever since. The first fast food restaurants in Japan were here. The younger generation just don't realise what they are doing.'

The 'Queen', I should clarify, is Kiyoko Yamashiro, a sixteenth-generation descendant of Shō Hashi, the first king to unify the Ryukyus (as Okinawa was once known). I should also point out that Kiyoko does not refer to herself as the Queen of Okinawa although she has a decidedly regal bearing with a straight back; her hair held in a tight, imperious bun; and bold lavender lipstick.

At her restaurant, Garamanjyaku, Kiyoko is serving us a multi-course 'detox' lunch. She had been inspired to develop this healthy alternative when a thirteen-year-old friend of her daughter's dropped dead from a heart attack while playing baseball. This alerted her to the dietary horrors consumed by young Okinawans, which she has vowed to change.

'I noticed teenagers eating all this fast food and additives. They looked healthy enough but they were not healthy inside so, over the last years, I started to use more and more herbal medicine in my cooking, and going back to the traditional diet,' she tells us as we sit around the open hearth or 'irori'.

Kiyoko's food uses only local ingredients and has its roots in Okinawan royal cuisine and the pre-war, Chinese medicine-influenced traditional diet of the islands in which specific foods are supposed to bring particular health benefits, or treat particular ailments (called *yakuzen* – or Chinese herbal medicine food). To this she has added her own, self-taught, Ayurvedic, macrobiotic spin. Okinawan royal cuisine usually features pork, but Kiyoko's food is vegan, for instance. Her menu includes items such as 'Enzyme juice of seaweeds' and 'Salad with lettuce, chia seeds and coconut oil' and okra. Gwyneth Paltrow would love it.

I am not at all convinced that any food has the power to cleanse or detoxify the body but, as I take a tentative sip of my purple foam drink, I grudgingly admit to myself that Garamanjyaku's food – Sanskrit for 'pure throat, good taste' – is as likely a candidate as any.

We had landed the day before, straight from Tokyo, and woke that morning heavily jetlagged. Though it is a thrill to be back in Japan, some of us are feeling a little tired and emotional, but the approach to this traditional Okinawan wooden house via a steep pathway overhung with plants and trailing flowers somehow transforms our mood before we even reach the door. The building itself is all but engulfed by rampant greenery. It feels like the nest of some great flightless bird. Inside, it looks more like a private home than a restaurant with shelves full of mementos, toys and old magazines, and a random jumble of wooden furniture, some Japanese, some Western.

'Are you sure this is a restaurant?' Asger had whispered as we entered. But after a long-haul flight in economy seats designed by the Spanish Inquisition it felt like exactly the kind of first meal on Japanese soil we should be eating.

Okinawa is usually depicted as a subtropical paradise of golden beaches, turquoise seas and verdant jungles, but the main island, Okinawa Honto, is a bit of a mess. In the hasty rebuild following the devastation of World War II, quality architecture was not a priority and the ensuing cheap, concrete development means that, today, urban Okinawa is pretty much an expanse of irredeemable eyesores. Garamanjyaku is located amid the worst of it, above the town of Kincho Kunigamigun. Home to a massive US military base, its centre is a sleazy maze of bars and hostess clubs whose chief culinary highlight is the aforementioned taco rice – minced beef with white rice, in a taco.

Yet, as we now sit and talk and eat, I feel far removed from all that. We are presented with several intriguing vegetarian courses, all served on banana leaves. Unfortunately, the predominantly bitter, vegetal flavours do not hold so much appeal for my children and several times Lissen and I have to reassure Kiyoko that they are 'just not very hungry' as they toy with some unidentifiable clumps of matter. I struggle, too, I have to admit. Among the more challenging items is a tea infused with various leaves plucked from the garden, including mugwort and one called *chomeiso*, the 'long life' plant, according to Kiyoko. For me, the tea is borderline undrinkable. And then comes the foaming purple drink.

'It is fermented brown rice and beni imo, with a little black sugar,' Kiyoko says. Depending on the weather, the mixture is left for up to two weeks to lactate and bubble, she adds. It is one of the more interesting flavours from the meal – sweet and funky with the floral taste typical of beni imo, the magical, Okinawan purple sweet potato.

Lissen and I have been fascinated with this vivid-coloured tuber since our first visit; indeed, for my wife, over the years, the fascination has become a certifiable obsession. Whenever we had reminisced about Japan, Lissen would always return to the subject of the beni imo and, if anything, she clung even more tenaciously to the idea of one day growing purple sweet potatoes herself at home.

She would describe this in that misty-eyed way that some people talk about one day fixing up a hammock or learning how to meditate, never mind that growing her own Okinawan purple sweet potatoes in our garden was an improbable ambition for a woman who a) only ever ventures outside to drink coffee on a sunny day, and b) other than watering house plants to death has never shown the slightest interest in horticultural matters in all the years I have known her. But return she would, again and again, to the subject of her beloved Okinawan purple sweet potato.

I know of no other person who would consider a visit to a potato research centre as a 'treat', but Lissen is thrilled to the point of agitation the next morning as we have planned a visit to Yomitan, Okinawa's purple sweet potato capital and the first place potatoes were cultivated in Japan. And if she was excited before the visit, it was nothing compared to how she felt when we left . . .

On Okinawa, the beni imo is credited with all manner of health benefits, mostly on account of its high levels of vitamin C and betacarotine. Its history here dates back to the turn of the seventeenth century, and has become intertwined with that of islands themselves. The sweet potato arrived via a circuitous route from South America to Spain from where it was taken to the Philippines and then China. In 1605, a local government officer, Noguni Sokan, visited China with a trade delegation. He brought some sweet potatoes back and tried to grow them in his garden back in Okinawa. It was a great success and the crop spread rapidly throughout the Okinawan archipelago. Thanks to the English sailor William Adams (of whom more later), it reached mainland Japan in 1615 where it also flourished, particularly on the south-western island of Kyushu.

Noguni Sokan is still considered a great Okinawan hero; his sweet potatoes have been credited with saving the islands from starvation several times during their typhoon-ridden history, and there is a shrine and annual festival in his honour. Today, the sweet potato is the second biggest crop here after, oddly, chrysanthemums; it is a bona fide Okinawan icon. Kit Kat chocolate bars even make a purple potato version exclusively for sale in this part of Japan, and in Japan the fides don't come any more bona than that.

The last time we had visited Okinawa I had been led to believe that Okinawa's frequent typhoons meant that its soil was constantly being replenished by nutrient-rich water washed up from the surrounding, coral-filled ocean. The theory was that the calcium from the coral ended up being distributed on the farmland of Okinawa and *this* was why the Okinawan purple sweet potato was so delicious and healthy, and possibly also why the locals lived so long. It turns out that this is completely false.

'No, the soil is not at all rich on Okinawa, it is not fertile at all, I'd say it's about a third as rich as the soil in Kagoshima [the next prefecture heading north, on the island of Kyushu],' says Ichiro Shiroma, as we stand in the well-ordered greenhouse laboratory where he works. 'Also, sea water is really not good for sweet potatoes. The whole coral mineral deposit theory just isn't true.'

Shiroma-san is uniquely placed to pronounce on all this as he used to be an oceanic researcher but is now a soil specialist in charge of the purple sweet potato research project at the local government agricultural centre here in Yomitan. He carries out soil analyses for local farmers to help them adjust fertiliser levels, but his main mission is to create the ultimate Okinawan purple sweet potato: one which is both deeply purple in colour and rich in flavour. At the moment, the two goals seem, frustratingly, to be mutually exclusive. You either get a lovely purple-coloured potato with not much flavour, or something which tastes great but is orange or white.

The current crop of purple sweet potatoes grown on Okinawa are a recent variety, created only around eight years ago after a decade of experimentation. 'They were bred by the prefecture to stay purple even when they were cooked – most coloured potatoes lose their colour when you boil them – but they don't really taste of much,' Shiroma, in his early thirties and dressed in a pale-blue boiler suit and baseball cap, continues. 'Our customers locally, the bakers and people who make purple potato products, just wanted a strong purple colour but actually, the pure white potatoes they used to grow after the war had the best flavour. They add lots of sugar to compensate for the lack of flavour with the purple potatoes and mix in some of the better tasting, pale potatoes. The purple one, that's the special potato for Okinawa today.'

Shiroma collects thousands of seeds during a season but only about one in a thousand is suitable for propagation. He shows us a selection of locally grown potatoes, all of which look pretty much like the large, orange variety of sweet potato grown in the United States until he cuts them in half. Though some of them are off-white, others glow with that extraordinary bishop's-mitre purple we had come to associate with Okinawa.

We chat a little more about the challenges of growing purple sweet potatoes, and Shiroma shows us some test tubes, each containing a slender green sprout rooted in a centimetre of clear gel. With a slight catch in her voice, Lissen mentions her decade-long dream to grow Okinawan purple sweet potatoes back home.

'Here, how many do you want?' Shiroma says offering her a tray of test tubes.

My wife and I look at each other. One of the world's leading sweet potato experts is offering us some of his ... sprouts? Saplings? (Still not sure what you call them.) We cannot quite believe our fortune and, disregarding considerations of how we will transport and care for the plants while travelling through Japan, not to mention concerns about the legality of importing live plants – and potato plants at that – into Europe, we greedily accept eight test tubes, four of which Shiroma says ought to produce a purple crop and four light-coloured.

One day, some months hence, I imagine us blending the two to make the most perfect, sweet-tasting, luridly purple cakes and ice creams with which to dazzle friends and family but over the coming weeks these eight Okinawan sweet potato plants will prove some-what burdensome. Though we observe the strict instructions from Shiroma-san not to open the tinfoil that covers the top of the test tubes until the leaves have outgrown them, and not to water the plants under any circumstances, they struggle to cope with life on the road. One by one, the first four potato plants turn brown with stress, then curl up and die. Yet Lissen refuses to relinquish the four survivors.

'Once I get them home, we can get them in some proper soil and really care for them,' she insists a couple of weeks later on in our journey, holding a glass tube containing a sad little brown splodge up to the light. Sadly, when it comes time to fly home, Lissen will judge only two plants worth saving – two plants which must bear the hopes and dreams of a novice potato grower.*

---

* Today, as I write this, some weeks later, only one plant survives, a fragile pale green thread which, against all the odds, does seem to have a tiny spark of chlorophyll left in it. It hasn't grown since we came home, but we live in hope and, come the spring, it shall be planted and, through sheer force of will on the part of my wife, I should not be surprised if one day it bears either the best-tasting, or the best-looking, Okinawan sweet potatoes in Europe.

** Actually, it just died.

Chapter 3

Umi Budo

In the years since we first visited Okinawa, Japan's southernmost archipelago has assumed the status of some kind of Shangri-La in our family's collective memory, thanks to its seemingly computer-generated sandy beaches, cloudless skies and quite unJapanese, chilled-out vibe.

Our first few days reinforce this impression as we are now staying at the Busena Beach Terrace, a luxury hotel which once played a key role in that mythology. The first time we were in Okinawa we had been travelling on a very tight budget and had regarded this splendid, beachfront resort from afar, like medieval serfs outside the palace gates. One day, we had dared to venture up its lengthy, winding driveway – really we just wanted to take a sniff at how the others lived – but had been gently shepherded back down again when the staff spotted us and, quite rightly, judged us to be unworthy of their frictionless service, complicated swimming pool and array of fine-dining options. This time, though, we have managed to bag a room at a heavily discounted, off-season rate.

The first morning, we encountered an old friend at the Busena's vast and dazzling breakfast buffet: umi budo. One of the most surprising foodstuffs I have ever encountered, umi budo is a type of seaweed, nicknamed 'sea caviar' or 'sea grapes' – minuscule, fragile, green tendrils bearing tiny spheres, like a briny rosary. When eaten, the spheres make a satisfying, crunch-pop on the roof of your mouth – a sensation called 'puchi puchi' in Japanese – before washing your palate with a delicate, fresh flavour of the ocean.

I had only eaten umi budo a few times since that first visit to Okinawa, only in Japan, and always at posh restaurants as a garnish dressed with a little ponzu. I am entirely lacking in self-restraint so, usually, when I find a food I like, I gorge until I am sick of the sight of it, but scarcity had prevented this happening with umi budo. I am determined to rectify this oversight during our time on Okinawa, and also have many questions about this strange little plant. Why, I wonder, is such an amazing and distinctive product not more widely available? I'd imagine chefs everywhere would go crazy for its texture and flavour. How did it grow? Is it farmed, or wild?

Okinawa's centre for umi budo production – and therefore Japan's, and perhaps even the world's – is the island of Kume, a little under an hour's flight from Okinawa's main island. Kume-jima is both a gourmet paradise and an actual, real paradise, with lovely beaches, tropical coral reefs and forested mountains. As well as the umi budo, it is famous for its miso cookies, for its sea salt, its sugar cane, for a special type of prawn, for raising goats (rarely eaten elsewhere in Japan, goat meat is common on Okinawa) and its cows. Many of the cows which end up as 'wagyu' or 'Kobe beef' are actually born on Kume-jima or some of the other islands of Okinawa, where they benefit from the warmer climate at birth before being shipped to famous cattle regions on Honshu, like Matsukawa, where the chillier weather encourages them to take on the incredible fat marbling for which Japanese beef is renowned.

We have some spare time during our first morning on Kume-jima so borrow bicycles from our hotel and head out through the sugar cane fields. We ride along virtually empty roads for most of the way accompanied only by massive butterflies, passing a beni imo farmer just as he is pulling a big bunch of purple sweet potatoes from the thick, red soil. Then, suddenly, in the middle of this bucolic scene, a stadium comes into view, packed with people. It transpires that many of Japan's baseball teams are visiting Okinawa on their winter training break, and Tohoku's Rakutan Golden Eagles have been billeted on Kume. We sit and watch the players practising for a while, alongside groups of cheering schoolkids up in the bleachers.

(Much later in our trip, inspired by this experience, we go to see the two main Tokyo teams, the Yomiuri Giants and the Yakult Swallows, play at the Tokyo Dome. Sadly, our Kume-jima experience had misled us: baseball turns out to be extraordinarily dull. The scoreline that day was essentially binary code – 1:0, 0:1, 0.1, 0.0, etc. It made Test cricket look like cage fighting. But the food at the stadium was wonderful: elaborate bento, sushi, tonkatsu, curry rice and tako yaki, with beer 'girls' circulating with tanks of draft beer on their backs. Based on the food and the atmosphere we would definitely recommend a Japanese baseball game if you get to Tokyo, just don't go expecting any kind of sporting spectacle.)

For lunch we have been recommended an Okinawa soba restaurant, Kumejima Soba, in Nakadomari, the island's capital, a small, dense grid of breezeblock houses clustered around a harbour. The 'soba' is actually ramen – that is, not buckwheat noodles served with a dipping sauce as the name suggests, but wheat noodles served in a soup. This is not a mistake; in Okinawa ramen is called soba, and they are actually in the right. It's the rest of us who are wrong. In the time before ramen came to Japan from China in the late nineteenth century, 'soba' was the generic Japanese word for all kinds of noodle. So it was natural that when ramen arrived in Japan, probably via the port of Yokohama, it was called 'shina soba', or 'Chinese soba'; indeed, some places in Yokohama still call it that. And, so, even though Okinawan soba noodles are made with wheat flour rather than buckwheat, they still stick to the old name.

More importantly, I discover that Okinawan soba ticks all my personal ramen preferences. The noodles are almost udon-thick and the broth is typically made with things from the sea rather than just pork bones boiled for days: things like konbu (dried kelp), katsuo-bushi flakes (bonito fillets, smoked and dried) and niboshi (dried sardines). There are some pork bones too, this is Okinawa after all; there's always some pork somewhere in the mix. I could definitely see Okinawan soba becoming the next big thing in the ramen world, although it will probably have to change its name.

Kume-jima has other surprises in store. It is a rock-pooler's paradise; we spend most of the rest of the day marvelling at the tropical fish which get trapped in the petrified coral beach on the north side of the island. That night, we enjoy a traditional Kume dinner at our hotel featuring satisfyingly large quantities of umi budo, served with a ponzu gel (ponzu – the dipping sauce which blends soy sauce with citrus juice, typically yuzu), and also as a garnish for steamed chicken and rice. It is the perfect hors d'oeuvre for our visit the next day to the Kume-jima Deep Sea Water Development Company (KDSWDC), a rather boring name for a rather extraordinary place, just a twenty-minute taxi ride from our hotel.

Here, in hundreds of tanks of water, they nurture great forests of bulging, ripe sea caviar – 180 tons a year. Each tank contains three tons of chilly deep-sea water pumped in from a couple of miles off the coast. This water is the secret to what is probably the best umi budo in the world. Unfortunately, the chances of the rest of the world getting hold of some remain low, at least for the time being.

'It is incredibly fragile, it doesn't keep much longer than a week. Our biggest challenge is trying to keep that freshness, that amazing popping texture.' Plant manager Tsukasa Nakamichi is giving us the lowdown on the tribulations of being the world's leading sea caviar farmer. 'If you freeze it, it liquefies. If you brine it, or dry it and rehydrate it, you lose the flavour.' Umi budo also needs to be kept relatively warm, so air-freighting is difficult. Nakamichi simply cannot meet the demand and, yet, the more the world gets to taste his umi budo, the more it wants. Already in Tokyo they are paying over ¥10,000 per kilo (£62), and though the demand is going global, so far the furthest he has been able to export is Hong Kong.

A dozen or so women in sun hats and elbow-length rubber gloves are sorting and hand-trimming harvested strands. The air is filled with a bewitching briny aroma.

Nearly all umi budo consumed by humans is farmed. The only place in Japan where it grows wild – in tiny quantities and during the summer only – is in the waters around Miyako-jima, which falls into the same climate band as parts of the Philippines, Malaysia and Indonesia, where umi budo also grows. In the wild it usually grows three to five metres underwater in the sand-filled hollows of coral or rock, although it has been found thirty metres down. Umi budo is very tricky to harvest from the wild because it grows amid a dense cloud of its own waste. You have to dive blind to pick it – one reason why, in olden times, fresh umi budo was considered a highly prestigious gift.

It was only twenty years ago, after many years of trials, that an Okinawan man called Mekaru finally developed a technique to farm umi budo on land, growing it as the kind of filling of a sandwich of one-metre-square rubber nets suspended in the sea water, and fed with fish food. The idea was that this new industry would give older Okinawans less physically demanding work to do compared to traditional farming or fishing, but initially it could only be farmed during the winter when the water was cool enough – which is where the deep sea water comes in. This production plant, which opened on Kume-jima eleven years ago, is the only place where they can harvest year round, because it pumps in that chilly deep-sea water during summer maintaining an optimum 25°Celsius in the tanks.

'I see it every day so I don't eat it very often,' Nakamachi laughs when I ask how he likes to eat it. 'It's great with just a little shiku-wasa juice [a tiny, mandarin-like fruit indigenous to Okinawa].'

As we talk, I notice a wall of photographs of dignitaries who have visited the plant, including the Emperor and Empress and the former US ambassador to Japan, Caroline Kennedy, daughter of JFK.

'I tried to stop Mrs Kennedy eating it before we had cleaned it,' says Nakamichi, looking at the photo. 'But she said she had a strong stomach, and took some anyway.'

I understand her impatience. Standing here, surrounded by tons of glistening, fresh umi budo, larger and more bulging and vital than any I have seen before, it is all I can do to stop myself scooping up handfuls of it and cramming it into my mouth. Sensing this, Nakamichi-san prepares a plate piled high with umi budo, plus some sachets of ponzu to accompany it.

The texture is almost startling – slippery bubbles resist slightly before popping against the roof of my mouth, releasing their intense ocean flavour. Umi budo has huge potential as caviar's vegan cousin, a new, rare seafood delicacy to rank alongside bottarga or sea urchin. I tip back my head and shove great handfuls into my mouth, all notions of decorum cast aside.

Who knows how long it will be before I get the chance to taste umi budo again, I think to myself, and reach for the plate once more.

Chapter 4

Awamori

I shall never set foot in Australia, the wildlife is just too homicidal. You probably feel the same way. That's sensible. Best leave it to the Australians. It is odd, then, that I feel so relaxed in Okinawa as by all accounts it too is infested by poisonous snakes. Odder still, then, that my family and I are about to enter a dark, dank underground limestone cave, thirty metres deep, whose entrance is overhung with trailing vines that all but scream 'Lair of the giant serpent!'

The snakes of Okinawa are called 'habu'. A particularly aggressive type of olive-brown pit viper, habu resemble rattlesnakes but without the rattle and can grow up to eight feet long. With the exception of a couple of the smaller islands, they are found throughout Okinawa and, according to the websites I read open-mouthed and appalled before we left, they love dark, damp underground-type abodes precisely like this.

A habu bite can be fatal if untreated. A couple of hundred Okinawans get bitten every year, although only one or two die as a result. There is a bounty on the snakes on many of the islands. As one local put it to me, 'If you see a habu, you have to kill it.' A while ago someone hit upon the idea of releasing mongooses in a campaign to reduce the habu population, the Rikki-tikki-tavi solution. The problem is, the snakes are nocturnal while the mongooses sleep at night. Now, they are dealing with the twin problem of the snakes and a rampant mongoose population.

The last time we were in Okinawa we met several people with snakebite scars and encountered dead snakes ourselves in irabu jiru, snake soup, a memorably unpleasant dish with all too readily identifiable chunks of snake floating in it (they even left its skin on, all black and scaly). There were also dried snakes on sale in the market in Naha, dead ones squished on the roads, and, most creepily of all, we also saw dead habu coiled and poised as if about to strike in the bottom of bottles of the local spirit, Awamori. They looked like medical specimens in a veterinarian training school, but I had been curious ever since about what the snakes' presence in the bottles of alcohol actually contributed to its flavour.

Awamori came to Japan in the early fifteenth century not from China or Korea – the route by which most culinary and farming innovations arrived – but from Thailand, where they still make a similarly potent rice liquor, often home-made, moonshine-style, called Lao Khao. Long ago, when the production and sale of sake was strictly controlled by the Ryukyus' royal family, awamori offered Okinawans an alcohol fix which bypassed taxes and restrictions.

I had always vaguely assumed that awamori was just another form of shochu, the other, more popular, clear Japanese spirit, originally Korean and primarily produced on Kyushu from barley, rice or sweet potatoes. Both awamori and shochu are cheap and strong, and though awamori is indeed often classified as a shochu, it is a completely different drink. In fact, many awamori connoisseurs claim it to be the superior of the two on account of its richer, more complex flavour although, equally, others wrinkle their noses at its earthy aromas and sometimes medicinal flavour.

Awamori is still made from long-grain indica rice imported from Thailand. The rice is washed, steamed and fermented using koji, a type of fungus (Latin name: *Aspergillus oryzae*) used in the fermentation of several Japanese foodstuffs like sake, miso and soy sauce. Awamori uses black ('kuro') koji as opposed to the yellow koji used for sake, or the white koji more typically used for shochu, and the rice is crushed rather than polished, as it is with sake. These may seem like minor differences, but rice polishing is extremely important when it comes to the flavour and quality of sake; meanwhile, the black koji ferments better with the non-glutinous long-grain rice than yellow koji would. The ageing of awamori traditionally takes place in ceramic pots though more often these days it happens in metal tanks and, in a new innovation, sometimes in oak barrels, usually for around three years, often for much longer.

I had assumed the inclusion of a snake in the bottles of awamori was a tourist thing but in this, as I was to discover during a week in Okinawa in which I diligently tasted numerous brands of the drink, I was only half right.

Back to the cave. The opening is at the end of a narrow concrete path behind an electricity generating station. Old leaves cover the top steps and tree roots push through the rocks around us, lending it an abandoned mine-shaft feel. A metal staircase spirals steeply down between the jagged limestone walls into the darkness.

Emil leads the way followed by Asger, Lissen and me, our guide, slightly worryingly, following behind. For the first few steps, I focus on my feet and the main sensory input is the sound of dripping water, but as my eyes adjust to the light I can see that the walls are filled with shelves lined with bottles. Each bottle is covered in a thick layer of dust and has a postcard-sized white label dangling from its neck, like the O-mikuji, the fortune-telling notes written on pieces of paper and tied outside Japanese shrines and temples.

The cave is the storage facility for the Kin Awamori Distillery where, our guide tells us, they keep fourteen thousand bottles, the oldest of which has been here for twenty-eight years. Asger notices some of the labels bear the names of Japanese cities – Osaka, Sapporo, Tokyo and so on. 'It is a tradition for people from around the country to buy a bottle of awamori for a new-born child and leave it here until their twenties,' explains our guide. She tells us that the caves have always been used to store awamori because they maintain a steady temperature of around 18°Celsius.

During World War II the bottles were joined by the local population. Up to three thousand Okinawans sheltered here during the American bombing raids. 'One time, a baby was born down here,' she says. 'So three thousand people came down, and three thousand and one people left.'

Occasionally, amid the racks of bottles there are also locked, mesh-fronted cupboards stacked with white plastic tubs. These contain the notorious fermented Okinawan tofu, 'tofuyo' – firm tofu fermented using a red koji – which I had had the misfortune to encounter on our last visit to the islands. Tofuyo is a noxious, cheese-like substance usually served in sugar-cube-sized chunks with a toothpick on the side. You are only supposed to taste tiny morsels using the toothpick but, unaware of this, on my first encounter with tofuyo I had taken a whole cube in one go and instantly regretted it. It was a frightful mouthful, with a throat-burn akin to a Roquefort which has been left too long on its own in a warm cupboard.

I had wondered whether the caves imbued the tofu with special bacteria as happens with Roquefort, which is also stored in limestone caves, but clearly the plastic tubs would prohibit this. The real reason they are kept here is, as with the awamori, the caves provide a steady chill away from the subtropical heat above ground. The tubs usually remain underground for six months to a year, our guide tells us, but tofuyo can be aged for longer, for years, even. From the seventeenth century until 1868, the Ryukyus, as they were still known, had stronger ties to China than they did to Japan and tofuyo has obvious links to the still popular Chinese fermented, or 'stinky', tofu. Oddly, the practice of fermenting tofu doesn't seem to have caught on much elsewhere in Japan (although they do have a tradition for something similar in Kumamoto, a prefecture on Kyushu), perhaps because for a long time the technique for making it was kept secret among a few people here.

Understandably, given my previous encounter with tofuyo, I am a little wary about trying it again when our guide offers us a tasting in the Kin Distillery store after our (in the end, snake-free) tour of the caves but, eaten in the correct manner in dainty morsels using a toothpick, it is really not bad at all, with a miso-like, sweet, fermented flavour – perfect for accompanying awamori. Not everyone agrees with me on this.

Asger and Emil did not care for it, and made it very clear they hoped never to encounter tofuyo again.

The next stop on our awamori exploration is the Zuisen Distillery in Naha, the capital of Okinawa's main island. Zuisen is perhaps the most famous of all awamori makers with a history going back over a hundred years – it is probably not a coincidence that the Thai honorary consulate is on the premises.

The sweetly cloying aroma of distilled rice fills the air as we pass the red porcelain dragons on the gateposts outside and are met by Gaku Sakumoto, the company's CEO, who shows us the black koji used for his awamori – it looks like mouldy black rice – and explains the special 'couth' method they use during the ageing process by which evaporated awamori is topped up with the previous year's batch, similar to the way grappa is made.

Sakumoto has kindly arranged for me to try a few of their awamori.

The three-year-old has what I believe oenologists would call an 'aggressive nose' (it stank). Those aromas dissipate when awamori is aged in the traditional, porous clay pots but the fatty acids responsible for the smell tend to be trapped in the new-fangled steel tanks and glass bottles. The six-year-old awamori is still a little rough for me; it is as if someone has taken the water left over from cooking white rice and used it as a vodka mixer. But the ten-, and seventeen-year-old awamori are progressively better, until we reach the twenty-one-year old, which is lovely, smooth and chocolatey, rather like a single-malt whisky.

Asger is keen to hear more about the mystery of the habu and why Okinawans put them in bottles of awamori, but Zuisen doesn't use them, Sakumoto says. The snakes are indeed a tourist thing, it turns out, aimed specifically at Chinese visitors – the usual nonsense to do with phallic potency. According to Wikipedia, a habu's mating habits make even Sting's sessions seem a bit premature, lasting for up to twenty-six hours. The Chinese believe that if one drinks a spirit infused with habu, their sexual stamina is transferred to the drinker.

Only around half a dozen of the islands' forty-six awamori producers add snakes to their bottles to make what is technically known as 'Habushu'. It is quite an uncomfortable process for the snakes. First, they are starved for a couple of months to purge their intestines, then they are killed and gutted before being pickled in the alcohol, although in some places they freeze the snakes while alive to render them immobile, remove their intestines – again while they are still alive – and then sew them up. When the snakes revive they are understandably none too happy about this turn of events and die in an aggressive spasm – the pose the awamori habushu producers are aiming for as it looks nice and dramatic in the bottle. Whichever method is used, the snakes are then placed in pure ethanol for a few weeks to preserve them and neutralise any remaining venom, before being added to bottles of a special awamori with added 'medicinal' herbs and honey. Several thousand habu end their lives in a bottle of awamori each year, apparently.

By this stage it has become apparent to me that researching awamori provides a legitimate excuse for drinking during the day, so I arrange for one more stop on our awamori familiarisation tour: a date with yet more Okinawan royalty, this time the Awamori Queen.

We meet Miyu Oshiro, as she is also known, at the offices of the Okinawa Awamori Distillers Association in an industrial zone of Naha City. She has kindly put on her 'queen' outfit for us: a pink skirt, peacock-patterned jacket, matching pillbox hat, Miss World-style sash (proclaiming her awamori royalty status) and white gloves, all made from polyester. She looks not unlike a 1970s Cathay Pacific air hostess and is presumably highly flammable.

She was chosen, Oshiro-san says, because of her love of awamori and her knowledge of its history. 'I want to tell more people about how wonderful it is,' she tells us, smiling. 'It is usually thought of as a man's drink but there has been an awamori queen chosen every year for the last thirty years.'

Awamori is experiencing a decline due to competition for younger drinkers from beer and wine, as well as the dreaded rival, shochu, from Kyushu (our next stop). The Distillers Association's response has been to promote awamori cocktails; Oshiro-san recommends one featuring coffee. She also says that the richer, funkier flavours of aged awamori are becoming more appreciated. 'And awamori is usually cheaper,' she adds. 'I drink it almost every day!'

It is time to go. I enjoyed some of the awamori I had tried on Okinawa but I still have a suspicion that it might be one of those location-specific alcoholic beverages which foster fuzzy memories when you taste them on holiday but perhaps don't travel all that well, like that bottle of limoncello bought in Amalfi after a gorgeous meal on a terrace in Ravello but which tasted like bubble bath once I got it home, or that bottle of ouzo, so lovely in a beach-side taverna on Chios, but which was not much better than rheumatism tincture a thousand miles north.

KYUSHU

Chapter 5

Pork

The main island of Okinawa had more than lived up to our happy memories from that first visit and, on Kume-jima, we found that rare thing, an idyllic subtropical island which still felt like an authentic, everyday kind of place. I suspect I could spend several happy years pottering around Okinawa's smaller islands, especially as some of them don't even have any snakes. But it is time to move on. A live volcano, the world's weirdest (and most wonderful) amusement park and the best pork we've ever tasted awaits us just an hour's flight north on the island of Kyushu.

We land at Kyushu's southern city of Kagoshima, which is also the capital of Japan's pork industry. The prefecture's Kurobuta black pigs – a cross between Japanese black pigs and Berkshires – are famed throughout the land and, increasingly, beyond.

While the rest of the world associates the Japanese with raw fish and, perhaps, bits of chicken grilled on sticks, pork is by far the most popular meat in Japan. The Japanese eat almost more pork than beef and chicken combined, in among other things tonkotsu ramen (the soup made by boiling pork bones, with a slice of chashu, braised pork, on top), or gyoza (Chinese-style pork-filled dumplings), or tonkatsu (breaded pork cutlets), all of which, from what I have seen over the last ten years, are only increasing in popularity.

From around the eighth century and the introduction of Buddhism to Japan, up until the Meiji Restoration in 1868, the Japanese supposedly did not eat any meat. This is the common perception, at least, but it isn't true. Though virtually no one openly ate beef, wild game continued to be hunted and eaten throughout the centuries, and in Kyushu and Okinawa in particular they never stopped eating pork (even in Tokyo pork was sometimes prescribed, as per my grandmother's late-night Scotch, 'for medicinal reasons').

The Asian black pigs came to this part of southern Kyushu – then known as Satsuma – about four hundred years ago from China via Okinawa. The region's ruling Shimazu clan, which also governed Okinawa at the time (to this day, Kyushu is viewed as a former colonial power by many in Okinawa), were a notoriously combative bunch. Its leaders early on recognised the importance of protein in the diet of their warriors, and a herd of pigs would accompany their armies wherever they fought. The fact that the Satsumas called pigs 'walking vegetables' perhaps indicates that they still felt some sensitivity about eating meat, but eat them they did and Kagoshima has been Japan's pre-eminent pork prefecture ever since. Today, Kagoshima Prefecture is the porcine equivalent of Kobe and its beef (although 'Kobe beef' is just a brand, and the cattle are raised elsewhere).

The modern-day Kurobata pig supposedly evolved when a Berkshire pig was sent to Japan as a gift from Queen Victoria's Windsor estate in the nineteenth century. It probably entered Japan via the port of Nagasaki in north-western Kyushu, and ended up pairing off with the local Asian black pigs. (Someone really should write a biography of that pig.) The island became Japan's main pig-breeding region because there was more land for raising animals here compared to mountainous Honshu, Japan's main island, and the climate was perfect: warm enough for piglets to flourish, cold enough in winter for their fat to accumulate. For the same reasons, southern Kyushu is today also a prime region for raising chickens ('Satsuma chickens' are also a major brand in Japan, the equivalent of Poulet de Bresse in France).

Kyushu's Kurobuta breed almost died out after World War II because they required too much time and effort to raise during what were straitened times but, slowly, as Japan grew more prosperous, the market for a super-pork grew and, over the last decade or so, strict rules for the raising of pigs that carry the Kagoshima Kurobuta label were defined and regulated. The pigs are slaughtered at around

250 days, weighing about 80kg; by comparison, in Europe, factory pigs are slaughtered at around 180 days, yet can weigh 115kg. Should you ever need to, you can identify an authentic Kurobuta pig from their six white patches – one on the tail, one on the nose and one on each hoof. Breeding, combined with unique feeds (often sweet potatoes, apples, or, in the case of one particularly avante garde Kyushu pork farm, strawberries), and a freedom to roam, has created a superior swine, its sweet, juicy, tender flesh boasting unusually high levels of tasty amino acids. Kagoshima pigs are also said to have a higher pH level which makes for darker, more delicious meat and a higher melting point for the fat, which in turn gives a purer flavour.

While we are in Kagoshima I really want to visit a pork farm and learn about the special methods that make Kurobuta pork so lusted after. Some weeks prior to our arrival, I had made contact with a famous pork farm in the region, and began to negotiate a visit.

Dealing with corporate Japan is always tricky. One of the main challenges is that, whether you are making a formal approach to a company or just asking a convenience store assistant if they sell chocolate mochi, it is rare ever to get a blunt 'no' in Japan. If your request really is literally impossible, you will most likely receive a head tilt and an expression of regret, followed by something along the lines of 'That's difficult at the moment', or 'Mmm-hmm, I am not really sure if that's possible.' I have several theories about why the Japanese find it impossible to say 'no' to one's face: it could be a facet of their famed service culture, 'omotenashi', in which the customer is not merely always right, they are properly cherished and respected; maybe it is born from an excess of sheer politeness, or just a genuine reluctance to disappoint; perhaps it is because I am a foreigner – I really don't know.

Neither am I any the wiser about what happened in what I came to think of as 'the mysterious case of the reluctant pork farmers'. It was clear early on that the people at the farm didn't want me to visit for reasons never specified during our initial correspondence but, equally, they couldn't quite bring themselves to refuse outright.

Using the incredibly helpful local tourist board as an intermediary, I repeated my request. It did the trick, and what I believed to be a firm date for a visit to see some Kurobuta pigs in the *Fleisch* was finally arranged.

Except, I wouldn't be able to see the actual pigs, they informed me in a later email.

That was the whole point, I replied. I really need to see some pigs.

Oh, OK, then, you can see the pigs, they wrote back.

Fast-forward a few weeks and we have arrived in Kagoshima, and checked into our hotel, the Shiroyama. Our room, with four single beds arranged in a line like something from *The Waltons*, has stunning views across the bay to Sakura-jima and its gently, smoking, very live volcano. I am unpacking. Lissen is tending to her sweet potato test tubes, lining them up on the window sill so that they can get some light and, I think, yes, she is actually singing softly to them. Asger and Emil are looking at the photos they took at Okinawa's aquarium of the three astonishingly graceful, gigantic whale sharks held in captivity there.

I check my emails. There is one from the pork farm. They have cancelled the visit tomorrow. Apparently, local authority rules forbid such visits to pig farms. Presumably these rules have been in place for a while but they have only now decided to tell me. When it came down to it, a concern about breaking rules *finally* trumped disappointing the foreigner. I ping back a virtual foot-stamp and angry pout, but they politely explain that foreigners, or indeed anyone who has been abroad, cannot come within sight of the pigs. A few years ago a foreign agricultural student visited a farm elsewhere on Kyushu and inadvertently brought foot and mouth disease with him, resulting in the slaughter of hundreds of animals. Aside from the fact that this seems to imply that anyone who works in the pig industry in Japan is never allowed to go on holiday abroad, I completely understand their concerns. I will just have to make do with eating some pork instead, which we do that night at a famed local restaurant, Ajimori.

Not only is Ajimori, an upscale place in downtown Kagoshima, *the* place to eat pork in this southern capital, it reputedly invented pork shabu-shabu. More commonly associated with beef, shabu-shabu is such a convivial, civilised way to eat I always feel, and healthy too. In the middle of our table is a large metal pot, atop a portable butane gas burner, or 'konro'. Inside the pot is a delicate, translucent konbu-infused broth into which we swish super-thin cuts of the local pork belly. The slices are more fat than meat and have been beautifully presented on a platter, bunched into pink and white striped roses, alongside shiitake mushrooms, cabbage, negi (Japanese leeks), enoki mushrooms and, finally, udon noodles, all of which are also to be cooked in the pot. The pork is extremely sweet, gently porky rather than the full-on barnyard you get with tonkotsu ramen, and it is so tender that it only requires a few seconds in the hot broth. The local shochu pairs perfectly with it, cutting through the fat and cleaning the palate ready for the next swish. All in all, it is a much more enjoyable introduction to the best pork in the world than a visit to a pig farm would have been.

Japanese hotel breakfast buffets present a strange culinary landscape, an improbable smorgasbord of incongruous delights. There is always tofu, seaweed, miso, rice and pickles, of course, but usually a salad with Italian dressing, maybe some fried chicken, various cakes and pastries, and often the dreaded natto (snot-textured, fermented soy beans which smell like a tramp's wet woollen socks). In a hotel in Kanazawa at breakfast I once faced the twin challenges of pickled fugu roe and the siren song of a morning draft beer, but the Shiroyama Hotel's breakfast buffet is perhaps the most extreme I have encountered so far, featuring a self-serve soft ice-cream machine, more draft beer, as well as lasagne, 'tuna lung' and wagyu croquettes. Along with the usual condiments of soy sauce and ponzu, there is also the fabulous local black vinegar, made from brown rice and fermented outdoors in ceramic pots for up to five years, plus I spy a display of another of Kagoshima's great local delicacies, 'satsuma-age', deep-fried hockey pucks of finely minced fish paste, sweetened with mirin.

We try a few more satsuma-age later that morning at the city's most famous satsuma-age shop, Agetateya. I get a bit carried away, and order mushroom, sweet potato, green pea, carrot and cheese versions. In each, these various ingredients are added to a basic fish paste, made with a blend of cod and mackerel with a little flour and lots of – perhaps too much – mirin (a kind of sweet sake, for cooking). Satsuma-age are extraordinarily sweet for something that is supposed to be savoury but at least Agetateya's, being freshly made, are a little less rubbery than they can be.

Agetateya has been doing business for around half a century but across the street is an even older store, Akashiya, founded in 1847, selling another Kagoshima sweet treat, karukan, a type of wagashi, or Japanese confectionery. These are ethereal, spongey-soft, snow-white cubes made from ground yam, egg whites and very finely ground rice flour, along with lots of sugar. They are utterly moreish. I have a mental list of Japanese foods and products which I would sell in my imaginary Japan-themed store, and karukan is definitely on that list.

Later, we take the ferry across Kagoshima Bay to the volcanic island of Sakura-jima. Emil excitedly points to a group of dolphins a little way off in the bay. We assume they are an everyday occurrence but another passenger, a local, tells us she has never seen dolphins here before. Some in our party appreciate our good fortune, but others among us interpret the dolphins' appearance as an omen of impending tectonic disaster.

I am wrong, at least that day, but Minami-dake, the southern peak of Sakura-jima's range of three volcanoes, does erupt frequently; news of its most recent outburst had, you'll remember, filtered through to Europe just as we were leaving for the airport to fly to Okinawa. About 4,500 brave souls actually live on the island, many of them farming the local type of orange, the Sakura-jima komikan, and the Sakura-jima daikon, which, thanks to the unusually fertile volcanic soil, can grow to the size and shape of a medicine ball and weigh over thirty kilos. Though their island erupts less often than it used to, kids go to school wearing yellow hard hats, every home has a shelter and every street a special rubbish bin for the ash. According to contemporary reports, during the 1779 eruption 'the water in local wells boiled and the sea turned purple'; the largest eruption was in 1914 and created a lava flow so expansive it connected the island with the Kagoshima peninsula. The fallout stretched as far as Kamchatka in Russia. Of course, virtually everyone in Japan lives with the threat of seismic activity to some extent, a fact which will be brought home just a few weeks after we passed through Kyushu when a 7.3 quake, and several large aftershocks, strikes the city of Kumamoto on the east coast. Two dozen people will die and thousands will be left homeless.

One place which makes the most of the region's volcanic activity is Ibusuki, a small town a little further south around the bay, back on Kyushu proper. This is where people flock to be buried – mostly, if they are honest, to be *photographed* being buried – in the black volcanic sands which are warmed by the local hot springs.

After visiting Sakura-jima, we drive down to Ibusuki to Hakusuikan Hotel where you don't even have to leave the luxury of what is one of Japan's most famous hotels to be buried up to your neck in hot sand for fifteen minutes; it all takes place in a specially built wooden shed next to the hotel's onsen baths.

The hotel's owner, Tadataka Shimotakehara, tells us people have been enjoying the health benefits of the hot sands here for 400 years, including his family. 'My father [who built the hotel over sixty years ago] is ninety-five, and my mother ninety-two, and they are both very well, so it must be good!' he says. The seismic activity which creates the hot springs also helps to create a special white clay found in Kagoshima, used for the celebrated Satsuma pottery. This is all very interesting, but then comes the bombshell: Sean Connery stayed at the hotel while filming *You Only Live Twice* nearby in 1966! 'A very nice man, very kind to me when I was a young boy,' remembers Shimotakehara.

Afterwards, we try the hot sand for ourselves but, far from being the relaxing if quirky spa-type treatment depicted in TV docu-mentaries, I find the whole experience to be more akin to a form of torture. The sand is heated by the hot spring water which runs just a few centimetres beneath the surface and reaches as much as 70°Celsius and, as teams of young people bury us beneath several kilos of the stuff covering our arms and hands, we must endure the unbearable tickles of sweat trickling down our forehead and face. After just a couple of minutes of this, if someone had asked me for my PIN number, I would have surrendered it gladly.

After rinsing all the sand out of our various crevices, we adjourn to the separate-gender onsen baths. This is the first experience of a Japanese onsen for Asger and Emil and though, having been raised part-Scandinavian, they have no qualms about public nudity, I note puzzlement and some alarm cross their faces as I explain onsen etiquette.

'First you need to sit on these little stools in front of that mirror and thoroughly wash yourselves with soap. Then you rinse. Take one of these tiny flannels and, using it to vaguely cover your private bits, you go into that room there, where there is a very large hot bath which we are going to share with a bunch of other men. We don't know them, no. When you get into the bath, it is important that neither the cloth nor your hair goes in the water, so you fold the cloth and place it on the top of your head, like this, right? And no swimming. And no diving, or splashing. The idea is, you just sit in the water. OK?'

Asger and Emil nod warily but follow my instructions. They are impeccable onsen guests but, later, there emerges a very clear schism regarding how the two felt about this most Japanese form of social interaction. Emil is adamantly opposed, claiming at another onsen we visited later on in the trip that he saw some 'poo' floating in the water.

'I hate sitting on the little plastic chairs to wash. If people like it, then good for them. I know what I saw. Even if it was algae or something, that doesn't make it any better,' he will say.

Asger, on the other hand, has always had a relaxed attitude to public nudity. He also happens to be very long-sighted. As he puts it, 'Without my glasses, I can't see anything anyway, so it doesn't matter to me if anyone has their clothes on or not.'

Chapter 6

Shochu

Can you name the world's most popular spirit? Vodka? Whisky? In fact, it is soju, the Korean distilled spirit, an ancestor of arak, the distilled drink made from grapes, which arrived on the Korean peninsula with invading Mongolians in the fourteenth century. Soju is usually made from rice and typically has around 20–25 per cent alcohol content (although sometimes much more), but it can also be made from potatoes or grains. The bestselling brand is Korea's Jinro which sold seventy-one million cases in 2014 and is promoted by Psy, of 'Gangam Style' fame.

Soju translates directly as 'burn liquor' and though I am sure different brands vary in quality, the only virtue of those I have tasted in Korean restaurants is that they were very cheap and very strong. Few other drinks can match up to kimchi, and soju at least induces a warm, fuzzy feeling in an efficient amount of time.

Japan's equivalent is shochu, whose distilling techniques were probably acquired during a Japanese invasion of the Korean peninsula in the sixteenth century, maybe even earlier. There are two main grades: otsurui, the more characterful, richer flavoured premium type, sometimes also called honkaku-shochu and made via a single distillation from whole sweet potatoes, or rice, or wheat (although I have heard of shochu being made from everything from carrots to chestnuts); and korui, a lower grade, lower alcohol, blander variety, distilled multiple times from a mash of sweet potatoes, often with various additives.

Shochu used to have a similar image to soju – it was something to be drunk with purpose, that purpose being to get drunk – but over the last decade a new wave of shochus has emerged in Japan that are smoother and dangerously drinkable. Sweet potato-based shochus in particular are even beginning to usurp sake as Japan's national drink.

Every time I try a good Japanese shochu – whether it is one of those fiery-fruity 'imo shochu', made with potatoes, or the smoother, korui grain varieties – I wonder why this clear spirit is not more popular in the West. I have become a bit of a shochu evangelist (if by 'evangelist' one can mean 'heavy drinker of'). I like it neat on the rocks but it is also great diluted with hot water (called 'oyuwari' – ideally mixed a day before and reheated in a clay vase), and is ubiquitous throughout the izakaya (a casual restaurant where the focus is usually as much on drinking as eating) of Japan as the mixed drink Chu-Hai (a truncation of 'shochu highball'), blended with lemonade, cold tea or other soft drinks – a kind of Japanese alcopop. Grape flavour chu-hai is good but the lychee one is insanely drinkable. Chu-hai is also sold in cans – never bottles for some reason – in all convenience stores in Japan.

Chu-hai is about as far as you can get from something a sommelier might get involved with, but the last time I drank a can of it, for some reason I started to think about *terroir* and wine pairings, the way wines in Europe often match the local cuisine – a flinty Sancerre with the chalky white local goat's cheese, for instance; a bold and fruity Côtes du Rhône with a meaty *boeuf en daube*; or a vinegary Alsatian *choucroute garnie* with a light, mineral Pinot Noir, and so on. This led me to wonder why there is no equivalent symbiosis between sake and Japan's regional foods. Of course, there are plenty of notable regions for making sake, places like Niigata or Kyoto where you are guaranteed a certain quality level, and there are also several bad sake regions (like Tokyo and Yamanashi), where you would probably be better off drinking the local beer, or even, as we will see later, the local wine, but sake always seems detached from the food of its region, from its *terroir*.

Perhaps the 'problem' is that sake goes with just about every type of food, Japanese and non-Japanese. Its acidity, sweetness and complex umami flavours make it a great match for just about anything savoury, but the real reason for the *terroir* disconnect, I think, is that the main ingredient in sake – rice – can be grown just about anywhere in the country. Indeed, sake producers in one part of the country will often boast that they get their rice from another prefecture, often Niigata, Fukushima or Akita, no matter that they are hundreds of miles away. Meanwhile, the other important ingredient in sake is water and, though I realise that Japanese water has special qualities, I am not convinced it is *that* different depending on where you are in Japan.

It occurred to me that maybe shochu was different. I knew it was particularly associated with Kyushu and its food so perhaps it reflected aspects of *terroir*. Already, we have discovered at the shabu-shabu pioneer Ajimori that shochu matches really well with the sweet, juicy pork for which this part of Japan is famed, but what other connections might there be between shochu and Kyushu cuisine?

Historically, the shochu industry has always focused on Kyushu precisely because of issues of *terroir*, namely its warmer climate and the fact that this has always been Japan's main sweet potato growing region. This is the shochu heartland also partly by default, as the warm, humid climate makes sake brewing tricky. Even in colder parts of the country, sake brewing takes place in the autumn and winter for this reason. To make sake here you would need to have powerful air conditioning running throughout the autumn brewing season, otherwise the yellow koji used for sake wouldn't survive. Hence, there are only a couple of sake brewers in all of southern Kyushu, while in contrast there are dozens of companies making shochu. The largest is Kirishima, the Kikkoman of the shochu world, which makes what are generally considered solid, mid-range, quality shochus in vast quantities. But as we were to discover when we drove there through the Austrian-looking alpine countryside from Kagoshima to Kirishima City, it also makes some intriguing and unusual premium brand shochus.

Kirishima is almost singlehandedly responsible for the extraordinary shochu boom Japan has experienced in the last few years. Around fifteen years ago it set out to change the classic demographic of the shochu drinker by targeting female drinkers with new, smoother, multiple-distillation shochus. These were sold in pretty bottles with lighter colouring on their labels and promoted with celebrity endorsements and female models in their adverts. It worked, at least if the sheer scale of the Kirishima Distillery is anything to go by.

Visiting a large Japanese company is always a special experience. You would expect it to be formal, and it is: both guest and hosts have clearly delineated roles to play. Over the years, I have learned that guests are expected to arrive about ten minutes before the agreed time, but no matter how early you get there a group of between four to six men and/or women in dark suits will already be standing silently waiting for you in reception (in Japan, if you are 'on time', you are late). There follows an awkward flurry as many, many business cards are exchanged simultaneously and deep bows executed. The entire group then follows you throughout your visit, even though only one or two of them will ever speak or in any active sense be involved in the tour.

This normally begins with the visitor being shepherded into a dusty, rarely used boardroom which always has a kind of trophy cabinet at one end and, no matter how prestigious or fancy the company, the same old worn-out, budget office furniture (this was even the case at Muji, the chic interior and clothing retailer, whose HQ I once visited in Tokyo: it might as well have been Wernham Hogg). In the boardroom, a corporate video, sometimes still actually on a VHS tape, will already have been lined up in the machine. The film will begin with a wobbly image of a sky- or seascape accompanied by some piano muzak, and continue with various scenes of diligent employees going about their work in factories and fields, before climaxing with another shot of a seascape and some slightly more stirring orchestral music. The video inevitably closes with a not-quite-right English slogan (in this case 'New Quality Wave: Kirishima'). After that you don disposable white paper hygiene-ware (stretchy hat, paper coat and comedy plastic slippers, always three sizes too small) and are shown a variety of production facilities featuring very large stainless steel tanks and complex piping, with a glimpse of a laboratory, before ending in a store selling the company's products. This is the case whether you are visiting a fruit company, a soy sauce factory or, in this case, Japan's leading shochu distillery. At least by now I know what to expect and am able to brief my family to muster their interested faces which, I have to say, they manage very well.

Kirishima is slightly different, though. It is *really* huge; it has its own golf course. Then there is the wonderful aroma of cooked potatoes which sets our nostrils twitching before we even enter the main building. And, this time we are accompanied by *nine* men and women in dark suits, as well as one or two in scrupulously clean overalls – a record. Then comes the final difference between the Kirishima factory tour and all the others I had experienced: our trip ends with one of the greatest meals I have ever had in Japan.

But first the tour. The scale of the output here is immense: 40,000 bottles a day. We learn the difference between Japanese shochu and Korean soju (the Koreans add sugar, while the sweet potato shochu Kirishima makes relies on the sugars in the potatoes to provide the alcohol). Kirishima makes some shochus using rice, buckwheat and barley, but most of their output is sweet potato shochu, which requires 320 tons of locally grown potatoes per day, 110,000 tons a year, making the company the largest consumer of sweet potatoes *in the world*; in one vast hangar we watch endless broad conveyor belts of yellow-skinned potatoes the size and shape of rugby balls being sorted prior to steaming. Shochu-making proceeds precisely as with sake-making for the first few stages. Rice is soaked in water, then steamed and inoculated with this mystical substance, koji, but hereafter the two diverge as cooked sweet potatoes are added and thereafter shochu is distilled rather than brewed with yeast. For most of its mainstream products Kirishima uses a whisky-style continuous distillation process which makes for a smoother, some would say blander drink with a broader appeal, but for the more complex, premium shochu, they distil only once.

Kirishima is currently run by three sons, the third generation of the founding Enatsu family. After the tour we are invited to have lunch with the second son and chairman, Takuzo Enatsu. An imposing man in his late fifties wearing a dark suit, he is the archetype of a Japanese CEO. We join him in the traditional tatami-covered dining room of the Enatsu family house where he was born within the factory grounds.

'Some years ago, I decided that shochu should be part of Japanese food culture,' Enatsu-san begins as we sit down at the table. 'So I created kuro shochu to pair better with Japanese food.'

This would prove a very smart decision. Today, Enatsu's brainchild – shochu made with 'kuro' or black koji is the bestselling shochu in Japan, but at the time it was a controversial move as this smoother, continuously distilled sweet potato shochu is made with the same koji that awamori producers used. But Kirishima's shochu is very different from the Okinawan spirit, Enatsu explains.

'Awamori is made with rice, of course, and it goes very well with Okinawan fried foods. I always drink it when I go to Okinawa. But when I bring it to Kyushu it just doesn't match with local foods here. So I wanted to make a shochu with a milder flavour. I was going against eighty years of tradition in this company when I changed the type of koji to black koji, and some of our older customers were angry when I changed it. But you can't keep on doing things the way they were done a hundred years ago. Nobody on the board believed me when I said I wanted to make this. I did it though, and the market loves it.'

This blockbuster shochu is one of the half-dozen shochu we are served during a dazzling lunch of local dishes. Another is Aka Kirishima, a seasonal shochu, made with purple sweet potatoes. It has a notably sharp aftertaste.

'Yes, exactly!' Enatsu beams approvingly when I mention this. That sharpness helps clean the palate between mouthfuls of food. 'You have ten thousand tastebuds, and when you take a sip of this, it resets them ready for the next flavours.'

The company is about to celebrate its centenary and to mark the anniversary Enatsu is breeding a new super-potato. 'I want to create a potato with a DNA unique to Kirishima, that no one else has or can copy. I will make something that nobody in human history has tasted. After you drink shochu made from it, I want you to feel like you've had a big hug. That's the taste I am after.'

Enatsu also has an eye on the health and beauty market. Because Kirishima doesn't add sugar to its shochu, it has fewer calories than many other alcoholic drinks; what calories it contains, he claims, are 'consumed by the body's temperature. It is good for beauty and eyesight too. There is a growing demand for foods that make you healthy and beautify you, and you can do this by drinking shochu.'

This is the best news I have had all day, to go with what has been an outstanding meal – an astonishing kaiseki lunch featuring abalone with fermented katsuo (bonito) guts, beef tongue, grilled bonito, vegetable nigiri and a lobster miso soup the umami power of which shall haunt me for many years to come. It is not an obviously child-friendly menu, but I watch, amazed, out of the corner of my eye as my two sons devour the lot.

I focus my increasingly blurry attention on tasting more Kirishima shochus. There is an Astaxanthin shochu, whose alarming pink colour derives from the same compound as that found in crabs and salmon eggs; and a top of the range, limited edition, thirteen-year Misty Island Gyoku in a gold box. This last one is personally blended by Enatsu-san and includes Chinese herbs, birds' nests, Madagascan vanilla beans, mozuku seaweed and coprinus mushrooms. It retails for ¥9,500 (£60) compared to ¥1,000 for their basic shochu and has a strong, sweet vanilla aftertaste.

For dessert we are served a classic Miyazaki confection, 'kujira yokan', or 'whale yokan', a black and white azuki paste/mochi sandwich, so-named because its colour scheme supposedly resembles that of a killer whale (created for the fifth lord of the Shimizu clan, legend has it, so that he would grow up as strong as a whale). This is followed by a slice of a remarkable fruit, the hyuganatsu, a citrus which – I later look up – spontaneously evolved following the freak pairing of a yuzu and a pomelo in a garden in Miyazaki in the 1820s. The hyuganatsu looks like a self-satisfied yuzu, plump with a beautifully smooth complexion. It is not only blessed with delicious, sweet orange flesh, but also has edible pith which is neither bitter nor astringent like every other citrus fruit I know, but sweet and delicately fragrant. I have a kind of pith phobia but this is fantastic. I add it to my mental list of those obscure local citrus fruits with which Japan abounds, like the dekopon from nearby Kumamoto, the vivacious sudachi (like a kind of mini lime with orange flesh), or the sweet kumquat, the 'kinkan'.

An analysis of my liver function might have told a different story, but as I totter away from the Kirishima Distillery together with my family some time later, I have convinced myself that our meal has been a healthy introduction to this fabulous, friendly spirit shochu, and to the *terroir* of southern Kyushu.

Chapter 7

Nori

Something is troubling me. On our three-hour drive up the western Izumi coast of Kyushu we pass a pachinko parlour. Nothing unusual in that. There is at least one of these cacophonous cathedrals in every Japanese town, each of them filled with row upon row of vertical pinball machines providing a constant clattering of ball-bearings and flashing lights for their entranced victims. And the coast of Kyushu, though spectacular with its forested, mountainous cliffs, rocky islets and sandy bays, is no different. Wherever man has intervened in the precious gaps of flat terrain, he has hastily filled them with flat-pack retail warehouses and light industrial estates, strip malls and fast food drive-throughs. Only the occasional vivid green rice paddy relieves the grey concrete and rusty corrugation. You see this kind of almost wilfully dreary urban sprawl everywhere in provincial Japan but, actually, it fascinates me. There are few if any places in this country that I don't find interesting, few if any streets I can walk down without finding something to linger over, whether it is a crazy tangle of overhead electric cables, the precision parking of a tiny kei car in a space barely larger than it, or one of those ingenious life 'hacks' at which the Japanese excel (they call them 'urawaza') – water bottles dangling on fences to deter cats, and so on. Sometimes, though, even I have to concede things have gone too far.

In between the Mazda showrooms and endless parking lots, the biggest buildings are these pachinko parlours; 'parlour' – an oddly domestic word for such cavernous warehouses. But a slogan, in

English, on the outside of one especially vast pachinko place we have just passed intrigues me. It reads:

> 'Take your hat off to the past, but take your coat off to the future.'

What could this possibly mean? What aphoristic imperative was mangled here? This occupies me for some miles until we arrive by the concrete sea wall at the small fishing village of Izumi. In fact, it is only now, looking at my notes some weeks later, that I have come up with my own interpretation of the weird slogan. I reckon it is an ominous prophecy for the future of nori.

We are driving up the coasts of Kagoshima and Kumamoto Prefectures to find out more about nori, the paper-like black, dried seaweed used to make sushi rolls and also to enwrap the ubiquitous onigiri – or rice balls – the classic Japanese snack found in every convenience store and train platform kiosk the length of the country. Nori is also sold shredded as kizami nori, but best of all is furikake – shredded nori mixed with sesame seeds, various different types of dried fish, and chilli flakes. Furikake is one of those substances, like parmesan or bacon, which makes *everything* you sprinkle it over taste better.

Like shochu, nori processing was another sixteenth-century arrival brought back following military activities by the shogun's armies in Korea. Back then it was a precious crop; one sheet of nori was said to be worth 1.5 kg of rice. These days, of course, the most common variety, susabi nori, is as cheap as paper and sold in most supermarkets in Britain.

I had often wondered how they turned seaweed – in this case, *Porphyra* – into perfectly square paper-thin sheets, one side always slightly rough, the other shiny-smooth, but my curiosity turned to fascination after I visited a specialist nori shop on a busy street corner close to Tsukiji fish market, in Tokyo, a year or so earlier. I had asked the shop manager what was the ultimate, the *very* best type of nori.

'Definitely Asakusa nori,' he had told me. 'But we haven't had any this season, and I am not sure we will ever get it again.' I made a note of the name, 'Asakusa nori', and began asking about it whenever I spoke to chefs in Japan.

Did it really come from Asakusa, a central district of Tokyo? This seemed unlikely. Why was it so great? How could I get some? How much did it cost? I found no clear answers.

At one point, I was lucky enough to meet the legendary Japanese chef Nobu Matsuhisa, co-founder with his friend Robert De Niro, of the Nobu restaurant chain, and the man credited by many with bringing Japanese food to the global mainstream. I was introduced to Nobu-san by mutual friends at an event at the London branch of his eponymous restaurant chain. I asked him if he had heard of Asakusa nori. He thought for a moment, as if dredging up a long-forgotten memory. 'Asakusa nori is from Tokyo, or it used to be. It doesn't grow in Tokyo any more, and hasn't for a long, long time,' Nobu said.

Eventually, I heard a rumour that Asakusa nori was still farmed on Kyushu and, knowing we would be travelling through the island, I thought I would look into it. What I didn't count on, as we set off from the hot sand hotel at Ibusuki that day and headed up the coast, was that I would also discover an improbable tale of how the entire multi-billion yen Japanese nori industry as we know it today would not exist if it weren't for a discovery made by a remarkable English woman, long forgotten in her homeland but celebrated every April here in western Japan.

It looks like nori, but not quite the nori I am used to. Held up to the light, the raggedy looking sheet is a translucent apple-green, not the dense, inky-black of the nori sheets I buy at home or that wrap onigiri in the convenience stores. It is like comparing handmade paper to the stuff I buy in bulk for my printer.

I have in my hands actual, genuine Asakusa nori, the King of Nori. Not only that, this is the ultimate incarnation because it has been dried naturally, in the sun, instead of by machine. I take a sniff and get a subtle tang of the sea. I tear a piece off to taste. It evaporates on my tongue, leaving a sweet, toasted, briny flavour. Unlike the nori I am used to, it doesn't clump together and stick to my teeth, and there is no bitter aftertaste. It is the finest, most fragile and delicious sheet of seaweed I have ever eaten, the seaweed equivalent of white truffles or caviar. Except, it turns out this translucent green paper is far rarer than mere truffles because it is quite probably the last of its kind on earth.

The man who has been kind enough to give me a sheet of the nori is Yoshio Shimanaka, sixty-two, a nori farmer just like his father before him. He is one of seven still working in the small harbour town of Izumi in Kagoshima Prefecture, our first stop of the day. With his massive meaty hands and close-cropped hair, Shimanaka looks more like a retired boxer, but he has spent all his life growing, harvesting and drying nori, working twenty-hour days during the freezing cold harvest season from December to mid-March.

In its natural state, nori grows like a slimy, dark green curtain on rocks in tidal areas, benefiting from the nutrients in the sea when it is below the water and then, when the tide goes out, from the sun's rays. Farmed nori replicates this cycle; spores are cultivated in oyster shells which are tied to rigid plastic nets suspended horizontally between poles planted in the seabed.

About a decade and a half ago farmers in Japan began spraying their nori with different types of acid solutions to control pests. The acids were supposed to be closely monitored but in reality all sorts of nasty stuff has been used, including hydrochloric acid, and the surrounding seas have been badly contaminated. 'Chemicals are not allowed here in Izumi,' Shimanaka explains as we chomp on the nori. 'We have kids and grandkids, we don't want to put chemicals in the water here.'

Nori is high in amino acids, and an especially good source for vitamin B, he continues. 'And it is very, very healthy. You know, after the Fukushima disaster many of the locals there started eating more nori instead of the local vegetables. The best way to eat it is just lightly toasted over an open flame, with rice.'

We are standing in an open-sided corrugated shed next to his house beside the seawall. Over a dozen other people have gathered here to welcome us this morning: other nori farmers, Shimanaka's wife and the mayor of Izumi. A table has been laid with all manner of sweets and cakes which Asger and Emil are eyeing intently. We are offered tea and soft drinks and sit down in deckchairs to talk. Asger and Emil descend on the cake table like locusts.

Afterwards, we walk across the road, through a row of pine trees twisted by the wind, and climb the sea wall to look out over Shimanaka's fishing grounds. Hundreds of wooden poles jut in neat lines from the sea's surface.

During the harvest season, the fresh-grown tips of nori are cut every week or so, and the harvested purple-brown slime is brought back to the shore for drying and processing. Here in Izumi the bay is shallow for several hundred metres out, so farmers usually wade out into the freezing water during the winter time, often at night because the flavour is said to be better when the seaweed is harvested then. Sometimes Shimanaka will hand-harvest but mostly he will use a machine which automatically cuts the seaweed at the right length to leave ten centimetres still growing on the netting. Most is dried by machine, but Shimanaka does sun-dry some special nori, like the sheet we just tasted, for his own use.

Asakusa nori did indeed get its name because it was first farmed in Tokyo Bay, but it has always grown naturally in Izumi. 'There is no doubt it is the best nori,' Shimanaka says. 'The flavour is stronger, the aroma carries for a long way, and when you eat it you can taste it all the way down your throat. You can tell good nori because it is soft and has small holes when you hold it up to the light. The moment you put it in your mouth it is very sweet, but it doesn't stick. But in the last ten years it has been in decline. We don't know for sure why but the biggest problem, I think, is climate.'

The sea is getting warmer all the way up this busy volcanic coast of bays, peninsulas and islands, as far as Ariake Bay, the largest and most famous nori-producing area in all Japan. This rise in temperature is bad news because nori, even the hardy, commercially grown Susabi variety, struggles to germinate and grow if the water goes much above 15°Celsius. Asakusa nori is even more vulnerable. It is also more vulnerable to acid pollution, too, both from acid rain and the type of acid treatments used in susabi farming.

'Asakusa nori is in danger of extinction, if it is not already extinct,' says Shimanaka, turning to look me in the eye for the first time. 'It is just not maturing like it should be. This year, for the first time ever, there has been nothing to harvest.'

Asakusa nori production peaked eight years ago, and has been declining ever since. Though it typically fetches three times as much as susabi nori – ¥100 per sheet for Asakusa compared to ¥10–30 for susabi – its yield is much lower and Shimanaka fears that, with these new climate challenges, farmers are going to conclude that it is just not worth bothering any more.

So why not just move production to a cooler part of Japan? It is not that simple. The western coast of Kyushu is perfect for nori, thanks not just to the climate and sea temperature here, but also the circulation of the water aided by the extreme tides – on Ariake Bay the difference between high and low tide can be as much as six metres. Around a hundred rivers flow into the Ariake Bay area too, which means the water's nutrient composition is unusually rich and creates the perfect balance of salinity for the nori, which prefers less salty water. It is not, then, a case of upping sticks to Hokkaido.

'I am not going to give up,' says Shimanaka-san as we shake hands to say goodbye. 'I am going to keep trying to grow Asakusa nori, I will try again next year.'

Could the Japanese really let a food product as exceptional as this disappear without a fight? Few countries value excellence in their produce more, and no other people are more obsessed with perfection on their plates than the Japanese.

My next stop is Uto, a larger coastal town further north in the next prefecture, Kumamoto. My ever-patient family decide they have had enough of nori for one day, and head for our hotel in nearby Kumamoto City, so off I go alone to meet Fumichi Yamamoto. He has spent half his eighty years researching all aspects of cultivating nori, and has invited along Yoshinari Fujiyama, another thickset boxer-type nori farmer, to help fill me in on the plight of Asakusa nori.

We meet in the harbourside shed of Fujiyama's company which is filled with vast incubation tanks, each with a large metal spindle suspended above to roll up the nets of oyster shells on which the young nori grows. There are stacks of mats for drying the seaweed, like the maki mats I use to make rolled sushi at home but made of green plastic; wooden box-frames for forming the sheets of nori; and electric fans for drying the freshly harvested leaves.

'Yes, it is true, Asakusa nori is almost extinct,' Yamamoto nods. 'In the old days, it was the main type of nori harvested and it grew here and in Nagasaki and Saga Prefectures. But no one has managed to grow any this year. It is really delicious with a softer texture and longer lingering flavour. It melts in your mouth, I really hope we can get it going again, but I don't think it is economical.'

Susabi nori, on the other hand, is a reliable crop which can be harvested up to ten times in one season, compared to perhaps twice for Asakusa nori. Sales of susabi nori have grown 100 per cent since the late 1980s in line with the inexorable growth of the convenience-store onigiri. Susabi nori is stronger, so it doesn't tear so easily, making it perfect for the mass production of these snacking rice balls. In a double whammy, just as the onigiri market has grown, the once common practice of giving high-quality nori as a gift has declined by 90 per cent, so, while total consumption of nori in Japan has actually increased slightly over the last thirty years, this is all accounted for by the cheaper, lower grade susabi variety.

I wonder aloud whether the climate change that seems to have done for Asakusa nori might eventually wipe out susabi nori too?

'It used to be that we could harvest for five months of the year, now that is down to four,' says Fujiyama-san, a farmer for fifty years (I had guessed his age at around fifty, so this comes as something of a shock – it turns out that he is seventy-one). 'At that rate, I don't think all nori will completely disappear but the amount we harvest will definitely decrease. I worry about it constantly. The costs are getting very high, labour costs and machinery costs – a new nori boat costs forty million yen [£250,000], and young people aren't interested in this kind of traditional food industry.'

The farmers lead me across the street and over some railway tracks to the processing plant for Fujiyama's company. The warehouse is almost completely filled with a gigantic blue machine into one end of which goes newly harvested, rinsed nori, roughly formed in trays into squares, and out of the other end three hours later come the familiar, dried papery nori sheets – 150,000 a day.

I watch the machine in deafening action for a while until Fujiyama gets my attention. He is trying to say something.

'Of course, you will be wanting to go and see mmmblleebm mumble?' I can't quite hear what he is saying but smile and nod.

And, so, a five-minute drive later we arrive at the end of a natural promontory out in the bay where we climb a small, tree-covered hill to a Shinto shrine. At the top of the hill, I turn to look out at the bay which is covered with the wooden posts used for the nori nets. But there is something else here on the hill. In front of me is some kind of memorial. A granite monument with a brass relief featuring the bust of a Western woman. She is wearing round, wire-rimmed glasses; her hair is in a bun.

The two men look at me expectantly. I look more closely at the memorial. It reads:

IN MEMORY OF
MADAME KATHLEEN
MARY DREW, D.Sc.
MRS WRIGHT BAKER
(6 XI 1901–14 IX 1957)
RESEARCH FELLOW IN
THE UNIVERSITY OF
MANCHESTER ENGLAND
DISCOVERER OF THE
CONCHOCELIS-PHASE
OF PORPHYRA
ERECTED in 1963

I look back at the men, who now look at each other as if realising they must reassess the situation. They are going to have to explain. I am very glad they do because, behind the memorial lies a quite extraordinary tale.

In 1949 a research fellow at Manchester University, a phycologist, or seaweed scientist, called Kathleen Drew-Baker, published a brief paper, 'Conchocelis-phase in the life-history of Porphyra umbilicalis'. It was just a couple of paragraphs long, and appeared in the scientific journal *Nature*. While studying *Porphyra* growth, Drew-Baker noticed that what had previously been considered two distinct species of seaweed – *Porphyra* and *Conchocelis* – were in fact the same species. She observed one grow into the other in her petri dish. Big deal, you might think, but this discovery was to have massive consequences for a struggling industry and a starving people on the other side of the world because it turned out Drew-Baker had stumbled upon a method of cultivating nori on an industrial scale.

The paper in *Nature* was picked up some months later by a Japanese scientist, Dr Sokichi Sagawa, from Kyushu. There were chronic food shortages in Japan at the time and many people had been relying on nori to supplement their diet, but that year had been a bad one for the nori harvest and no one knew why. Drew-Baker's paper held the answer to more reliable and efficient nori cultivation because it solved the riddle of the early stages of its growth. Together with the local fisherman of Uto, Dr Sagawa set about implementing her new technique for growing nori spores on oyster shells. It revived the local nori industry within a season and ensured that, henceforth, crops would be more robust and reliable.

Within a few years, nori production in Kumamoto had increased by 40 per cent. The locals nicknamed Drew-Baker 'the Mother of the Sea', and collected a sum of money to erect this memorial in the Sumiyoshi Shrine Park in 1963. They also planted an oak tree to symbolise England, in the shade of which I am now standing.

Drew-Baker died in 1957 without ever making it to Japan and never earned a penny from her discovery, but more than half a century later the locals still hold a ceremony here every year on 14 April. Her old academic gown and cap are placed on the monument and they raise the Union Jack. Crowds of hundreds turn up, apparently. On the 100th anniversary of Drew-Baker's birth in 2001, her son and daughter visited the memorial and learned how their mother is still remembered and revered in this part of Japan. Schoolchildren are taught about her discovery and the impact it had here. She is considered a great scientific heroine.

'We appreciate her very much,' says Fujiyama, the nori fisherman, and, for some reason, my mind drifts back to that pachinko parlour slogan we had passed earlier that morning.

'Take your hat off to the past, but take your coat off to the future.'

It suddenly makes a weird kind of sense, at least in terms of nori. The fishing community of Uto 'take their hat off to the past' every 14 April when they commemorate Drew-Baker, and as for the future? The future looks warmer. You might indeed want to take your coat off …

Chapter 8

Obama

To get to Obama you have to take a ferry from Kumamoto City across the choppy waters of Shimabara Bay.

On board the ferry, a fellow passenger beckons to us. My family and I look at each other and for some reason we all dutifully get up and follow the young man, who is dressed in a bomber jacket and jeans, out onto the rear deck of the ferry. By now the ship has picked up a decent lick of speed so we are surprised to see a flock of seagulls flying fast and low right along with us, almost close enough to touch. Other passengers are feeding them packets of biscuits and the man kindly hands us a packet of our own and gestures that we should feed them too. Emil is our sanctioned go-between when it comes to wildlife, so he goes first, squealing as the birds' beaks nip at his fingers.

Obama is a popular holiday resort, named long before the former US president was elected, of course, although there is now a statue there in his honour and he features on the welcome sign. It turns out to be a cosy seafront town, its promenade lined with palm trees and hotels. With the mountains looming behind, there is a touch of the Italian Riviera about it, but Obama is an onsen town, so hot that steam spirals from the manhole covers on the streets and in the seafront park you can bathe your feet, or hard-boil eggs if you prefer, in sulphurous spring water. Best of all, nearby on the seafront is Mushigamaya, an onsen restaurant.

This turns out to be little more than a pine-wood shack, but it is the wooden shack of my dreams, and the reason why Obama is my new favourite town in all of Japan.

Mushigamaya may not have crystal chandeliers and linen table-cloths, it may not have an obsequious maitre d', a celebrity chef in the kitchen, or an impressive wine list, but it does serve truly amazing seafood, much of it still living until cooked to order, for about the same price as a visit to McDonald's in Leicester Square.

We select our lunch from an edible aquarium: abalone writhing indignantly in their upturned shells; twitching, glistening shrimp; scallops with vivid orange and purple shells which open slowly as if squinting at the world and then slam shut with an irritated hiss; and oysters and sea snails the size of my fist. We plunk them all in our plastic shopping basket and take them outside where a couple of young men are manning a range of steaming wooden hatches. They pull a rope to open one of the hatches, letting out a waft of eggy-smelling steam, set an electric timer and lower colanders full of the cross but doomed seafood into the hellish, earth's core waters, heated by magma deep underground as it makes its way to the sea from Mount Unzen high above us.

A few minutes later, the seafood is pulled up from the steamy depths of hell, no longer twitching. Served at a table inside, with a splash of soy sauce, it tastes like a fantasy of the ocean's bounty, perfectly seasoned from the salty steam. Admittedly, some of our party feel a little queasy about the process of selecting our lunch and having it killed in this way, but it doesn't stop them eating it. Some even return for seconds, and thirds.

Obama had recently become quite well known in Japan thanks to Chanponman, a character in a TV series based on the story of a fictional local tourist authority employee who is determined to make the town famous for a particular type of Chinese-style noodle soup eaten here in Nagasaki Prefecture, called Champon. There is a picture of the actor in character outside the restaurant by the small enclave of food stalls and shops that you find at every tourist destination in Japan; he is dressed in the classic superhero vernacular with tight Lycra suit and cape, except that he also has a large bowl of noodles strapped to his head.

You encounter this kind of thing often in Japan: a cultural phenomenon so peculiar and offbeat that it stops you in your tracks.

In a similar vein is Anpanman, one of Japan's most popular cartoon characters of all time. Anpanman is made out of cakey, adzuki bean paste-filled bread. If he encounters a sad or hungry child, he simply tears off a piece of his face and gives it to them – something I always think seems more likely to induce trauma than bring comfort. His enemy is Baikinman, or Bacteria Man, whose aim is to enslave the earth and all its people through the power of dirt.

This kind of cultural oddness isn't just limited to fictional or cartoon characters; indeed, aside from natural disasters, the international media's reporting on Japan seems to focus almost entirely on other such freaky cultural phenomena, like the vending machines that sell women's used underwear, or the passing fads like eyeball licking, on which the world's media reported a few years back. Both of those stories were nonsense, by the way. I suspect that, often, these kinds of rumours start when three people try something weird, once, in Harajuku, the fad-hungry teenage zone in Tokyo, and do so in the presence of a blogger or photographer knowing full well that the international press will pick up on it. Let's be charitable and assume that's what happened with Ganguro, the disturbing schoolgirl blackface trend of the 1990s. But occasionally the trends are both true and genuinely Japan-wide, like the comparatively recent tradition of eating KFC on Christmas Eve – a result of a successful marketing push by the industrial chicken fryer – or the horrifically graphic and violent manga porn read openly by men on public transport, which you do see everywhere if you are the type to read over people's shoulders (and if you are, then this ought to cure you).

I have to say, though, that having now myself been turned into a cartoon character* – a character which, at various times, has been

---

* In 2015–16, the Japanese national broadcaster NHK made a twenty-five-part animated series based on my book *Sushi and Beyond*, broadcast in both Japanese and, on NHK World, in English. Which was a bit weird. To be honest, I still don't really understand what happened there.

depicted flying naked through the sky in a tamago kake gohan (raw egg on rice)-induced ecstasy, and orbiting outer space with the 'Ramen King', among other indignities – I am now much more accepting of things like Chanponman and his noodle hat, or Anpanman with his edible face. 'Sure,' I think to myself. 'Of course, there is a noodle superhero. Why not?'

It is with this open-minded approach that I invite you to join us as we venture forth from Obama to our next stop, Huis Ten Bosch, a theme park nearby in Nagasaki Prefecture, which I suspect might well be a strong candidate for the most perplexingly bonkers place on Planet Earth.

Huis Ten Bosch is a full-scale evocation of an eighteenth-century Dutch city replete with canals, a full-sized replica of Huis Ten Bosch Palace – Holland's answer to Versailles – windmills, (of course, there's loads of windmills), as well as Renaissance-style redbrick townhouses and fields of tulips. About the only thing it lacks to complete the Amsterdam vibe are coffee shops selling pre-rolled joints and ladies of the night beckoning from red-lit windows. It does, though, have several hotels, including one staffed by robots, as well as a truly terrifying horror zone, and even a residential district where actual people actually live. What's more, quite by chance, in Huis Ten Bosch on the day we visit we even get to experience the very latest bizarre Japanese cultural phenomenon to have captured the global media's attention: Kabe Don.

This happens in the Chocolate House, which has a five-metre-high chocolate fountain and serves chocolate pizza. It is also temporary home to a tall young Japanese man dressed in a dinner suit and sporting the layered, spiky, androgynous hairstyle beloved of Japanese boy bands. Right now, he has my wife pinned to the wall. He is caressing her cheek with his left hand and leaning in as if to kiss her. He pulls back, unwraps a small chocolate, looks deep into her eyes and places it between her lips. Seeming to forget that she is a strong, independent woman of a certain age, my wife blushes and giggles. If she had a fan, I think there is a good chance she would now be fluttering it distractedly.

She is experiencing the full romantic force of Kabe Don. 'Kabe' means 'wall' and 'Don' is onomatopoeic, it is the noise the man's hand makes as it comes to rest, with a thunk, on the wall beside the woman's head as he leans in to seduce her. The practice originated in the realm of manga and seems, from where I am standing (a little tense next to Asger and Emil, who can barely breathe with embarrassment), to teeter perilously between assertive courtship ritual and non-violent sex attack. But Kabe Don has gained cultural currency in Japan as a 'thing' over the last few months, to the extent that it is being presented as just another of the many visitor experiences here in Huis Ten Bosch on the day we visit, which happens to be Valentine's Day.

The 'seducer' moves back, smiling. His Kabe Don work is done as far as my wife is concerned, but now it appears it is my turn. I am guided gently towards the man by the Huis Ten Bosch staff and enter his 'office' in the corner of the chocolate shop. This has been cordoned off and, for some reason, furnished Steampunk-style, like a Victorian doctor's surgery. I pass Lissen as she leaves. She is looking a little flushed and guilty, as well she might. The man now positions me against the wall. I assume it is a joke, that he will stop and everyone will start laughing but, without warning, he moves in again, pressing one hand on the wall beside my head.

'Ha, yes, this is all very jolly and funny, can we stop now?' I think to myself, but he begins unwrapping a heart-shaped candy and positioning it on my lips. I mean no offence to my beautiful wife but, clearly, you could have placed a dead halibut in front of this guy and he would try to seduce it. Blushingly, I find myself accepting the chocolate, trying not to feel like a cheap sex object. My dear children have somehow now forgotten their embarrassment and are filming all this on their cameras for future use.

'That was weird, wrong on so many levels,' says Emil afterwards. 'Is that seriously how Japanese people are like? They need to get a life. It's already weird enough to see you and mum kiss, but another man *feeding you chocolate . . .?*'

Kabe Don is definitely strange but I should stress that it was performed with the kind of relaxed humour typical of the Japanese but which rarely survives the translation via our media. Contrary to their popular image, the Japanese have a pretty good sense of humour (if I may generalise about an entire nation, not for the first time in my career). They are open, accepting, non-judgemental and fun, which is something to bear in mind when you see those crazy Japanese game shows, or Instagram feeds of people wearing cosplay costumes. Mostly, those involved get the joke and usually the broader Japanese viewing public tend to think it is all as mad as we do (it always helps, too, to attempt a cultural reversal: how must Mr Blobby, say, or the State Opening of Parliament appear to outsiders?).

As our blushes subside, it is time to move on from the Chocolate House to explore some of Huis Ten Bosch's other, more child-friendly attractions. I had planned this visit really as a thank you to Asger and Emil. Over the previous few days they have sat through endless technical discussions about seaweed husbandry and shochu distilling techniques which they probably did not find especially gripping. This is payback, so I didn't expect to enjoy Huis Ten Bosch at all, but, my Kabe Don assignation aside, I absolutely love it. I assumed it would be a chipboard and fibreglass mock-up of a Dutch city, but the buildings are constructed with absolute integrity out of proper materials and it is actually quite beautiful, right down to the detail in the brickwork and the ornate, cast-iron street lamps. Being Japanese, all is clean, ordered and relatively classy. The tulips are incredible, and not a little miraculous given it is February, and best of all there is virtually no queueing. On the rare occasion when there is the slightest risk of having to wait in line, 'Please Wait Slightly' signs are positioned at the entrance to the attraction.

The food is on a higher plane to the stuff usually served at Disneyland, too. In the countless gift shops dedicated to local foodstuffs you can buy mentaiko (cured, spicy pollock roe, a speciality of Kyushu), dried niboshi (sardines), and Dutch cheeses. Best of all, at night-time, the entire park erupts with astonishing 3D lighting displays which transform the buildings' facades into moving images. The sixty-six-metre-high town hall tower becomes a giant waterfall;

the surface of the canals turn into *Saturday Night Fever*-style pulsating dance floors.

We join an open-air 'Venetian masked ball' which turns out to involve communal dancing to ABBA hits. There aren't any roller-coasters or conventional thrill rides at Huis Ten Bosch. The closest you can come to visceral thrills is on a zip wire. To gain admission we have to sign a lengthy indemnity form pledging that we have no physical ailments and that we understand it brings a risk of 'emotional injury'. It all seems a little overcautious for something that can be enjoyed by six-year-olds and the precautions seemed odder still when, later on that evening, we visit a kind of haunted house, called the Prison Ward, which turns out to be quite the most disturbing thing I have ever experienced – either at a fun park or anywhere else. Far from the tame 'fright house' experience I was expecting, it involves full-on psychological terrorising which begins with the stomach-churning smell of formaldehyde as we enter (the theme appears more 'prison hospital from hell'); is followed by the graphic, gruesome exhibits of operating theatres and severed limbs which I have to scurry past with as much dignity as I can muster; as well as the suddenly rattling doors which make me jump out of my skin; and the horribly authentic moans and screams from hidden speakers. It is as if David Lynch directed *Casualty*. I leave the building a quivering wreck.

True to its billing, the front desk of the Robot Hotel on the edge of the park is 'manned' by a robot dinosaur and a robot woman. We elect to check in with the dinosaur but he doesn't seem in the mood, remaining motionless to our commands. While we wait for him to gather his thoughts and accept our reservation code, Lissen and I start a heated discussion about the last chocolate-covered macadamia nut in a box we have been sharing – a convenience-store staple to which we have lately become a little addicted.

Our raised voices at last prompt the dinosaur into action, and he begins to berate us in Japanese. Eventually, a member of staff is reluctantly forced from behind a curtain, like the Wizard of Oz, to check us in manually, which seems to defeat the point of all the costly animatronics. The 'robot luggage trolley' which accompanies us to our room is also a bit of a head-scratcher. It is glacially slow – it would have been quicker to carry our own bags; and yet another robot in our room doesn't really seem to work either. It squats on the bedside table and appears to serve no practical purpose other than to startle us by bursting into life in response to the TV or random movements. We can't figure out how to switch it off so it continues in this vein through the night, as if it has taken it upon itself to extract some information from us through Chinese secret police-style sleep deprivation torture techniques, abetted by the similarly random 'automatic' lighting system. At one point it occurs to me that we are the unwitting participants in one of those sadistic Japanese hidden camera shows, observed via a two-way mirror by someone operating the technology with the sole aim of nudging us towards emotional breakdown.

Never mind; as we leave the next morning I still proclaim Huis Ten Bosch the world's best amusement park. When I had first heard about it, I thought it sounded absolutely bonkers. A recreated Dutch city on the western coast of Kyushu seemed the most random thing imaginable. What on earth did the Dutch have to do with Kyushu? Why were the Japanese so infatuated with Holland?

Actually, it still seems pretty bonkers as we leave the next morning too, but then we come to Nagasaki and it all begins to make some sense.

Chapter 9

Sugar

The Portuguese were the first of the *nanban*, 'southern barbarians', as the early Europeans in Japan were called by the locals. A group of them arrived in Japan in 1543, having been shipwrecked on the islands of Tanega off the Kagoshima coast in southern Kyushu.

Famously, the Portuguese brought with them the method for tempura; less famously, they also brought the recipe for a type of sponge cake called Castella. I am sure the Japanese were grateful for the cake and fried stuff but after establishing a trading route from their bases in Goa and Macau to their new East Asian outpost, a small fishing village called Nagasaki, the Portuguese also helped fuel a civil war raging in Japan at the time thanks to their new-fangled firearms. And then the Jesuits set about their work. Within seventy years of their arrival, three-quarters of a million Japanese had converted to Catholicism but such evangelical zeal would eventually prove the Portugueses' undoing when the Japanese Christian farmers of the Shimabara peninsula staged a violent revolt against their rulers in 1637. The farmers were put to the sword, and the Portuguese were blamed for their rebellion. The remaining Portuguese traders were quarantined on a small, man-made island in Nagasaki harbour, called Dejima. Later, as he nervously regarded the rising influence of the Europeans in China, the ruler of Japan, Tokugawa Iemitsu (grandson of Tokugawa Ieyasu, the man who unified Japan), eventually kicked the Portuguese out of Japan altogether, making Christianity a capital offence in 1639. A notably hideous persecution of Japanese Christians ensued over the next few years, as graphically detailed in Martin Scorsese's 2016 film *Silence*.

Meanwhile, the Protestant Dutch had also arrived in Japan, in 1600. A ship, *De Liefde*, which had left Europe with 110 sailors a few years earlier arrived, again off the coast of Kyushu, with just twenty-four – this time red-haired – barbarians alive, the others having perished mostly from malnourishment and disease (astonishingly, you can see *De Liefde*'s figurehead of Erasmus in the National Museum in Tokyo). More Dutch arrived within a few years and settled in the town of Hirado, further north up the Kyushu coast from Nagasaki.

The British, too, followed their great rivals and set up their own trading warehouse in Hirado a few years later but, due to a combination of factors including more rewarding colonial activities elsewhere and sheer incompetence, they only lasted a few years before packing up and heading back to India. The Dutch stayed for quite a while longer, more than two centuries in fact. Their trade and knowledge became so important to successive rulers of Japan that they were granted a special exemption to continue doing business long after the country was almost entirely closed off to the outside world.

The 'Sakoku', as this period of Japan's closure was termed, began in earnest in 1651. During this time the Dutch were 'invited' to move to the island of Dejima, vacated by the Portuguese. Presumably, the Dutch imagined this would be a temporary sojourn, but they ended up staying confined to this tiny, crescent-shaped island until the American naval commander Commodore Perry sailed into Tokyo Bay in 1853 and forced the country to open up once again to foreign trade.

Two hundred years confined to an island measuring not much more than a single hectare: this is the curious story of the Dutch in Japan. During that time, the short, narrow wooden bridge connecting Dejima to Nagasaki's harbour-front was the only connection Japan had to the outside world, as far as Europe was concerned. No Japanese were allowed to leave, and no foreigners – at least no unaccompanied foreigners without very good reason to be there – were allowed to set foot on Japanese soil, on pain of very painful death. For Japan, most of the world was thus viewed through orange-tinted glasses, and Huis Ten Bosch is the bizarre, though in its own way quite logical, legacy of this Dutch–Japanese trading history.

Nagasaki has, of course, changed virtually beyond recognition since Dejima's construction, not least on account of the atomic bomb dropped by the Americans on 9 August 1945 but, remarkably, the Dutch traders' island enclave is still here, albeit surrounded by built-up, reclaimed land, and no longer inhabited by red-haired barbarians.

My family and I are standing at its entrance now, beside the two sea gates – one for import, one for export – which these days open onto a sea of traffic rather than galleons and junks. Through these gates first arrived an astonishing number of products, technologies and ideas which Japan now takes for granted.

After our discombobulating Huis Ten Bosch experience, today we are fortunate enough to be visiting Dejima with someone who can help us make sense of history. This is Junji Mamitsuka, director of Dejima's restoration office. He has overseen the restoration or re-creation of most of the Dutch buildings which grew up on Dejima during their residency in a motley assortment of styles and materials – some are wooden, others are clay-walled or clapboard – plus an allotment.

'For us Japanese, this island was almost like a foreign country,' Mamitsuka explains as we walk along Dejima's 'high street', stopping outside what was once the residence of the Dutch trading team. 'All of our trade with Europe came through this gate, and it was all controlled by Holland.'

In the next building are exhibits of the products which were introduced to Japan through those gates during the time of the Dutch. These included:

Nutmeg	Sloths
Cinnamon	Pumpkins
Black pepper	Orang-utans
Cloves	Wine
Ivory	Beer
Chillis	Vaccinations and stethoscopes
Chocolate	Tomatoes
Tobacco	Cheese
Coffee	Astronomy
Bread	Pineapples
Sugar cane	Photography
Elephants	Cabbages
Porcupines	Potatoes

I can't speak for the influence of porcupines on Japanese culture but modern Japan would be unimaginable without many of these products. Perhaps the most significant was sugar which the Dutch brought to Japan initially as sugarcane from South America via the Caribbean. Previously, sugar had only been imported in small quantities from China for medicinal purposes, but from the early eighteenth century onwards the manufacture of sugar from sugar cane increased rapidly, in part as a result of the development of the tea ceremony and its accompanying 'wagashi', or Japanese sweets (beet sugar, incidentally, also arrived via Dejima, in the nineteenth century).

Sugar was particularly influential on Kyushu's cuisine as the island's climate was ideal for growing sugar cane. To this day Kyushu's food is noticeably sweeter than that in the rest of Japan; the tares, or basting sauces – most commonly for eel – are much sweeter here than in Tokyo, for instance; the satsuma-age – the deep-fried fish cakes we had eaten in Kagoshima – are also sweeter; even the soy sauce is sweet on Kyushu, unpleasantly so, actually.

As we walk, Mamitsuka explains how, each year, the Dutch ships would arrive with their cargo in July and August, borne by the summer winds from Batavia (modern-day Jakarta) about a month away, and then leave in October laden with Japanese camphor, silk, pottery, precious metals like silver and copper, as well as sake. Of these, copper became by far the most valuable commodity to the Dutch. So rapacious was their appetite for it that, in the end, the Japanese had to ration them to two ships a year.

Apart from rare, closely monitored trips to meet the Tokugawa in Tokyo, for the rest of the year the resident employees of the Dutch East India Company (who ranged from several dozen in the seventeenth century to under twenty towards the end of the Dutch period), had little else to do but play billiards and badminton, and enjoy the semi-legal visits of the local prostitutes, resulting in numerous mixed-race children being born in Nagasaki, *Madam Butterfly*-style (Puccini's opera is set in the city, but features an early twentieth century American–Japanese liaison). And so, for most of the time, a captive Dutch community lived here on this fan-shaped piece of dirt, their only view of the outside world through the windows overlooking the harbour from where they would watch the less restricted comings and goings of their Chinese rivals in the silk trade.

The Dutch attempted as much as possible to live as they had done in Amsterdam, raising, slaughtering and consuming their own pigs, for instance, something severely restricted on the mainland, although they respected the ban on Christianity by celebrating the 'Winter Solstice' instead of Christmas. Some of them stayed for up to a decade at a time, going slightly mad in the process, one suspects. Their suffocating community is brilliantly evoked in David Mitchell's 2010 novel *The Thousand Autumns of Jacob de Zoet*, the characters of which are loosely based on real residents of Dejima; it has a denouement which also mirrors a real incident in which the British Royal Navy frigate HMS *Phaeton* sailed into Nagasaki harbour in 1808 to attack the Dutch. (France then annexed the Netherlands and for three years Dejima was the only place on earth where the Dutch flag was still flown.)

Today, the Dejima museum attracts almost half a million visitors a year and Nagasaki has turned its origins as an international trading centre, a city open to the world when virtually all others in Japan were closed, into a core element of its brand. But, as well as celebrating its Dutch connections, the city also acknowledges the considerable influence of the Chinese.

There was some contact with Korea elsewhere in Japan, but China was the only other nation permitted to trade with Japan during the Sakoku, which it did from its own, much larger enclosure, home to two thousand Chinese traders and staff, adjacent to Dejima in Nagasaki harbour. The Chinese were seen as less of a threat by the Japanese and were free to enter and leave their trading zone which is perhaps why, these days, their influence in the city is much more evident than that of the Dutch. We happen to be visiting during the Chinese New Year when Nagasaki's China Town erupts with spectacular festivities and feasting. The manager of the hotel where we are staying is part of the team that carries the dragon during the elaborate dragon dance. The dance is due to take place that night, and he invites us along to watch.

The celebration is set in a kind of makeshift open-air theatre in one of the city squares. Though it is freezing, the place is packed. Even after the Technicolor overload of Huis Ten Bosch, this is quite some spectacle with thousands of coloured paper lanterns, illuminated dragons and, in pride of place, a fifteen-metre-high light sculpture depicting the legend of the Monkey King. The skill of the dancers as they manoeuvre their dragon, mounted high up above their heads on long poles, through a complex choreographed routine is breathtaking, particularly when, after the dance, our new friend lets me try to hold the dragon's head: it weighs ten kilos and feels like carrying a small fridge.

Afterwards we walk back through packed alleyways illuminated with yet more lanterns, stopping on the way for a pork bun or two.

We sample more of China's culinary influence on Nagasaki at lunch the next day. This is Shippoku ryori, a multi-course banquet which blends Japanese, Chinese and, supposedly, Dutch influences although, perhaps fortunately, I can't spot anything Dutch about it. Radically different from the Kyoto style of kaiseki ryori, Shippoku ryori features more seafood, as well as pork and sugar, and is served in a less formal atmosphere. Once fashionable as far away as Tokyo, Shippoku ryori fell out of favour after World War II when the influence of American food grew and it was deemed both decadent during times of hardship, and too imitative of the Chinese. This is a shame, I think, as this may well be the world's first ever example of fusion cooking.

The meal is served for all four of us to share at a Chinese-style red lacquer round table at an historic ryotei, Hashimoto (ryotei are a type of traditional-style inn, usually with a restaurant attached). It begins with the ohire – a clear soup made from sea bream, with one of the fish's fins floating on the surface. Just as our spoons are poised at our lips, our host, Yumi Hashimoto, the third-generation owner of the restaurant, coughs loudly. It is explained that Shippoku tradition dictates that no one can take so much as a sip until the host or hostess says 'Ohire wo dozo', or 'Please enjoy the soup'.

Once she does, we tuck into the soup, followed by slow-simmered pork belly (the Chinese-influenced 'buta no kaku ni'); a stunning tempura course in which the tempura batter is made in the Nagasaki style with yolks only; a classic Shippoku cold starter, or 'shosai', of white beans; and 'umewan', or 'plum bowl', an adzuki bean and mochi 'soup' for dessert, also very sweet.

Pace is important to a Shippoku meal. Things begin quietly with the soup being consumed in silence alongside the cold dishes which are already on the table, then the sake starts to flow, toasts are made and there is a burst of action as special dishes are brought out. It ends with a sweet dessert which is also not a very Japanese way to finish a meal: the Dutch influence, perhaps.

The highlight for me is the chance to taste 'kue', a fish, known as 'ara' in Nagasaki, which is one of the few places where it is caught. This is 'longtooth grouper', rarer and more expensive than bluefin tuna, and a winter highlight of the menu at the absurdly expensive Manhattan sushi restaurant Masa, where dinner can cost upwards of $500 per person. I've read that the restaurant has it flown in directly from Kyushu at vast cost. Hashimoto-san whispers to me that it costs ¥500 per slice; the richness of flavour apparently comes because it feeds on konbu. I notice both Emil and Asger have left most of theirs so, when Hashimoto-san leaves the room, I swiftly vacuum up the remaining slices of the fish, which has been slightly poached – perhaps, again, in deference to the Chinese, who traditionally don't eat raw seafood.

The cost and complexity of a Shippoku mean that the locals in Nagasaki would rarely make it at home. Hashimoto is the kind of place to come for milestone celebrations, like weddings or birthdays. In the 1940s this traditional wooden house with its ornamental garden, sliding paper walls and *engawa,* or deck, stretching all the way around the outside, was a residence for the officers of the occupying US Army, and today it is one of the few places still to host geisha in Nagasaki (there are eighteen geisha remaining in the city: should you be interested, the going rate is ¥21,000 – £155 – for three hours of their company).

As we eat, as if arranged perfectly to complete the *Madam Butterfly* mood, a few snowflakes begin to descend delicately into the carp pond in the garden. A geisha would have been quite a nice addition, actually.

With its slow-cooked pork and sugary flavours Shippoku ryori reminds me a little of the food in Shanghai. Both cities have a notably sweet tooth, something also evidenced by Nagasaki's most famous cake, Castella, another of those *nanban* imports dating back several centuries.

Castella is either Portuguese or Spanish in origin depending on who you talk to (the Portuguese were said to offer it to potential Christian converts as a bribe) but, as usual, the Japanese have taken things a step or two further, refining the recipe over the centuries to create a super-moist slice of pale yellow spongy perfection, dense with tiny air holes and a thin, browned, soft crust on the top and bottom. It is a genuine Nagasaki icon, familiar in convenience stores the length of Japan, where it is sold by the slice. In Nagasaki long, rectangular boxes holding an entire Castella are a popular gift. Locals like to eat it with milk or green tea for breakfast and, slightly more improbably, the manager of Shokando, the best Castella shop in Nagasaki and supplier to the Emperor of Japan, assures me when we visit that the cake is especially loved by marathon runners because it gives them energy.

Asger, Emil and I are visiting the Shokando store in central Nagasaki, right by the iconic Megane Bridge (the oldest stone arch bridge in Japan, dating from 1634), to learn the secrets of their beautifully airy sponge. They make several varieties, all hand-baked in special wooden frames about a metre square. The premium product – the one sent to the Emperor's palace in Tokyo – uses a ratio of five egg yolks to three whites, along with rice syrup and Japanese sugar, which is unusually moist and I suspect a key ingredient. They use no raising agent, other than the egg whites. The key to that dense but light pound cake-style sponge is the 'awagiri' technique whereby the mixture is stirred three times during the baking, with steaming temperatures closely monitored by the highly experienced Castella baker.

Shokando's manager claims that the first documented recipe for Castella in Japan dates from the late sixteenth century but he knows little more of its history. For that, I will have to travel further north along Kyushu's western coast to Hirado, Japan's westernmost port, where the Europeans first settled. Leaving Lissen and Emil in Nagasaki, I drive there with Asger the next day in search of an edible history lesson which, he and I later agree, is the very best kind.

'The first Portuguese ships landed here in 1550, and they brought many cakes, including Castella. It came literally all the way from Lisbon.' As he explains the origins of his iconic cake, Toshiyuki Matsuo, the master baker of Tsutaya, the legendary Hirado confectioner, is preparing their special version of Castella, called Casdous. Casdous is even lighter and even sweeter than Castella because Matsuo beats even more air into the batter and, after baking, the sponge is cut into slices, dipped in egg yolk, dropped into hot sugar syrup and rolled in yet more large-grain sugar. It is unbelievably, almost intolerably, sweet, although its magnificently light texture somehow redeems it.

Tsutaya has been making Casdous here in Hirado for almost five centuries, but the company dates even further back, to 1502, before the Portuguese arrived in Japan. Matsuo is the twenty-fourth-generation owner. Hirado was, then, already a centre for confection before the arrival of sugar in Japan, back when they would have made jellied confections from adzuki beans or rice flour, the sweetness coming from fruit or honey. The ruler of Hirado throughout the period of Dutch and British trade was the head of the Matsuura clan, whose descendants remain prominent in the town. The family grew unusually rich by Japanese standards thanks to the trade with the newly arrived foreigners, while their remoteness from Tokyo afforded them an unusual autonomy. With this wealth and isolation, it seems, there also came a certain amount of self-indulgent thumb twiddling, and thus Hirado developed its own version of that ultimate time-frittering exercise, the tea ceremony.

The apogee of Hirado's tea preoccupation came in 1841 when the Matsuura ruler of the day demanded that Tsutaya make him one hundred different types of cake and wagashi for the tea ceremony to end all tea ceremonies. According to the records, Casdous was one of those cakes.

As Matsuo-san explains all this, it occurs to me that what came to Hirado all those years ago was more likely some kind of ship's biscuit: hard and dense and probably riddled with maggots. Though presumably named after the Spanish region of Castilla, Castella – and also Casdous – closely resemble a bready type of Portuguese cake called Pão de Ló. Obviously, there is no way a cake like that would have lasted a journey of many months. Rather, the Portuguese will have brought knowledge about oven-baking techniques which were new to Japan, and maybe the idea of baking with eggs too, but in their simplicity and almost artificial perfection the contemporary Castella and Casdous I tried during our days in

Nagasaki seem to me to be entirely Japanese creations, not least because the rice syrup and Japanese sugar were crucial in keeping the sponge moist.

Matsuo-san shows us how the wooden frames in which he bakes the Casdous are lined first with newspaper, then baking paper, with a final scattering of sugar over the surface, before going into his ovens (which I notice are made by a brand called Nanban). 'This has so much history, I can never change the recipe. It has been passed down by word of mouth over the years. My job is just to use the best ingredients I can, and respect that tradition.'

I give Asger a significant 'regard how deeply Matsuo respects history and tradition' look, but he is busy scoffing the pale yellow offcuts from a fresh-baked loaf of Casdous which another baker is expertly trimming.

I am curious about something. My question is not really related to cake and I hesitate as it is perhaps too personal. Given the fact that Matsuo was the twenty-fourth generation of a five-centuries-old company, did he ever have a choice over his own career?

'No, I had no choice! I was working here from when I was little. Then I went to train in Fukuoka and Tokyo but I realised how important Hirado had been in the tradition of sweets in Japan. It's a small town, but because it was the first town to get sugar it has a long history of sweet things. I started to feel a responsibility to keep Casdous going and the best quality I can make it, because it represents the history of this place.'

Matsuo has taken the family firm from strength to strength. Nine years ago, Tsutaya moved into a new, rather auspicious address down on the high street in Hirado. This was the former home of one of the most remarkable foreigners in Japanese history, an Englishman who was among the twenty-four 'red haired barbarian' survivors of *De Liefde*, the first Dutch ship.

William Adams of Kent was the ship's pilot and a skilled ship-builder. After a tricky initial period during which the Japanese confiscated all *De Liefde*'s weapons and the Protestant survivors were entirely at the mercy of hostile Portuguese Jesuit translators, Adams

managed to avoid execution. More than that, over time, in the kind
of yarn you might find in a rather implausible romantic novel, he
became a valued adviser to the great ruler and unifier of Japan,
Tokugawa Ieyasu – equivalent to a random, shipwrecked Japanese
sailor becoming the left hand of Henry VIII. Adams grew wealthy
through his connections, married a Japanese woman and became
the first foreigner to attain the level of samurai. And his life was
indeed the loose inspiration for an implausible romantic novel, James
Clavell's blockbuster *Shogun*, so in my head he is always played by
Richard Chamberlain.

Thirteen years after he had settled in Japan, Adams – who became
known by the Japanese name Anjin Miura – would be the first
contact for the British East India Company when, decimated by
scurvy, dysentery and cannibals encountered along the way, the
surviving crew of its galleon, the *Clove*, staggered ashore here in
June 1613. They had been at sea for over two years, despatched to
the part of the globe literally marked 'Here be dragons', bearing a
letter from King James I requesting permission to trade.

As we've seen, the great enemy of the English, the Dutch, were
already successfully established in Hirado and they would endure
here long after all other foreigners were driven out. Still today, 400
years later, every fourth Sunday in the month the local ladies of
Hirado dress up in Dutch costume and parade up the high street.
But when I first visited the town back in 2013 to research a story
about the 400th anniversary of British–Japanese trade for a British
newspaper, Union Jacks had adorned the main drag.

'You feel like you've come to the end of the world, don't you?'
my contact on that visit, ironically a Dutchman, Remco Vrolijk, said
as we had clambered aboard his titchy Daihatsu. Hirado certainly
felt like the end of Japan that day. 'If you want to experience a more
authentic side of Japan, this is the place,' beamed Remco, towering
above me in that irritating way the Dutch have.

Remco was a genial fellow obviously well liked in Hirado judging
by the greetings he received as we walked down the high street. He
took me to see the site of the original English warehouse, now a

noodle shop; we also saw Adams' house – now Tsutaya's gorgeous new showroom – and the place where Adams was buried in 1620, on a hill overlooking the town.

'You see that house,' Remco said pointing behind some trees as we stood on the hill. 'The family name is Miura, the name Adams took.' Relatives? Remco shrugged. 'Maybe. When Christianity was banned in Japan anyone with foreign blood hid their traces.'

To gain permission for the newly arrived English to trade, *Clove*'s captain, John Saris, needed to secure an audience with Tokugawa Ieyasu, which meant travelling to Shizuoka, at that time the Tokugawas' home city. Saris was accompanied on the four-week journey by Adams. Bear in mind Adams had been in the pay of the Dutch for years, even before arriving in Japan, and was clearly prospering personally. Thus, Saris and his crew had not received the effusive welcome they had expected from their countryman whom they had assumed to be unhappily marooned on the other side of the globe. The two men grew justifiably wary of each other. Saris distrusted Adams, describing him as 'a naturalised Japaner', while the English historian and expert on Adams, James Murdoch, likely echoed Adams' view of Saris when he described him as 'a mere dollar grinding Philistine with a taste for pornographic pictures'. The captain exasperated Adams by ignoring his advice on points of courtly etiquette, insisting on delivering King James's letter to Ieyasu himself along with a gift of the first telescope to leave Europe, but refusing to prostrate himself before the Japanese ruler as courtly etiquette demanded. But the journey also gave Saris time to observe the Japanese. In his journal he recorded that he liked their 'cheese' (tofu), and that the women were 'well faced, handed and footed' although he was somewhat put off by their practice of dyeing their teeth black.

Ieyasu lavished hospitality upon the new English visitor, perhaps out of respect for Adams. This time, though, it was Saris' turn to be exasperated as he learned that they would still have to travel to Edo – modern Tokyo, more than 600 miles from Hirado – to beg final permission to trade from Ieyasu's son, Hidetada.

Permission was finally granted, but the ensuing story of the English in Hirado is hardly bathed in glory. Though they learned to enjoy onsen and green tea, and fathered several children in the town, the Englishmen left behind to run the East India Company's trading station at Hirado went slowly mad on a diet of drink and whores.

In charge of English trade efforts towards the end, long after Saris had departed, was Richard Cocks, a man for whom the word 'hapless' might have been coined. Thanks largely to his naivety and indolence, the East India Company's Japanese adventure ended in unmitigated disaster. The English never did figure out what goods the Japanese wanted to buy or how to sell the products they had to offer. Cocks died on the journey home after the Hirado warehouse closed in 1623.

Back in Hirado, Remco and I had stopped by a bronze statue in Cocks' memory. I took a closer look and noticed that the plaque read 'Richard Cocs' (sic). Even in death, ignominy stalked the Englishman. He must have cursed the day he was not born Dutch.

I am happy to report that the British would eventually redeem themselves on the island of Kyushu. After Japan reopened to the world in the mid-nineteenth century, a Scot, Thomas Glover, arrived in Nagasaki, aged just twenty-one, bringing with him the many innovations of the British industrial revolution. He was the first man to drive a steam engine on Japanese soil; was heavily involved in the founding of the country's first Western-style factory, the Nagasaki Ironworks, which would eventually become the Mitsubishi Corporation (still a huge presence in the city); as well as the Japanese Mint and a coal mine. Perhaps most happily of all though, he helped to start the company which would become Kirin Beer.

So, beer. The Portuguese brought cake and tempura. The Dutch brought everything else of significance. But we British, we British gave the Japanese beer.

And then came the Americans …

Chapter 10

Burgers

There are eight US military bases in Japan, located the length of the country from Okinawa to Hokkaido and home to around 50,000 servicemen, 40,000 members of their families and 5,000 American civilians employed by the US Department of Defense. I have no particular view on this – it is none of my business – but I do find it quite astonishing that Japan is for now still, in a sense, an occupied land.

Particularly striking is the continued existence of the US military's Sasebo base, because it is located a little more than an hour from Nagasaki where the American Air Force dropped 'Fat Man', the second nuclear bomb, in August 1945, the first having been dropped three days earlier on Hiroshima.

Reunited with Lissen and Emil after Asger and I had taken our detour to Hirado, we all spent the next morning visiting the Nagasaki Peace Museum, close to the epicentre of the bomb.

Whatever the justification for the bombing of Nagasaki, the fact remains that American bombs killed tens of thousands of civilians here, devastated a city and contaminated the land for years afterwards. So, in that sense, the last thing one would perhaps expect to find is that, within a decade, a nearby town would embrace that most American of foods, the hamburger, to the extent that, today, the two – town and burger – have become synonymous. But this is precisely what happened in Sasebo which proudly proclaims itself the first city in Japan where burgers were served, and is known throughout the land as 'Burger City', complete with a burger-ish city mascot, drawn by Anpanman artist Takashi Yanase.

It could be argued that it was here, in this otherwise nondescript port town, that the invasion of Japan by the American fast food revolution began. This was where the Japanese began their inexorable – and some would say calamitous – move away from their traditional, relatively parsimonious, low-fat, vegetable-, soy-and fish-based diet to the current, meat heavy, deep-fried, fat-filled, fast food frenzy.

Here is Hideo Miyauchi, the Sasebo City tourist boss, in his cramped and cluttered office overlooking the concourse of the train station. We have come along to hear him tell the origin story of the Sasebo burger.

The Korean War brought many American servicemen to the city during the 1950s, he tells us, and, to cater for them, local restaurants started serving cheap beer and French fries. Soon, burgers were added to the menu, but no one, Miyauchi says, knows exactly when or who was the first to make them here. Actually, he admits sheepishly, the branding of Sasebo as Burger City didn't start until they were looking for a way to mark the city's centenary in 2001.

'We realised that the burgers were special for our culture here,' says Miyauchi. 'In daily life, everyone eats burgers but people from other prefectures thought what was unique here was that we eat them after drinking, when other Japanese might have a bowl of ramen.'

A map of all the burger places was duly drawn up, a burger festival organised and, aided by Takashi's mascot and a mention in Sasebo-born novelist Ryū Murakami's* novel 69 and the movie based on it, the branding of Sasebo as Burger City took off nationally.

---

* Ryū Murakami, sometimes referred to as 'the other Murakami', is as well known and respected in Japan as his friend, the internationally better known Haruki Murakami. When I once interviewed Ryū Murakami, we met at the suite he keeps just for writing in a posh, high-rise hotel in Shinjuku. (He keeps a hotel suite just for writing. I often think about this.) He was an intimidating figure and our encounter was even more awkward than it might have been due to an unfortunate misunderstanding: he thought I was there for a heavyweight profile which would examine the social issues he wrestles with in his novels – homelessness, poverty, inequality and so on. I just wanted his restaurant recommendations. He later refused to be photographed for the piece. I hope I can make up for it with this description of the excellent burgers of his home town.

At peak burger a few years back, there were nearly forty burger places in Sasebo; 50,000 people attended the city's burger festival; and a satellite Sasebo Burger 'theme park' opened in Tokyo. Today, the theme park has closed and there are thirty burger joints. I wonder aloud if the whole burger thing is running out of steam. Perhaps there is a movement away from fast food. Could the gourmet burger be the way to go?

'The Sasebo Burger is an icon. It is good quality, not fast food. It is cooked to order, it takes time,' replies the tourism chief, slightly tetchily. 'We don't call them *gourmet*, but we have special burgers all the time, like some made with Nagasaki beef, which won best beef in Japan in 2014, or there is one that is the size of a pizza and another with waffles. One restaurant is in an air raid shelter, you know.'

The interview is at an end, but that is OK. The tourism man seems actually to know very little about the origins of the burger in his town. We head off, clutching our Sasebo burger map, to the oddly named Log Kit, a small, first-floor restaurant decorated like a Wild West log cabin, just a couple of minutes' walk from the entrance to the US base. It seems to be one of the older burger joints, if not the oldest. Perhaps this is where the Sasebo burger phenomenon has its roots.

'My parents started this place when I was three, back then it was a laundry for the [US] base and we did some bike rental too. Then, when I was older, I was volunteering on the base teaching yoga and I saw how they made burgers there.' Nobuyo Maruta, a tiny woman in her late sixties, dressed as if for a rodeo in matching red shirt and stetson, is explaining how she did, and didn't, invent the Sasebo burger. 'McDonald's had started in Japan but I saw that the servicemen wanted a different kind of burger from that. They wanted the taste of their mothers' burgers, these big home-made burgers, a burger as a whole meal, so I improvised a recipe. I started the Sasebo burger!'

So, *she* was the one, the inventor of Sasebo's signature dish?

'Ha! Yes, I was thinking of getting it patented! No, no,' she continues, confusingly, from behind the bar where she is flipping burgers for our order, 'I'm not the one who started it. There were many diners serving the hamburgers back then, many American bars.'

Our burgers arrive. Mine is a Special Burger, a gigantic, towering affair featuring lettuce and onion and thick-cut bacon. It is a challenge to eat tidily but is very good, and does indeed remind me of the burgers my mother used to make. Asger, Emil and Lissen go for two bacon double burgers and a chicken avocado burger respectively, and tuck in with gusto. Emil says it is the best burger he has ever eaten.

I hesitate to turn to more sombre matters but ask Maruta-san how she explains the enthusiastic embrace by Sasebo of a dish so synonymous with the nation that had virtually destroyed nearby Nagasaki just a few years earlier?

'Since I was born I have been close to American people, like everyone in Sasebo. I had personal experience of them. Of course, because of the bomb some older generation said, "We can't eat burgers", but when I heard them say that, I said, "Shall we eat Americans instead then?" '

I suspect something of this last aside was lost in translation, but I take it to mean she felt that it was time to move on, despite the fact that her mother's family was from Nagasaki and several of them perished there in 1945. It sounds extraordinarily magnanimous but I don't think this attitude is so unusual in Nagasaki Prefecture. A couple of locals I spoke to described the essential difference between how the people of Hiroshima and Nagasaki reflect on their respective atomic disasters: Hiroshima, they said, stood for protest, while Nagasaki, perhaps because of the Christian history of the region, stood for prayer and reconciliation.

As Maruta-san and I chat, a tall American in his thirties with a buzz cut enters and starts looking at the take-out menu. Obviously a serviceman from the nearby base, I ask him what he thinks of

Log Kit's burgers. He mulls over the question with appropriate gravity for some moments before answering.

'This burger has much more pepper in it, and there's lots of dressings, mayo and ketchup and egg,' he says. 'I'll definitely be putting the fried egg in my burgers when I go home to the States. It's not really American style, though, it's American with a Japanese twist.'

Chapter 11

Arita

'It requires a strong personal commitment to become a craftsman here.' Atsushi Sakaida is very much not joking. Atsushi is the fifteenth-generation descendant of Sakaida Kakiemon, the most famous potter in Japanese history, and the son of Sakaida Kakiemon XIV, until his death in 2013 one of Japan's officially designated Living National Treasures. 'We believe that you should take your time to master all the techniques when you start your career as a potter. It is a lifetime commitment.'

Atsushi is showing Asger and I around the 344-year-old company's exquisite collection of vases, plates, cups and pots housed in a small museum at the entrance to the neatly kept factory compound.

We have stopped off for the afternoon in Arita, a small town with a big reputation, while Lissen and Emil continue on from our lunch in Sasebo, across the top of Kyushu, to our next overnight at Yamaguchi, on the next island east, Honshu.

Wedged in a steeply sided, forested valley in north-west Kyushu, the town of Arita is Japan's unofficial porcelain capital. This is where many of the plates and bowls I have eaten from in kaiseki restaurants up and down the land have been made, items of fragile, translucent beauty decorated with scenes from nature and the seasons which played a sometimes annoyingly allusive role in supporting and enhancing Japan's traditional multi-course meal. Of the more straightforwardly symbolic pairings, for instance, I remember a bowl with an autumn scene bearing chestnut rice, and a plate decorated with a seascape for sashimi, but more often the decoration would reference an image from traditional Japanese art which in turn would contain a visual pun which referenced back to one of the ingredients, or the month or the moon's phase, and so on. What hope did I have of solving these kinds of riddles? But even when I failed to interpret their symbolism, Arita pottery, with its almost Chinese-style bold reds and royal blues, was always distinctively, exquisitely beautiful.

I was drawn to the town itself by a chance encounter at the event I had attended a few months earlier at restaurant Nobu in Mayfair, London, the same one where I had asked Nobu about Asakusa Nori. Nobu-san, the stiff-backed, hamster-cheeked elder statesman of Japanese food in America and Europe, had been launching a new range of tableware co-created with the artisans of Arita, and I was lucky enough to be invited along to the celebratory dinner to mark its launch.

Before we sat down to eat in the private dining room of the restaurant, we had been shown a documentary made for the Discovery Channel about the collaboration between Nobu and the potters of Arita. It followed Nobu's quest to commission new pieces from them, as he explained the brutal realities of a professional kitchen's dish-washing regime on their fragile, decorative pieces. The subtext of the documentary was a hoped-for revival of a declining market for these makers of ornamental porcelain by getting them to create more everyday, usable pieces.

Some of the potters had travelled to London for the launch of the new tableware. I'd been introduced to this group of rather shy men with the air of country mice in the big city (for some of them it was their first time, not only in Europe, but abroad), and, when I realised that on this trip we would be passing Arita on our way across Kyushu, I asked if I might stop and see one of the famous workshops. Happily, they agreed.

Arita was the birthplace of Japanese porcelain. Korean artisans, who had learned porcelain-making techniques in China where the technique had existed for several centuries, had been captured during one of Japan's expansionist periods in the early seventeenth century and started making their wares on Kyushu. Instead of earthenware, which is made from clay, porcelain uses a type of white stone, kaolin, which is turned into powder and then mixed with water – traditionally by kneading with bare feet – to make a special clay. Following high-temperature firing, this produces far finer pieces. The Koreans had been making pottery in Kyushu for some decades when one of them discovered a source of kaolin in the hills of Izumiyama close to Arita, and production began of, initially, simple pieces decorated with indigo patterns and depictions of nature similar to, but more impressionistic than, those made in China.

It was here, too, that Sakaida Kakiemon (1615–53) began making overglazed enamelled porcelain in 1643, supposedly having learned that technique from a Chinese craftsman in Nagasaki. As the name suggests, the technique allowed Kakiemon to paint over the glaze and introduce more colour to his designs. He defined what remains the company's signature style, called 'iro-e' – literally 'a colour picture' – featuring predominantly red, yellow and green depictions of trees and birds, with plenty of white space in between.

The Dutch East India Company began exporting Arita porcelain from Dejima in 1659 to fill the gap left by a decline in the availability of Chinese porcelain because of their war with the British. As a result, the pieces produced in Arita, and later also those made further south in Kyushu's rival porcelain district of Satsuma, would become famous in Europe, cherished by monarchs and noblemen. They were among the first Japanese cultural artefacts to make it to Europe and were a source of immense fascination, but the canny Dutch also influenced the style of Arita-ware in the other direction, requesting Chinese themes and patterns to satisfy the European tastes of the time. By the late seventeenth century, Arita porcelain was more valuable than gold and it directly influenced the nascent porcelain industries in Meissen, Delft, Sèvres and Spode. Marie Antoinette's mother, Maria Theresa, ruler of the House of Habsburg, was a fan, as was Augustus II of Saxony who owned 20,000 pieces of Arita porcelain. He once reportedly swapped 600 soldiers for 100 pieces. Today, decorative art museums from the Topkapi Palace in Istanbul to the V&A in London have some of the five million Arita pieces said to have been brought to Europe by the Dutch, the ones which had survived a one-year voyage around Africa. Though these days the market for Arita-ware – sometimes called Imari-ware after the west Kyushu port from where it was exported – is nothing like as inflated as that for Chinese porcelain, pieces can still fetch tens of thousands of pounds at auction.

Atsushi Sakaida has agreed to show us behind the scenes at Kakiemon to areas usually off limits to the public. First, we are led to the workshop where pieces are hand-formed in ghostly white clay by men who have dedicated their lives to maintaining this rare craft. (I actually prefer the undecorated pieces to those that have been painted and glazed, but don't mention this.)

'If you become a Kakiemon apprentice you can expect to wait ten years before you actually get to make a finished piece,' Sakaida-san tells us. 'It takes thirty years to train properly before you can teach the next generation.' Some of the craftsmen have been there for over forty years. Ten years practising. Another twenty refining your skills. Graduating as a brain surgeon takes less time. I send a meaningful glance towards Asger who has been listening intently.

If Asger has a fault (and it's a big 'if', he is an amazing young man, and I say that from a position of complete impartiality), it is that, like many teens, he has less enthusiasm for sustained effort when it comes, say, to acquiring the complex motor skills required to play musical instruments, or doing the washing-up properly. I have brought him along today because I hope that Kakiemon will offer an inspiring insight into what one can achieve with intense focus and long-term dedication. As it turns out, the Arita motivation model is turning out to be more offputting than inspiring.

'The first few years they spend learning how to prepare the clay,' Sakaida-san continues. 'Then they practise on the wheel for some years. Only at ten years are they allowed to form something, usually something small and round like a tea cup.' Apparently there is no great 'coming of age' ceremony at this point. The satisfaction, Sakaida says, is all internal, personal. What's more, Kakiemon strongly discourages any artistic expression on the part of its 'shokunin' (directly translated as 'working person' or more accurately, 'artisan').

Continuity is always subservient to creativity. Despite this glacial career progress, Sakaida claims there is a zero drop-out rate for apprentices. I wonder if, given the time it takes to train, whether they have trouble finding new apprentices – something which had been a common concern when I had spoken to people within the food world in Japan. 'No, we have no problems. We always have plenty of enthusiastic young people wanting to work here.' Presumably it pays well? 'There is a strong personal commitment to being a shokunin. They are prepared that this career will have no end.'

I take that as a no.

Making Kakiemon-style enamelled ceramics is an extraordinarily involved process. A simple dinner plate, for example, will go through eleven stages including moulding, drawing, painting, firing, glazing and firing again, at any point during which a minuscule flaw might emerge meaning the piece must be destroyed. Pity the poor person in charge of the kiln: the local Izumiyama stone they use creates a clay with a distinctive kind of milky white colour, called 'Nigoshide'. This differentiates it from other white porcelains which can have a blue tint, but it is infuriatingly tricky to fire. Around half of the pieces entrusted to the kiln do not survive the process and so the kiln guy is presumably held responsible for the destruction of pieces over which people have slaved not just for days, but, in a sense, for years. 'Yes, there are moments of conflict, not exactly fights but ...' Sakaida trails off.

Though it is a Saturday, the Kakiemon craftsmen are still at work in a dozen or so workstations sunk down into the bare clay floor in a row beneath the windows so that the craftsmen's eyes are level with our knees. Just above their heads are planks of wood balanced across the beams, laden with the fruits of their work: stark white unpainted cups and pots and vases. Each worker sits hunched on a white cushion on a wooden bench over a potter's wheel. Beside them is a small barrel of water and an array of strange implements, guides, scrapers, callipers and something that looks like a small, padded cricket bat, all to regulate forms and sizes.

All the potters are men but in the painting workshop there are several women diligently decorating pots and vases beneath the focused light from Anglepoise lamps. They use thick brushes made from deer hair, with short, chunky bamboo handles. 'Preparing the clay is very physical, hard work,' says Sakaida by way of explanation for the gender split between the two disciplines. 'Painting is not so.'

There are two types of painters: one does outlines, the other fills in. We watch them through the window of their workshop which is arranged like a classroom with several rows of three painters sitting in silence, none of them, Asger points out, wearing headphones.

I hang back to ask Asger what he makes of all this. Could he imagine spending ten years learning a craft? 'Nooo, I don't think so,' he says. 'I think I'd move on pretty quickly somewhere else. I'm more a man of action.' I don't blame him. I suspect it requires a very specific mentality to flourish as a Kakiemon potter.

As we go to leave, I see one of the potters inspecting a freshly thrown cup. He holds it up to the light at different angles for a minute or so. He taps it to check for the correct thickness, then takes out a measuring gauge to check its dimensions. Though his expression remains neutral, clearly something has displeased him. He crushes the cup between both hands, and throws it in a bin.

Chapter 12

Tare

I had one final task to carry out while we were on Kyushu. One last puzzle I wanted to solve which, naturally, would involve one last meal that I wanted to eat. This particular dish would be the culmination of a year-long quest to find the oldest continuous tare still in use in Japan. What is a 'continuous tare'? Allow me to explain, but first a bit of a rambling introduction ...

There are two golden rules for journalists in the modern era: never comment online on another journalist's article, and never read the comments on your own. I routinely break both rules but occasionally the comments can be enlightening. I remember reading one beneath an online piece in the *Guardian* newspaper, for instance. The piece was about the wonders of Osakan cuisine and I had written it. The comment said something to the effect of, 'Well, I lived in Japan for a year and I can tell you Japanese food is all the same – everything's cooked in soy sauce and sugar.'

There is some truth to this. A lot of things do get simmered in soy and sugar in Japanese kitchens, with perhaps some dashi (the Japanese 'stock' made with an infusion or konbu and, typically, katsuobushi, with dried shiitake mushrooms) or ginger or garlic, or mirin – sweet cooking sake – as a sugar substitute. When I have been in Japan for more than a couple of weeks, I do sometimes yearn for a splash of lemon juice or vinegar to cut through the sugary umami flavours, but soy sauce and sugar provide such a potent combination of sweetness and amino acids that, for most of the time, they are hard to resist.

The apogee of the soy–sugar genre is tsukudani but, far from being monotonous, properly made tsukudani is, I think, one of the minor yet-to-be-discovereds of Japanese cuisine. It is made with a variety of ingredients, from the konbu left over after making dashi, to clams, to tiny squid, all of which are simmered, separately, in soy sauce and sugar to make different types of tsukudani. With a rich, fermented, almost beefy base note from the soy sauce and that addictive sweetness from the sugar, tsukudani is great for giving heft to rice or salads, to nibble alongside a bento box, or just with sake.

The sweet–savoury aspect of tsukudani is particularly intriguing to me. Ferran Adrià's brother Albert was probably the first modern-era European chef to push the boundaries of sweet and savoury with his desserts featuring olive oil, beetroot and bay leaf, all of which were considered quite radical back in the 1990s (macaron master Pierre Hermé should also get an honourable mention here, although his ketchup macarons have not stood the test of time). But Japanese cooking has long mixed sweet and savoury in this way – sugar is added to simmered vegetables, or the simmered beef dish sukiyaki, for instance, and it is in many of the tares, the sauces used to baste grilled foods. Often during a traditional kaiseki meal you will get something sweet early on when you might otherwise assume everything would be salty, or a course that mixes sweet with savoury (at a contemporary soba restaurant near Harajuku I recently had a great combination of prawns with persimmon as a starter, for instance). Tsukudani does something similar, it is simultaneously sweet and savoury.

It is possible to pinpoint the exact geographical location where tsukudani originated. The name of the place helps: Tsukuda-jima, a man-made island in Tokyo Bay. Tsukudani is still made here in three ancient shops not far from the lively street of okonomiyaki (a western Japan dish often described as a thick, savoury pancake, although it's so much more than that) and monjayaki (a sloppier, Tokyo version of okonomiyaki) restaurants for which the island is better known. The tsukudani district still feels like the fishing village it once was. I am told there are families who have lived here for generations and they tend to hold on to their homes and pass them down. Perhaps this is why it hasn't yet been swamped by high-rise apartment buildings, despite being within sight of the tower blocks of Ginza. Washing still hangs from the balconies, and there are little grocer shops and shrines dotted along the canals. The morning I had visited, a year prior to my family's trip to Japan, a shopkeeper was hosing down the pavement outside his door and kids played in the street, a rare sight in central Tokyo. At the point where I reached the wall which keeps this patch of reclaimed land safe from the Sumida River beyond, the air was rich and heavy with the smell of sweetened soy sauce. The island's three tsukudani shops are all on the street here by the river wall and one of them, Tsukugen Tanakaya, a seventh-generation business dating back to 1848, had agreed to let me visit.

The women who serve in the shop sent me round to the back of the building where, in a dark cave of a kitchen, I found Tsutomu Ebihara dressed in white waterproof dungarees and hunched over a large vat of bubbling black liquid on his stove.

'This was once an island of fishermen,' Tsutomu told me when I asked about tsukudani's origins. 'They used to stew the fish to preserve it, then, as preservation became less important, they began to concentrate on the flavour.'

These weren't just any old fishermen, though: they had been commanded to move from their original home in Tsukuda Mura in Osaka to the new capital, Edo, by Tokugawa Ieyasu, Japan's seventeenth-century shogun. Some say that one of the fishermen had saved the shogun's life, others that they were simply the best fishermen in Japan and they were needed to keep the fast-growing city of Edo supplied with seafood. They settled on this island in the bay just a couple of miles from Edo Castle, and were granted special fishing privileges.

'The smaller fish they couldn't sell, they would boil in sea water to preserve them,' Tsutomu said. Later, by stewing meat, fish, vegetables or even insects in soy sauce, they could not only preserve them but make them tasty and, with the advent of cheap sugar from home-grown sugar cane, that too went into the pot. The fishermen also realised that you could even reuse ingredients this way, like the konbu which had been simmered once to make dashi, which could then be turned into a tasty condiment for rice.

Today Tsukugen Tanakaya sells twenty different types of tsuku-dani, including my favourite which is made from tiny clams. When I visited, Tsutomu was busy making their best-seller, konbu, which is also the trickiest to get right (it burns easily, apparently).

'You boil konbu for three to four hours, cut it into bite-sized pieces, then simmer in soy sauce and sugar for an hour and a half,' he explained. It is hardly a complex process, and the soy sauce doesn't even need to be anything special – I noticed he was using catering-sized cans of Kikkoman – but there is a huge difference between cheap tsukudani and the good stuff: the latter will have a rounded flavour and still taste of the original ingredient rather than just sweetened soy sauce. A cheap one will taste like something burnt, with added salt.

Tsutomu's favourite was goby fish, a bottom feeder, in truth rather a smelly creature which usually tastes to me of soil. It changes into something deliciously savoury when simmered as tsukudani, but not delicious enough, apparently. As with so many traditional Japanese foods, tsukudani is in decline. 'It's not something you make at home because, well, the smell. And the people who eat it are dying off' was Tsutomu's bleak diagnosis. 'People eat more bread, more than rice these days, I'm sad about it of course but I can't really do anything about it.' There used to be half a dozen tsukudani shops on the island, back when a little mound of tsukudani was a regular feature of every schoolchild's bento box, but as consumption of rice has dropped, so has its accompanying condiment. 'Some younger sake drinkers are rediscovering it. Maybe one day all Japanese people will come back to it,' Tsutomu said unconvincingly.

Tsutomu had been rather wary at the beginning of our meeting but eventually he felt at ease enough to reveal the secret of great tsukudani: the tare, or basic sauce, which he said had its origins back when the company was founded in 1843. Every day, he said, he put the leftover sauce to one side and then, the next morning he would use it as the base for the next batch of tsukudani. This 170-year-old, continuous 'mother' sauce was the secret of the special Tsukugen Tanakaya flavour.

In Japan tare – pronounced 'tah-ray' – is ubiquitous. Or, rather, 'they' are ubiquitous, as tare ingredients and their ratios vary. Tare is basically a multi-purpose, savoury-sweet, dark brown sauce. As well as providing the base for tsukudani, it is used in numerous other dishes. Tare is, essentially, soy sauce sweetened with mirin or sugar, sometimes augmented with garlic or ginger, sometimes reduced or thickened. It can be brushed over yakitori or unagi (freshwater eel) prior to grilling. You see types of tare thinned for use as a dipping sauce for sukiyaki or shabu-shabu, or as a trans-lucent glaze ('nikiri') brushed on nigiri by sushi chefs. Confusingly, tare is also the word given to the super-intense flavour base of ramen soup – another potent, brown, soy-based liquid usually added to the bowl before the broth (though, sometimes it comes after), kind of like its essence, or as some ramen chefs I have spoken to like to claim, 'its soul'. It is also a close relative of the super-addictive, thickened Terikayi-style sauces which are slathered on tako yaki (savoury octopus doughnuts), and okonomiyaki. Those tare can have everything from fruits (apples, tomatoes) to sesame oil, herbs or spices added; basically, you could brush okonomiyaki sauce on the seat from an old railway carriage and it would taste great.

As I walked back to the Metro station that day on Tsukuda island my thoughts kept returning to the tare. Could Tsutomu's sauce really have had its origins in the mid-nineteenth century, before the internal combustion engine, before the electric light bulb, before the telephone? I had long been fascinated by this practice, widespread among Japanese chefs, of using a tare during the day, putting the leftover sauce in the fridge, and then simply topping that up the next morning and continuing – as if this absolutely did not constitute any kind of health hazard – for many years. I had eaten at yakitori joints where they had been doing this with the same tare for decades. Sometimes, when a new apprentice leaves a master yakitori chef to start up on their own, the master will donate some of his own tare as a kind of 'starter', much as a baker might with a sourdough starter. Once, I visited a small, hole-in-the-wall yakitori place which claimed their tare was over *sixty* years old. I had heard of another which claimed theirs could be traced back through continual usage to before World War II, and now this one, at Tsutomu's Tsukudani kitchen, which supposedly went all the way back to the mid-nineteenth century.

This set me thinking about what the oldest continuously used tare in Japan might be. And thus my quest was born, a quest which eventually took me on another detour while we were visiting Kyushu on this latest trip. As with the nature of much that I do, this 'quest' was not especially focused, nor indeed all that taxing. It was more an excuse, in this case to eat some great unagi at a restaurant which by chance lay en route from Arita to our next overnight stop in Yamaguchi. It was here that I believed I had tracked down a tare whose longevity could beat all the others, even Tsutomu's, by quite a few years ...

I can smell my quest's end, the oldest tare in Japan, before I have even entered the doors of Motoyoshiya, a three centuries old unagi restaurant in Yanagawa, in Saga Prefecture, northern Kyushu. Beside the quaint thatched entrance to the restaurant is a massive industrial air vent blackened with a thick layer of eel grease. It is sucking cooking fumes from the kitchen and expelling them straight out onto the street and is a far more effective promotional tool than any sandwich board, neon light, or ten foot sign could ever be. Asger and I stand there a while, hungry after our Arita pottery tour, savouring the meaty aromas of grilled eel and what is presumably that ancient sauce. Dear God, it smells good. You can almost *eat* the air.

Asger hastens through the door and I follow him. We are met by the restaurant manager, Ken Ichiyasu, husband of the daughter of the Motoyoshiya family which has owned the restaurant since it opened over 335 years ago.

'We serve exactly the same dish that they did when they opened in 1681,' beams Ichiyasu, a jovial, chubby fellow dressed head to toe in Champion sportswear. The dish is unagi no seiromushi, grilled freshwater eel on rice with shredded omelette – the omelette being a special addition of the region. The rice itself is covered in the magical tare and steamed in a wooden box, known as a 'seiro'. Meanwhile, eel fillets are grilled over charcoal and intermittently dipped in the sauce (a technique called 'kabayaki'), before being placed on top of the rice with the shredded omelette scattered down the middle. The whole box gets one final steaming prior to being served in a gorgeous lacquered box.

Before we get to taste it, we must pay homage to the tare. Through the kitchens Ichiyasu leads us to a separate alcove where a chef is busy tending to white-hot coals and flayed eels.

'This is the most important treasure of this restaurant,' says Ichiyasu, pointing to a very large ceramic mixing bowl brimming with a glossy black sauce. I place my nose inches from its brooding, mirror-still surface and breathe deeply of its fishy-caramel aroma. 'Nobody can copy this tare or make it at home. We have been making it, without stop, for over three centuries.'

Wrestling with an almost overpowering urge just to lap directly from this mythical liquid like some ravenous wolf, I am nevertheless aware that I have to present Ken with some awkward scientific truths about his tare. I tell him about the analysis that was carried out by a Japanese TV show a year ago, which proved that every single molecule of a tare used in this continuous manner will in fact be entirely replaced within a few weeks' use.

To my surprise, Ken agrees: 'Oh, no, no, we also don't believe there is 330 years of flavour in this. Of course not. But there is a secret ingredient.'

The two main ingredients of Motoyoshiya's tare are simply soy sauce and sugar syrup, but after a little more gentle probing the 'mystery' third ingredient turns out not to be so secret after all.

'The secret ingredient of the sauce is the eels that are dipped in it!' says Ken. 'The more eels are dipped in it, the better. This is where the flavour is. So, you can imagine, it tastes *really* good at our busiest time in July and August. We can serve up to three hundred eels a day then. But,' he adds, suddenly serious, 'the method for making the tare is secret.' (I'm guessing 'gentle heating'.)

As Ken says, summer is the traditional eel-eating season in Japan, the, to me always rather odd, logic being that hot, oily, grilled eel dipped in a sweet brown sauce and served on a large mound of cooked rice somehow 'cools' you and 'gives you energy' to combat the muggy heat of a Japanese summer. The truth is, as Ken admits, eel actually taste better in winter because they take on more fat to insulate them against the cold. He also claims that Kyushu unagi, in particular those from around Yanagawa City which is criss-crossed by canals and lies close to Ariake Bay, are the best in the world.

Yanagawa was once a prime habitat for eels, in particular 'hoshi-ao', a type of white-spotted eel found in this zone between the rivers and the sea, but today there are very few of any kinds of Japanese wild eels left (proper name Anguilla japonica). The population has declined by 90 per cent over the last thirty years and the unagi have belatedly been placed on the government's 'Red List' of endangered fish. (It's a similar story in Europe, where the eel population has decreased by over 80 per cent since the sixties, dropping off especially dramatically in the eighties to the extent that the eel is now also officially an endangered species there.)

Just as we are getting to know the freshwater eel, it is disappearing. Until the early twentieth century when research began to throw light on this strange creature's life cycle, the reproductive cycle of the eel was a dark mystery which had piqued the interest of some of the greatest minds in history. No one had the faintest idea where they came from or how they reproduced. Aristotle believed they were a type of earthworm; Freud spent ages studying their genitals. Today, it is understood that half of the world's population of eels spawn in the Sargasso Sea, while the other half spawn in the Western Mariana Trench area, Japanese eels coming from the latter. They wriggle their way thousands of miles across the oceans to freshwater rivers and lakes, where they can live for ten to fourteen years.

Japan consumes around three-quarters of the total global eel catch; these days most eels consumed in Japan are imported from farms in China. Wild Japanese eels are increasingly rare and expensive; their scarcity has forced prices up as much as tenfold in recent years, leading to the closure of several venerable eel restaurants across Japan.

'It is a big, big problem,' says Ken of the Japanese unagi's decline. 'There are two reasons: climate change, and because their habitat has been taken by industrial farming.' The global eel population has also been struck by a devastating parasite while other manmade obstacles, like weirs and locks on rivers, block their migration.

These days, all of Motoyoshiya's eels are farmed on Kyushu, down south in Miyazaki and Kagoshima Prefectures. Farming produces fatter eels with smaller bones and a more consistent flavour, and they also don't smell quite so much during cooking. But merely breeding baby eels, or 'glass eels', which have been caught in the wild is no solution to the impending extinction of the species. For that, someone needs to find a way to actually breed them in captivity sustainably. Until then, researchers at Kinki University have recently developed faux-unagi, using catfish fed a special diet to make them more oily and counter their characteristic soil flavour. Their eel-ish catfish had recently gone on sale, pre-grilled, in limited quantities.

'We would never use that,' says Ken. 'But I think someone, one day, will figure out a way to breed unagi in captivity. It will happen, but it will be very expensive, I'm sure.'

Back to the tare. What if I offered him fifty million yen for the entire bowl? He laughs, and shakes his head. Fifty billion? Nope. The sauce is the source of the restaurant's repute and wealth. What about the hygiene issues of an everlasting tare? In the West, the restaurant would likely be closed down for all sorts of health and safety violations. 'We warm it through every day and the whole box of rice and eel is steamed, so that is not an issue.'

I stand and watch the chef tending to a dozen or so eel fillets in his smoke-and-tare-encrusted cocoon. Every surface of the alcove is coated with a thin layer of brown gunk. He dips one fresh-grilled fillet, now glistening with fat, into the tare then places it back on the grill. A few drops of that precious sauce drip down onto the hot coals and catch light, turning the air deliciously smoky. My mouth is a waterfall. Time to eat.

In one of the restaurant's private dining rooms, kneeling on the tatami mat before a low table, Asger and I are each served our own red lacquer boxes of rice topped with two fillets of tare-encrusted eel. The eel are the colour of creosote, their tare coating shimmers in the light. They taste of fish fat and sugar, soy sauce and, yes, I do believe, in their depth and richness, I can also detect an echo of centuries past, of the residue of a million eels. I just hope there are a million more to come.

CHUGOKU

Chapter 13

Clams

The test tubes are lined up along the train window and, though it is true that Lissen's Okinawan sweet potato plants are not quite as vivacious as they once were, the small green sprouts are at least still alive and enjoying the light. There is plenty of it as the snowbound landscape reflects the morning sun into the carriage of our Limited Express stopping train from Yamaguchi at the western tip of Japan's main island, Honshu, along the Sea of Japan coast.

The Limited Express is no Shinkansen, but that's OK. I have deliberately chosen this route through Shimane Prefecture to slow our pace. On Kyushu we hurtled from town to town like hungry Pac-Men gobbling up sights and flavours, but in this part of Japan, which I have not only never visited but never even considered visiting, I have heard that life moves at a more sedate pace.

This is the 'Other Japan', as the Japanese refer to it, the dark side of the moon, a place of spirits and legends, ghosts and demons, where many of the country's myths and fables arise. Shimane is the least densely populated prefecture in Japan; there are fewer people here than even Hokkaido, and it is depopulating the most rapidly, too. Not only is there no Shinkansen line here, there are no plans for one either, there are few main roads, and the only major town is the 'City of Water', Matsue, home to 200,000 people and our destination today. For an hour, I see not a single person from my window, only bamboo forests, mountains and rice fields on one side, white waves on the other.

Shimane attracts the fewest foreign tourists of all Japan's regions but it does have one major attraction, a shrine, perhaps the oldest in the country (no one knows exactly when it was built), called

Izumo Taisha, which draws several million people a year – not just Japanese visitors, but also Chinese and Korean. Izumo Taisha is dedicated to Okuninushi, the god of marriage, who is also god of the harvest, of business and of health. Oh, and he also created Japan itself. But mostly this is the shrine for single women to come and pray to find a partner and so, as you might imagine, it is also quite a draw for single men: a kind of spiritual speed-dating site, although there is not much evidence of anyone pitching the woo when we visit. It is, though, an extravagantly serene place, surrounded by massive cedars, with a vast inner sanctuary, off-limits to the public, and public prayer halls, the entrance to one of which is bedecked with a monstrous-sized *shimenawa* (the braided rice straw rope meant to purify buildings), the largest one in Japan. It hangs there like the cable for a straw suspension bridge.

Matsue has another cultural claim to fame. This was, for a while, the home of Patrick Lafcadio Hearn, the late-nineteenth-century, one-eyed, Irish-Greek journalist, who moved here in 1890, married a Japanese woman, the daughter of a local samurai (she was his second wife: his first was a teenage ex-slave, whom he met during his time in Cincinnati – an interesting man, Mr Hearn). Alongside a career as an English-language teacher, Hearn wrote numerous books about Japan, often decrying what he saw as the westernisation of the country following the end of the period of national closure. Though he and his writings are largely forgotten these days, Hearn was witness to a fast-vanishing, feudal Japan with which he was clearly enchanted. As he wrote towards the end of his life: 'What is there, finally, to love in Japan except what is passing away?'

At the exquisite ex-samurai house, built in 1868, where he lived for fifteen months when he first moved to Japan, we meet Yumiko Tane, head of the Lafcadio Hearn Memorial Museum.

'Everyone in Matsue learns about him when they are growing up,' says Tane-san, a petite, middle-aged woman with close-cropped hair. 'I like his writing because he has such a strong sense of the five senses. When I read him, it's like I see the images in my head. He really brings to life the colours, sounds – perhaps because he was partly blind. And as a Japanese person, it's always interesting to see the things he noticed that we wouldn't.'

Hearn particularly cherished the ghost stories and legends which abound in Shimane. In *The Chief City of the Province of the Gods*, the book he wrote about his first home in Japan, he retells a legend concerning Matsue Castle in which an anonymous maiden of the city was interred alive under its walls during construction 'as a sacrifice to some forgotten gods. Her name has never been recorded; nothing concerning her is remembered except that she was beautiful and very fond of dancing.' Hearn records that, since the castle was finished, there has been a law in Matsue prohibiting girls from dancing in its streets. 'For whenever any maidens dance the hill Oshiroyama would shudder, and the great castle quivers from basement to summit.'

Hearn also records a fondness for the sunsets over Lake Shinji, Japan's seventh largest lake beside which Shimane is situated: ' ... the light is gentle as a light of dreams: there are no furies of colour; there are no chromatic violences in nature in this Orient. All in sea or sky is tint rather than colour, and tin vapour-toned.' The Shinji sunsets are still famous in Japan, although the sun does not put in an appearance during our stay.

Hearn left Matsue for the warmer climate of Kumamoto on Kyushu as soon as he could (I noticed his house had only paper screens, no glass), and the locals apparently gave his wife a hard time for marrying a foreigner, but it is in this forgotten-feeling city that his memory is most cherished in Japan today.

If you ask Japanese people for Matsue's most important contribution to the culture of Japan, they will more likely mention the tea ceremony. The city's particular 'school' of tea ceremony is considered one of the three greatest, along with Kyoto's and Kanazawa's. My limited tolerance of Japan's tea ceremonies is a subject of record but I want to experience Matsue's own version of this archaic and belaboured ritual because the city is the biggest consumer of matcha in the country and so I assume they are quite good at making it.

Matsue's tea ceremony was created by the city's late-seventeenth-century feudal lord, Harusato Matsudaira (also known as Fumai). As well as the pedantic and tediously overcomplex preparation of matcha, the ceremony features three specific types of apparently rare and valuable wagashi – wakakusa (which is coloured green), yamakawa (pink and white sugar blocks) and Natane no Sato (coloured yellow by rape seed flowers) – about which Fumai was inspired to write special poems.

We sample both the ceremony and the wagashi at Fumai's own tea house which, remarkably, still exists up on a wooded hill overlooking the city.

It is a thin line between serene and mind-numbingly boring and I am afraid once again, for me at least (and I feel confident that I speak for my family too), this tea ceremony crosses that line pretty much within the first minute as our instructor, a stern, bespectacled woman, explains the absolutely vital importance in observing the difference in the pitch of the thatched roof of Fumai's tea house compared to the angle of pitch in the roofs of other tea houses of the same vintage. The entrance, she continues, is 70 × 70cm, in order to force guests to bow upon entering. This supposedly renders all visitors equal but also, I can't help feeling, perhaps undermines some of the basic principles of hospitality. Meanwhile, a toilet, built around the same time as the tea house, is located nearby to reassure guests during the endless bladder-bursting ceremony. However, our guide notes that it was built as a *non-functioning* toilet. It could be that I got this wrong, but after repeated questioning we are assured that it is, and always was, a purely decorative lav which also seems unnecessarily sadistic, even by the standards of the tea ceremony.

The matcha – when we finally get to taste it after the instructor invites us, first, to appreciate the smaller bubbles on its surface and note how they contrast with other tea ceremony frothing techniques which encourage larger bubbles, and then to spend an appropriate amount of time admiring the beauty of the bowl in which it is served, turning said bowl 90°clockwise, and lifting it to our lips in the prescribed manner with the palm of our left hand beneath it, then turning it back 90° – is nice enough, but the wagashi are almost intolerably sweet.

Afterwards, we are in need of simpler, quicker fare. A local Izumo soba restaurant supplies it. Izumo soba is unique in that the entire buckwheat seed is ground to make the flour (usually the husk is polished off), and the noodles are served in the liquid in which they are cooked. It is a dark and satisfying bowl of noodles, a proper winter dish, but, as good as it is, the local soba is not among the legendary 'Seven Delicacies' of Lake Shinji, which are the real reason we have come to Shimane.

Around twenty-eight miles in circumference, Lake Shinji is separated from the sea by a thin sliver of land which, on a map, makes the lake look more like a lagoon. Matsue sits between Shinji and an even bigger lake, Nakaumi, to the east. Nakaumi is salt water, Shinji is 'brackish', meaning it mixes salt- and freshwater. This delicately balanced ecosystem is what makes it so special for the tasty creatures which dwell in it but, it turns out, it has also left them extremely vulnerable to environmental changes.

It is six o'clock the next morning and Emil and I are swaddled in all the clothing we have brought with us to Japan. We are sitting in a small dinghy with an outboard motor, piloted by Masaki Kawabara of the Shinji Fisheries Cooperative Association, rocking gently on the waves in the middle of the lake alongside another boat.

Junichi Yano, the man in the other boat, has been a shijimi fisherman for over a decade. The black, thumbnail-sized shijimi clams are the most famous of the lake's Seven Delicacies. As we chat, Junichi lifts up a large metal, cage-like scoop on the end of an eight-metre pole, or 'joren'. The pole itself I would struggle to lift, but the cage apparently weighs another 15kg: loaded with clams it can total over 25kg. The cage is deliberately weighted in order to plunge effectively into the lake bed to scoop up its precious prize: the umami-rich clams which are sought after the length of the country. As everyone in Japan knows, shijimi clams make the best miso soup.

'You have to learn to use the energy from the currents to help you move the joren,' he explains. The fisherman lowers the cage into the freezing water and a few moments later empties its contents with an almighty clatter into a sorting machine on his boat.

Junichi-san's daily quota has been slashed by 40 per cent in recent years, but he still struggles to achieve it. He worries about the future of the clams because the lake's delicate balance of salinity and oxygen is highly variable, depending on season and climate, and is being affected by increasing temperatures and pollution.

Later that day we taste the clams at Omoigawa, a near-hundred year-old restaurant known for its Seven Delicacies menu. The delicacies are seasonal so we only get to sample five – suzuki (sea bass), unagi, koi carp, shirauo (whitebait) and the shijimi clams, of course. Late summer is the time for moroge ebi, a type of shrimp, and amasagi, or smelt, a small, silver fish, the other two delicacies.

The carp is the best dish: the raw fish fillets have been sliced to resemble noodles, then dusted with fish roe. The whitebait are also excellent in an egg dumpling served in an oddly sweet dashi. And the shijimi-based miso soup is absurdly rich with a deep, meaty umami flavour.

Chef Nagao Tadashi prepares all this for us in a corner room of the restaurant looking out over the lake. After the meal we chat about the delicacies. He is not optimistic for their future as he confirms the lake has been hit by a triple whammy of recent warmer winters, dire pollution from local industry and pesticides from rice paddies, which has been happening since the 1960s.

'Just about everything is declining,' he says. 'Especially the amasagi, because it needs cold water. The lake is only about six metres deep at most, so it is more affected by the heat because the fish can't go deep to keep cool. The local authority has tried to revive the stocks, but it isn't working. This year the shirauo, which usually start in November, didn't turn up until the New Year, and only in small amounts, and then in dribs and drabs in January.' The unagi we had eaten wasn't from Shinji as they no longer grow large enough to eat.

There seems to be a contradiction in the way the Japanese approach their natural surroundings. Most Japanese I know deeply appreciate nature and the seasons, and the natural world is of course inextricably intertwined with their national religion, Shintoism. My Japanese friends spend as much time as possible in the countryside and speak wistfully of one day perhaps retiring to Hokkaido or Okinawa, or walking the temple route on Shikoku. At the same time, I was hearing these stories of the desecration of Japan's nature by its industry and farming. This is by no means exclusive to Japan, of course, but there is something distinctive about the Japanese's relationship to the natural world. As Alex Kerr writes in *Dogs and Demons: The Fall of Modern Japan*, though worshipping nature and the seasons, the Japanese also do everything they can to control the natural world: channelling rivers, concreting over hillsides and cluttering their coastline with billions of those jack-like concrete sea defences. Though some of these measures might be misguided, they are a perfectly understandable reaction to the earthquakes, eruptions, tsunamis, landslides and floods with which these islands are regularly and fatally beset, but there seems to be a curious tension in relations between man and nature in Japan.

I was determined to find a more positive story about Japan's natural resources, a story of regeneration, sustainability or good husbandry. It came sooner than I expected, and on the shores of another of Japan's great lakes, although this particular delicacy did have a bit of a stinky sting in its tail.

KANSAI

Chapter 14

Rotten Fish

We have left Matsue and taken the train to Kyoto where we are staying in a *machiya*, one of the city's historic merchant townhouses. These atmospheric wood- and earthen-walled buildings are distinctive for being far deeper than they are wide on account of an ancient tax on shop fronts; this one also happens to house a working weaving factory so every day from nine to five we have the pleasure of watching the weavers work through the floor-to-ceiling window of our first-floor living room.

From Kyoto, the morning after we arrive, I take a local train alongside the western shore of Biwa, Japan's largest lake, fifteen miles north of the city. I travel not in hope but in trepidation for I have a date with possibly the most feared and notorious foodstuff in Japan.

One of the things that surprised me the most when I first began learning about Japan's food culture was the vast array of fermented or 'rotten' foods that have existed there for centuries. For some reason, I had got it into my head that, because the Japanese did not have a tradition of eating bread, cheese or dairy products (though they certainly do eat all of these things these days), or kimchi, they didn't like *any* pungent or stinky foods.

I could not have been more wrong. Just how wrong had been confirmed by my first encounter with shiokara – salted and fermented seafood, guts included. Shiokara is typically made from squid, crab, or sea cucumber flesh and their innards, but anything fishy goes where shiokara is concerned, it seems. Initial encounters confirmed that shiokara was exactly what you would expect from rotten fish

guts: slimy, stinky, putrid, fetid and gag-worthy, a substance so repel-
lent it made *andouillette* (French pork colon sausage) or *casu marzu*
(Italian maggot cheese) look like baby food. But at least now I had
reassessed my preconceptions about 'Japanese people only liking
things that don't taste of much and are preferably white'.

Of course, one moment's reflection on the methods used to make
soy sauce, miso, katsuobushi, sake, the various types of pickle, mirin,
konbu and the fearful natto (fermented soy beans) ought to have
alerted me to the fact that the Japanese are masters, perhaps *the*
masters, of the preservation of foods and the enhancement of their
flavour through the use of microorganisms, bacteria, fungi, yeasts
and enzymes. Less well known is the fact that the Japanese have
been making fermented fish sauce for centuries too (by the way, it
is the best in the world) and, so, now, as young chefs with beards,
tattoos and leather aprons in the West are suddenly becoming
obsessed by all things 'rotten', it is to Japan that they are turning
for inspiration.

I have worked hard to acquire, if not an appreciation, then at
least the ability to stomach the more aggressive of Japan's fermented
foodstuffs, but this new openness was sorely challenged during one
recent meal. I was visiting Tokyo alone this time and had taken up
an invitation to dine with Muneki Mizutani, the former editor of
Dancyu magazine, Japan's most popular food monthly. Towards the
end of our meal the chef at the izakaya where we were eating
started bringing out a few of his home-made fermented delights –
crab, squid and sea cucumber ovaries. I considered making my
excuses but it turns out that, as with everything else, there are also
good and bad fermented fish guts, and these were genuinely excellent, the kind of thing you would eat even if you weren't under
unavoidable social pressure as a guest of one of Japan's greatest
gourmets. Of course, the sake helped, and I don't mean that sar-
castically; shiokara is made to pair with sake. The salty, yeasty, umami
flavours created by converting fish protein into super-tasty amino
acids harmonises especially well with sake, plus the booze cuts through
the gloopiness of the guts.

These are the kinds of experiences I have come to expect when I dine out with Mizutani-san. He is easy to spot in a crowd with his thick head of prematurely white hair (he is in his early forties) and penchant for lumberjack shirts. A man of few words carefully chosen, he seems to know everyone in the Japanese food world which is why he gets to taste the special stuff, the off-menu stuff, the stuff food lovers crave.

That evening, as we tucked into the small dishes of rotting fish innards the conversation turned to what was, for me, a mythical dish in the same category, and supposedly the origins of sushi itself: funa zushi. This was an ancient method of preserving carp by salting them then packing them in cooked rice. The salt kills any dangerous bacteria and, as the rice decays, the fish are preserved by the lactic acid which this generates.

Generically, the technique of using rotting rice this way is known as 'nare zushi'. It is said to have originated in Thailand or perhaps Vietnam but also has relatives in China. There are records of it being used in Japan dating back to the eighth century, to preserve not just carp but different types of seafood and also game meat. Funa zushi, ideally made with pregnant female carp with their roe intact, was these days rare but still a speciality of Lake Biwa, fifteen miles east of Kyoto.

Funa zushi is typically left to do its thing for up to three years during which time the fish's bones soften and the flesh is said to take on a cheesy texture and flavour, but Mizutani casually mentioned that he had in his fridge some ayu – sweet river fish – which had been fermenting in this way for *eight years*.

'Eight years?' I said.

'Eight years,' he nodded.

'That I would love to try,' I said, not meaning it *at all* and never thinking for a minute that such a frightening eventuality would ever come to pass. But then, some days later, I received a message that Mizutani had a surprise for me. That's how it works with him. He never contacts you directly; communications always go through an intermediary. He's like the Pope. But if you are at all interested in food, an invitation from him is not to be ignored. If he sends word, you come running because you are guaranteed a meal to remember. And so it was that he and I met at Utou, a little wooden cave of a restaurant hidden away on the first floor of a building in Ogikubo, a quiet part of western Tokyo. It belongs to Aomori-born chef, Satoru Kon, who served us from behind a wooden counter dressed in monk-like, brown robes. Muneki had also invited along Chieko Fujita, another prominent food writer who specialises in all things fermented.

We started the evening's journey into the funky world of fermented Japanese foods with a glass of unfiltered sake the consistency and colour of wallpaper paste, which Chieko had brought along.

'I was sent to write about a sake brewery about twenty-five years ago,' Chieko told me when I asked her where her obsession with fermented foods started. 'And I became fascinated by it. Young people were not interested in sake at that time, but I started to realise that my child, when she gets older, she won't be drinking sake. I grew more and more worried about Japanese food culture. I saw it changing, with more fast food, mothers working and not cooking for their families. But I realised these [fermented foods] were the real Japanese fast foods. They may take months to make by the artisans, but you can cook with them in seconds and, if they are good quality, then you will make good food.'

After her Damascene visit to the sake brewery, Chieko began to specialise in writing about sake and then moved into other fermented Japanese foods, realising that the two paired so perfectly, and were very healthy. 'People often talk about Japanese food as being very salty, but the good part about dashi is that, because it is made with fermented products it helps your body get rid of the salt.'

As we talked, in the background I could hear the sound of dripping water and assumed the place had some plumbing issues. It was a while before I realised the dripping water was coming from the speakers; it was a CD called *Soundscape of Suikinkutsu*, which Chef Satoru clearly felt provided the perfect contemplative ambience for the enjoyment of his fermented offerings.

He passed across the counter a bowl containing what looked like a large marshmallow. 'This is the most famous hanpen in Japan,' smiled Mizutani. Hanpen are dumplings made with ground fish and mountain yam, lightened to a cloud-like density with egg white. This soft, gently-flavoured dish lulled me into a false sense of security which, looking back, was probably the intention. The next appetiser was a spoonful of pungent pickled rice with red cabbage, the grains of rice having decomposed into a mushy whole. This jolted my tastebuds awake, and then the heavy weaponry was unleashed. On a gorgeously patterned, rectangular ceramic plate, Satoru offered us the first nare zushi dish, ugui, a freshwater fish from Ishikawa Prefecture, packed in similarly part-liquefied rice with chilli and carrot.

Glistening malevolently, it looked like something half digested then regurgitated by an ailing Labrador. A couple of other friends had joined us by this stage and, of course, everyone was waiting for the guest of honour to try it first. I reached over with my chopsticks, plucked a slice of this fishy mush, sniffed it, instantly regretted having done so and then tasted it.

Actually, it really wasn't bad, with a sour, yeasty flavour and a pleasant chilli kick. Was it healthy? 'Oh yes, very,' said Chieko, her eyes amused behind a long dark fringe. 'If you were sick, this is the kind of thing your granny would give you because the lactic acid kills the bad bacteria.'

I'm not sure how I would have reacted if, suffering from flu, my grandmother had served this at my bedside, nor some of our next dishes: Pacific mackerel marinated in nuka (the rice bran left over when brown rice is polished into white) and sliced thickly like cold-smoked salmon, and then a small bowl of chopped raw herring aged in koji for three weeks and with a troubling firm-slimy texture.

And then came the dish I had been anticipating with a mix of excitement and terror: Mizutani's freshwater ayu which had first been salted for six months to extract all its moisture, then packed in steamed rice and left for eight years to age in his fridge. It was presented by Satoru on another exquisite rectangular ceramic dish in seven slightly squashed slices, still coated in its semi-liquefied rice. I nibbled a corner of one slice. It had a fearsome flavour, for sure: powerfully acidic, again yeasty, with astonishing umami and an aftertaste of … what was it exactly. I *knew* that flavour. It tasted remarkably like an incredibly tangy, aged parmesan. And, simply by telling myself that was what it was, I was able to happily nibble away at several pieces.

I suspect had I eaten it a decade ago I would have gagged on nare zushi but one's tastes change and, just as I acquired a serious blue cheese habit some years back, I had by now begun to understand the appeal of Japan's long-fermented fish dishes. Seeing my facial expression change from raw fear to wary curiosity and then bemused pleasure, Mizutani said: 'That's nothing. I know someone who aged some nare zushi for thirty years. It was almost like a liquid.'

It was an astonishingly generous act for him to have shared this with me: who'd have imagined one could be so touched by a gesture involving rotten fish? But then the evening took a turn for the worse as Chef Satoru presented us with some fermented fugu milt, made in Ishikawa. Bluntly, this is the rotten sperm of the infamous poisonous fish, another gift from Chieko-san.

'Two hundred years ago they fermented fugu in rice and rice bran,' explained Chieko. 'They would leave it for three years and the rice would extract all the poison. These days they breed the fugu so they aren't so poisonous any more.' Putting aside thoughts of the presumably high rate of attrition involved in the research phase of this, I examined the plate of 'matter' before me. The rice bran had turned the fugu milt from white to muddy brown. It looked like a flattened piece of clay, smelled like an abandoned caravan and had a texture like overcooked liver. Instead of the moreish, lactic-umami savour of the fermented ayu, this was sour and bitter. It really was a fearful substance.

All of which makes it inexplicable that, some months later, having left my family for a day in Kyoto, I find myself on the train to Lake Biwa, spiritual home of funa zushi, the mother not just of fermented fish of the kind Mizutani had subjected me to, but of all the broad – now truly global – culinary category we think of as 'sushi'.

I had never tried funa zushi before myself, but my cartoon had. I found it a little discombobulating to be turned into a cartoon character for the NHK TV series based on my book: it was how I imagine a dog might feel when it looks in a mirror. Whenever I saw my avatar there would be some kind of vague recognition but only enough to create confusion: an unsettling cognitive dissonance. Sometimes it was all I could do to stop myself barking confusedly at the screen. (I should add, cartoon Michael is a neurotic, pig-headed, irrational idiot, prone to hysterical outbursts and a great deal of pompous pontificating. He drinks too much, and eats to grotesque excess. He is obese and wears a green polo shirt. This is clearly ridiculous. I have never owned a green polo shirt.)

I don't imagine it is easy to turn real people into anime, so some fictional licence was required. We did not meet a ghostly okonomi-yaki cook on our travels those years ago, for instance, nor a twenty-foot-high gothic Lolita. At no time have I communicated telepathically with a sexy cow either, but all of these things occur in the cartoons. And there was also an entire episode of the NHK series in which I was challenged to try funa zushi and, though terrified, I finally did and pronounced it 'delicious'. That never happened. We never visited Lake Biwa where funa zushi is made. If I am honest, I deliberately avoided it, but now it was more than a little embarrassing that my cartoon avatar had tasted it and pronounced himself a fan on my behalf without me ever having tried it. Clearly, it was time for a trip to Lake Biwa, time to taste proper funa zushi at source. Lissen and the kids are less than enthusiastic about a trip on a dark and rainy winter's day to taste some rotten fish, so I head off alone from the *machiya* in Kyoto to Omi-Takashima Station on the western bank of Biwa.

The version of nare zushi made using a special type of crucian carp (Nigoro buna) evolved on the shores of Biwa simply because the region had the carp from the lake, salt from Wakasa Bay not far north (the road which passes from there to Kyoto, at the time

the capital, was once known as the Salt Highway) and good rice.
For centuries funa zushi from the shores of Biwa was a highly prized
gift, rather like the posh Hokkaido melons are today, and though
those days are long gone, funa zushi is still presented by the region
to the Emperor each year as a gift.

Even among the Japanese, funa zushi always seemed to be talked
about as one of those 'dare you?' foodstuffs. I imagined it to be a
little like surströmming, the Swedish herring fermented in a can, or
Icelandic hakarl, pieces of shark buried underground for two years
or so, both of which I have had the misfortune to taste and whose
rancid-acrid flavours I will never quite forget. So I approach the
premises of Kitashina warily. The company was founded in 1619
and is now the last shop in Japan which specialises exclusively in
making funa zushi. It is on a charming flagstoned street lined with
traditional, mostly wooden houses and isn't difficult to find: I just
follow my nose which detects a haunting odour, acidic, like soured
cream, but with a cloying sweetness.

Inside Kitashina's shop and café I am welcomed by the owners,
Mariko and Atsushi Kitamura, a shy but friendly married couple in
their thirties. Atsushi is wearing immaculate grey overalls and cap.
He presents me with my own disposable smock and paper hat
which I must put on before I can enter the fermenting chamber.

'Don't worry,' Mariko says, sensing my apprehension as we move
closer to the source of that ungodly smell. At this stage I am genuinely concerned at my ability to master my gag reflex. 'We don't
mind if you don't like it, we know it is a special smell. The process
of making funa zushi derives from home cooking, so we like to
leave it to natural temperatures and humidity and light.'

Takashima is one of the great fermentation capitals of Japan. As
well as the funa zushi, some of Japan's best miso, sake and vinegar are
all also produced here. The climate by the lake remains relatively humid
even in winter with lots of snow and rain, both of which are good for
fermentation. I imagine things must get pretty funky round here in
the summer but there are always some who can't stomach funa zushi.
The folks at Kitashina are used to wrinkled noses, Mariko says.

We leave the café at the front of the premises and move towards the source of the smell out back. I am now getting overripe Camembert, horse manure and drains. Frankly, I am regretting my curiosity in the matter of funa zushi. Also, I am keenly aware that after my tour of their fermenting room I am going to have to taste some while under the gaze of those who have dedicated their lives to making it.

Why, I wonder aloud, do we need hygiene clothing to look at a product that is by definition rotting? (I don't put it so rudely.)

'Only family members are usually allowed in here,' says Mariko as she opens the door to a cold, half-timbered, barn-like room. 'That has been the rule, passed down from generation to generation because we value the movement of each bacteria in here and are careful not to destabilise the balance of the bacterial ecosystem, not only the bacteria in the barrels but the ones that are alive in the rafters and walls too.' I am suddenly keenly aware of my bacteria. I hope they behave themselves.

The floor of the fermenting room is almost completely covered with gnarly old cedar barrels, some bucket-sized, others like wine barrels. All have wooden lids weighed down with circular granite stones, like mini-millstones. Seeping up over the lids is a cloudy, reddish-grey liquid with mould growing on its surface. Mariko asks that any photos I take are for my own use; she is concerned that the barrels look unappetising. She is not wrong.

Atsushi explains how they make funa zushi. The carp are scaled and cleaned, then their guts are pulled out via a small hole in their belly using a chopstick, a process which requires great skill to avoid splitting the fish's skin. This happens in April and May when the females are pregnant because funa zushi with its roe still intact looks prettier when sliced, and fetches a higher price. The fish are then layered in salt in the barrels where they are left for two years to enable the salt to kill any dangerous bacteria.

Atsushi has kindly readied a barrel which was prepared two years earlier. He is going to show me the second stage of the process. Wearing blue rubber gloves he opens a barrel, scrapes the salt layer away from the top and pulls a fish from the reeking, oozing liquid. It looks more like something archaeological than culinary. I can feel my body engaging fight or flight mode. My pulse begins to race. Buttocks clamp.

'Now we rinse the fish, and hang them in the sun to dry. We replace the salt with steamed rice and put them back in the barrel for another year,' he says. It is special rice, of course, grown here in Shiga Prefecture, hand-harvested and sun-dried. Usually when making sake, soy sauce and miso, koji is used at this stage to start fermentation but with funa zushi the rice itself takes care of that as lactic acid bacteria begin to flourish, converting the protein in the fish into the amino acids responsible for its 'special' aroma and sour flavour, as well as softening the bones.

Mariko is the eighteenth-generation owner of this 400-year-old company, which was originally founded as a ryotei. She grew up surrounded by stinky fish; when she was a baby her mother would work packing the funa in the barrels with her daughter on her back. Mariko's husband, on the other hand, comes from Nagoya which has its own famous fermented product, hatcho miso, a dark and pungent miso paste, traditionally fermented in cedar barrels the size of grain silos weighed down with large stones. Atsushi had never encountered funa zushi until he met his future wife, which happened while the two were working in the kitchen and front of house respectively at the fabled Kyoto kaiseki restaurant, Kitcho.

'I never really knew about it before, I certainly did not know what it smelled like,' smiled Atsushi. 'But once I was allowed to join the company, I learned a lot, then I understood the smell.'

'I remember him having his first taste of funa zushi,' recalls Mariko. 'It was like electricity ran through his body, he was thrilled.' Her husband nods bashfully. The couple had intended to spend their working lives learning about the endless complexities of kaiseki ryori in Kyoto, but in 2000 Mariko's father became ill and the two moved back to her home town to take over the company.

Kitashina has faced existential challenges in recent years due to the familiar story of declining demand and ever more scarce natural resources. In its heyday in the 1930s, the company had branches in Tokyo, Kyoto and Nagoya but, as with so many traditional Japanese food products, tastes changed, particularly after World War II and the influx of Western foods. Then came the environmental pressures.

'My father almost closed down the company because it became more and more difficult to get the fish,' explains Mariko. In recent decades the southern part of Lake Biwa has become more heavily industrialised and populated; elsewhere the shores have been concreted over and the carp's reed habitat has been lost. The fish used to migrate to paddy fields via rivers to lay their eggs and then return to the lake but now numerous man-made obstacles block their path.

'Compared with their heyday, the numbers are down and the fish are smaller, but ten years ago the local government made a big effort to recover the population, which has helped,' says Mariko.

At one point not a single carp was caught in Biwa for an entire year but the local authority started a campaign to increase the fish population and once again they have a steady supply. Mariko explains all this as we move back in to the café. The moment of truth is fast approaching.

'People have this mindset that funa zushi is smelly,' says Mariko. 'But we change the rice after six months for new rice, so it's not so bad. If you keep it in the same rice, then it's really bad.' By this stage I hear Mariko's voice only as a distant muffled noise. My world has crash-zoomed onto the glistening, part-decomposed fish in front of us, its flesh sunken and wet, the year-old rice now a homogenous, off-white paste.

'Some people around here still make this at home,' Mariko continues as her husband scrapes the part-liquefied rice from the fish. 'Each one tastes different depending on the bacteria that live in their homes and whether they rinse their hands in sake when they are packing them, or in mirin, like we do.' I am watching Atsushi intently as he now begins to slice the funa zushi with well-practised precision, fanning out the pieces in a perfect spiral around the plate. The cross section of bright orange roe in the fish's belly contrasts prettily with silver skin and the gleaming white rice. It looks like some kind of weird, avant-garde necklace.

Much has been made in the Western media recently about the health benefits of 'good' bacteria on everything from our digestion to obesity and even our psychology (our so-called 'thinking gut'). These 'good' bacteria are especially abundant in fermented foods. Had funa zushi's time come, I wondered? Could it be the next health food fad?

'The lactic bacteria are definitely healthy,' says Mariko. 'They are researching it at the universities in Osaka and Nagahama. I do think that when more people learn about how good lactic bacteria are for you, they will realise its health benefits. Some research already says it lowers blood pressure, reduces allergies and helps the intestinal environment, but if you like funa zushi you probably drink sake with it, so that might counter-balance the health benefits,' she laughs. 'In this region, when people get a cold or stomach problems, they eat funa zushi as medicine – and locals eat it with rice, not so much with sake.'

I have run out of questions; I can filibuster no longer. We might as well get this over with. Atsushi offers me the plate, I pick up a slice of funa zushi and put it into my mouth.

Now, wouldn't it be wonderful if at this point I can report that funa zushi tastes so much better than I feared, that actually I really enjoyed it and it was nothing like as bad as its smell. But it is awful. The sourness especially takes me by surprise. It is cheek-puckeringly sour, sour to the power of ten lemons, and the sourness is swiftly followed by an unpleasant bitterness which I can feel is actually making my cheeks flush. Then there is the texture – the sliminess of the flesh and the graininess of the roe together make it a colossally challenging mouthful.

To be fair, it was stupid of me to take a whole slice. As with my fermented tofu misadventure on Okinawa ten years ago, it would have been wiser to begin with a tentative nibble. Also, a rinse of sake helps. Mariko, sensing my distress, offers me a cup, and it instantly softens the acridity of the funa zushi, which sells for ¥8,400

– £63 – per fish. 'This one is actually less sour than one that is only matured for six months,' says Mariko.

Kitashina's newest product is funa that has been fermented with sake lees – the leftover fermented rice from making sake – instead of plain, cooked rice. Now deeply wary, I taste this new product, which is sweeter and milder. It is really rather good – I might even eat it again.

'For local people, *this* is the traditional funa zushi,' says Mariko. 'But all our customers, from all over Japan, have different memories of funa zushi as a part of their personal and cultural heritage. Our products remind them of all these things.'

Mariko and Atsushi hope Kitashina will continue its nare zushi traditions for another 400 years. Their son, Masaki, fifteen, is already showing a keen interest. 'It is up to him but I hope he will take over,' says Mariko. 'He is already learning more about fishing and farming the rice. In 2013, he prepared fifty fish in his own barrel, cured only with salt, no rice, so it lasts longer. It will be ready for the 2020 Olympics. I have customers waiting for him. He will be the nineteenth generation, they want to eat his funa zushi while watching the Olympics on TV!'

Chapter 15

Osaka

While my family and I are staying in Kyoto, *Amakara Techo*, the leading food magazine of western Japan, has invited me to Osaka, a half hour or so away by Shinkansen. The editors have kindly offered to show me around and get me to sample some local delicacies. I need no further invitation. Every time I visit the city I taste something new, surprising, delicious or enjoyably weird. Osakans seem to live for their stomachs. Plus, accompanying us will be my old friend Hiroshi Sakurai, a television writer, musician and legendary bon viveur, and the man who first introduced me to the wonders of Osakan food a decade ago. Like me an unashamed glutton, Hiroshi has an intimate knowledge of the best places to eat in what I have long suspected is the best city in the world in which to do this.

We begin our tour of Osaka with a visit to the Tsuruhashi market. In the fish section I enjoy a lesson in fish processing from fishmonger Hirohisa Hayakawa, master of ikejime. This is the special Japanese method of preventing lactic acid build-up and blood spoiling the fish's flesh by first severing its spine and main blood vessel then forcing a stiff metal wire down the unfortunate creature's neural canal, which runs along the top side of its spine, nullifying its nervous system. This can slow the effects of rigor mortis and keep a fish fresh for ten to fifteen hours, Hayakawa says, adding proudly that it was a Kansai (western Japan) invention. I had only heard of ikejime being used in small to medium-sized fish but he tells me it can be an effective treatment for fish as large as tuna.

He now moves to a nearby case from which he plucks a live octopus and, as he juggles it expertly, he explains how to sex an octopus: you look at its suckers. On a girl, they will be arranged in two neat rows, with boys they are more randomly distributed (I have yet to find any scientific corroboration for this, but it sounds convincing).

I have been especially looking forward to our lunch appointment in the Tenma district of the city. When I had visited Osaka for the first time years ago while researching *Sushi and Beyond*, Hiroshi and a friend of his had taken me on a memorable food crawl to some of their favourite places, ending many beers, sakes and shochus later, at an udon restaurant called Tenma. The udon there, and in particular the fresh-made dashi which accompanied it, had made a huge impression on me. The dashi was made with katsuobushi and dried mackerel and was hair-raisingly savoury. At the time, I had described it as the most delicious thing I had ever tasted, and wrote as such in my book.

Some years later, after *Sushi and Beyond* had been published in Japanese, I heard through the grapevine that the owners of Tenma had hit hard times. The husband, who ran the kitchen, had fallen seriously ill and been unable to work. His wife was about to close the restaurant when one of her customers told her about my praise for their dashi in my book and – at least this is what I'd heard – this had given her the strength to continue. The book had apparently brought many customers to her door.

Naturally, I was keen to revisit Tenma to find out whether any of this was true, and get the free bowl of udon that was my due.

Owner Sachiko Yamasaki welcomes us warmly when we arrive at her noodle restaurant in a side street in a business quarter of the city. She explains that they had indeed experienced a torrid time since I had first visited. Following a long and ultimately unsuccessful legal battle with their landlords who wanted to redevelop the building which housed the restaurant, her husband, Yoshinki, then only in his mid-forties, had had a stroke. He was paralysed down one side of his body and could no longer work in the restaurant. To make things worse, they were evicted from the restaurant at the end of the following year. Sachiko was pregnant with their first child.

'We were going to close the restaurant, that's what my husband wanted,' she says quietly. Her parents found an alternative location for the restaurant, still in the Tenma district; her brother volunteered to help out in the kitchen. They reopened just as Sachiko's husband was discharged from hospital. He struggled on in the kitchen for a year but eventually the work became too tough for him, and he now lives with his mother. For a while, Sachiko's brother was in charge of the all-important dashi, the basis of the soup that drove me wild all those years ago, but now she takes care of it herself.

Sachiko, a shy, young-looking forty-eight-year-old with a heavy fringe, seems quietly proud of all she has achieved, but catches herself and adds modestly, 'When I get into trouble, I call my husband.'

All of this had clearly happened *before* my book was published in Japanese, so the story about me 'saving' Tenma was not quite true, but the book had at least brought customers from across the country.

'I had seen your book in the bookshops, but I didn't know our restaurant was in it at all,' Sachiko tells me. 'Then a reader came in a couple of years ago. She'd been trying to track our restaurant down through clues in the book. All she had to go on was that it was an udon place in Tenma. I later realised that people from all over Japan had been trying to figure out where the restaurant was. Then the first TV crew came here when Japanese food was given UNESCO [World Heritage] status. I really wanted to meet you, I am so happy to have been in your book. I've been awake all night, so nervous about making dashi for you and whether it would meet your expectations.'

I was also a little worried that I had somehow exaggerated the soup's deliciousness, but it was everything I remembered: sweet but with a slight bitterness, and a wondrous smoky-savoury flavour that lingered satisfyingly. It was simple, but a testament to top quality ingredients and perfect technique. Firstly, Sachiko steeps the highest grade of Hokkaido konbu in soft, cold water overnight before bringing the water almost to the boil to make the dashi fresh every morning. 'The soft water helps extract maximum umami,' she confides. Having heated the water and removed the konbu, she then adds three types of dried fish – sardine, katsuo (bonito) and mackerel – lets them infuse a little, and then strains the liquid to make the primary dashi. To that she adds sugar, soy, sake and mirin.

'No MSG,' she assures me, wagging an index finger. 'MSG makes you thirsty, natural dashi doesn't.'

I have no doubt that thousands of restaurants across Japan make a dashi as good as this one every day. Tenma is a humble, everyday, local restaurant with no airs or pretensions. The decor is plain; my bowl of udon costs just ¥600 (£4). But I guess you never forget your first time, and Tenma was one of my first experiences of proper, fresh-made dashi. It will always hold a special place in my heart and, I should add, the udon noodles were pretty great too.

On to our next stop of the day: tako yaki.

I had eaten Osaka's most iconic dish many times. This is tako yaki, or 'octopus balls': savoury doughnuts with a chunk of octopus in the middle cleverly cooked on a special hob with semi-circular hollows, and served with a super-savoury brown sauce. But I had never tried to make them.

I got the chance at a small tako yaki stand in one of the city's wonderfully evocative *shotengai*, the Japanese covered shopping arcades. I love these places; they are the perfect antidote to the modern retail plague of the shopping mall, and Osaka is particularly famous for them. Mostly free of chain stores, let alone international chains, these covered, ground-level retail corridors typically boast an array of 'mom and pop' stores, tiny restaurants and community spaces. As well as proper fishmongers and green-grocers, there is almost always a fresh tofu place, someone selling dried seaweeds, a mochi café, someone grinding coffee beans, a proper old-fashioned ironmongers and low-cost clothing shops selling complex-patterned knitwear and trousers made from highly flammable material.

The *shotengai* my Osakan friends have brought me to has an exceptional tako yaki place, Umaiya. We watch chef Taizo Kita pouring the batter into the semi-spherical indentations in his hot plate, then deftly turning the dough once it has set, gravity ensuring that the still-liquid uncooked portion of the dough forms the other half of the 'yaki' ball. I appreciate his skill all the more after I am invited to try my hand at making my own tako yaki. The resulting doughnuts I make look decidedly ragged but still taste terrific.

In the taxi afterwards we talk about the amazing quality of Kita-san's tako yaki but a thought, perhaps slightly sacrilegious, has struck me: why did no one ever try to put something *else* inside tako yaki? I realised you would have to lose the 'tako' (it means 'octopus'), but what about a nice chunk of pork belly, slow-simmered in sake and mirin? Or some lightly pickled mackerel, something sour to cut through the doughy exterior? Or what about a sweet tako yaki with a chunk of fruit inside or some chocolate? *

This set me off on a chain of thought. Was this perhaps the great weakness of Japanese food? For all the beauty and seasonality, the glorious regionality and refreshing simplicity, did it not rather lack innovation? Was that why the younger generation of Japanese chefs and their diners were so attracted to Italian cuisine, or Western fast food, or ramen, with its Chinese origins? Perhaps they felt freer to experiment with foreign forms of cooking. There do appear to be quite a few other genres of Japanese food which seemed immune to change or reinvention, untouchable even. The rules for everything from the kaiseki meal, to the few accepted ways to serve soba, or yakitori and okonomiyaki, all seemed to be written in stone, immut-able, simply not up for discussion. All the innovation was happening in ramen shops, or burger restaurants with their squid ink buns, or with freaky pizza toppings at Italian places, uni sauce on spaghetti, or whatever. As we have heard, there are always plenty of Japanese chefs who strive to perfect a particular form of cooking, to source

---

* Months later, at dinner with some Japanese friends in France, I mention my frustration. It turns out, there *is* a chain of tako yaki restaurants that does mix things up a bit with, for instance, a chocolate version. But I think my point still stands as these have hardly gained a wide currency.

better ingredients and hone their technique to make a better bowl of udon or piece of nigiri than anyone else and, of course, that was one of the things that I loved about Japan's traditional food culture, but I was curious – where were the Ferran Adriàs or Heston Blumenthals of Japan? Where were the revolutionaries who were prepared to play with traditional forms and reinvent classic dishes, or for that matter the René Redzepis who were searching for new and original indigenous ingredients to reinterpret in a modern form?

Kozue Chizo, one of the journalists from *Amakara Techo*, has a kind of answer. I blurt out my frustrations about tako yaki to her in the taxi on our way to the station to catch the train back to my family in Kyoto. Why must it always have octopus in the middle, why not a bit of eel? I say. She turns to me on the back seat of the cab.

'We don't change the way we make tako yaki,' she smiles, mildly. 'Because we have found the ultimate way, the best way to do it. And when you've found the best way, why would you change it?'

She has a point, and I do think Chizo-san's views reflect those of many, many Japanese, but another whirlwind food crawl in Osaka showed me that there is plenty of innovation left in Japanese cuisine, if only you know where to look for it.

Chapter 16

Osaka Take Two

There was once a small, local restaurant in the old garment district of Osaka. Since 1935, through four generations of the same family, it had served homely, affordable yoshoku dishes – Japanese interpretations of Western food – 'omurice' (rice and omelette), hamburgers and suchlike, to a loyal clientele who were fond of what they liked.

Ten years ago, after a lifetime of serving this simple home cooking, the elderly owner handed the restaurant over to his then twenty-nine-year-old son, assuming he would continue in the same vein, but the son had spent time working as a chef in Europe, falling under the spell of the mysterious multi-sensory 'neuro-gastronomer' Dr Miguel Sánchez Romera, a neuroscientist turned autodidact chef infamous for trying to serve flavoured waters to New Yorkers (unsuccessfully, as it turned out). Under the tutelage of the enigmatic Romera, the son's approach to cooking had been irrevocably enlightened. The son had plans, grand plans, and once he had taken the reins in his father's kitchen, he began to implement them. The problem was, no one had asked the regulars whether they wanted things to change and they were less than impressed with the son's new, avante garde, contemporary European cuisine. Father and son quarrelled. In the end, the father was forced to return to the stove, and opened a new restaurant around the corner serving the same old dishes to keep his established clientele happy. Meanwhile, the son continued doggedly with his vision and gradually word spread that here was a chef worth watching. Eventually, he won a new clientele and international acclaim. A decade later, his restaurant was awarded its third Michelin star.

That's the story of chef Tetsuya Fujiwara, current owner of Fujiya 1935, one of the most talked-about restaurants in Japan and beyond. I ate at Fujiya ten years ago on our first trip and I was staggered. Back then, Fujiwara was still in thrall to the molecular movement and my meal featured wildly inventive, deconstructed dishes with foams and gels. I remember some kind of space-agey white capsule which burst in my mouth releasing something terribly delicious; it was so good I asked for seconds.

Fujiwara's reputation has only grown since so I was keen to return during this trip and made a reservation a few days after my tako yaki experience. But on arriving at the restaurant, nothing is recognisable from my previous visit. The interior has completely changed – the dining room has now moved upstairs, there is no open kitchen and the food is completely different: a fusion of contemporary European and Japanese, with New Nordic elements.

'When I took over my father's restaurant I was just back from Europe so that was the biggest influence,' says Fujiwara, a tall, slender man with a look of utter exhaustion about him common to all the best chefs. 'But now, over time, I have had lots more experience with Japanese food, it's been a slow evolution. Now, my creativity is more about a sense of the seasons, of nature.'

He tells me one of his greatest inspirations is the legendary chef Hisao Nakahigashi, famed for his foraged ingredients and his emphasis on rice, and whose restaurant, Sojiki Nakahigashi, is in Kyoto. 'When I eat there I feel the mountains and the field,' says Fujiwara. 'I never really learned authentic Japanese cuisine like that, but it doesn't matter. These days I am creating something with more of a Japanese sense. I am remembering the food and the seasons from when I was a child.'

To go from omurice to three Michelin stars in less than a decade is a very Osakan trajectory. Things move very fast in Japan's second city. Unlike the people of Kyoto, Osakans are not ones to preserve the past in aspic. They do not merely embrace the future, they race towards it. The rapid and radical transformation of Fujiya 1935 from omelette and burger joint to high-concept modernist gastro temple is par for the course here. This city is set permanently on fast forward. People walk faster talk faster and eat faster. It is the birthplace of instant ramen, the standing bar (sitting down? Waste of time!), and the first beer in a can in Japan. Tellingly, both the travelator and conveyor-belt sushi were also invented here: one to move humans quicker, the other to move food more quickly to the humans.

In truth, there isn't much else to do in Japan's second city besides eat and shop. You could visit the Instant Ramen Museum – and I thoroughly recommend you do – but apart from that there is little by way of culture, virtually no parks or open spaces. Even the castle is a recreation; there is nothing, then, to distract you from the quintessentially Osakan practice of 'kuidaore', or 'eating yourself bankrupt'. My kinda town.

It is true that Osaka is famed for its fast foods, so-called B-class stuff like tako yaki and okonomiyaki. As a local once put it to me, 'The essence of Osakan food is that it is cheap, fast and delicious.' But this is not just a fast-food paradise. It is also home to some of the most creative and refined restaurants in Japan, as well as the origin of a particular type of restaurant, the 'kappo', which in recent years has radically transformed the high-end dining landscape from New York to Paris and London.

You can see the influence of kappos in Joël Robuchon's L'Atelier chain (first opened on the Left Bank in 2003, and now rolled out globally); or at Momofuku Ko in New York; or, of course, in those now omnipresent chef's tables. 'Kappo' means literally 'cut and cook' but it defines a counter-style restaurant where the chef and his assistants work in view of the guests, usually serving a fixed, multi-course menu. Some say the tradition dates back to feudal times when samurais took great pride in demonstrating their culinary skills to their guests while making the food to accompany the tea ceremony, but it is generally acknowledged that the kappo developed in Osaka in the nineteenth century.

While the quasi-spiritual overtones of kaiseki restaurants can be a little intimidating – I recall with a 'there but for the grace of God ...' sympathy for a confused Australian diner I once saw who mistakenly opted to enter a classic kaiseki restaurant in Kyoto on her knees – kappos are friendly, informal places. The food is still refined and beautiful, but chefs chat with their customers, customers chat with each other, jokes are exchanged, sake cups mutually refilled.

When I last visited Koryu, one of my favourite kappos, in the Kitashinchi night-life district in Osaka, a dozen or so guests sat chatting at the counter as chef Shintaro Matsuo and his assistants rustled up dishes which were somehow simultaneously classic and contemporary, serious and playful, and occasionally challenging – things like wild boar bacon with mustard and shrimp, or poached slivers of monkfish liver, a largely forgotten ingredient in Europe but highly prized in Japan. The meal started with a landscape of sashimi, featuring a china house dusted with fake snow and some astonishingly tender squid. One dish, a small, heavily vinegared, bony fish, served cold, pretty much summed up many people's worst fears about Japanese food, but as I watched the chefs prepare the next – a clear soup with a spine-tinglingly tangy dashi-based broth – the anticipation soon distracted me.

Afterwards, I emerged into the maze of Kitashinchi's hostess bars not a little dazed. As per the sashimi plate, it was snowing gently but there was still plenty of life on the streets of what was once Osaka's geisha district, although I am told only around ten geisha remain here. There were shops selling stockings and gift fruit. Men in dark suits with earpieces loitered on every corner. Occasionally, a door would open releasing a plume of cigarette smoke and smooth jazz. Out would totter a girl in a slinky pink dress on the arm of a short, fat, older man in a suit, and together they would tumble into a glossy black Toyota Century idling outside. An archetypal Osaka scene.

I was looking for a bar called Flute Flute, recommended to me by a local friend. Finally, I spotted the sign and descended the steps to a classic Japanese basement bar like hundreds of others, narrow, low lit, with a few stools and more mellow jazz playing on the sound system. But there was one major difference: instead of bottles of spirits lined up behind the bar, there were over a hundred different types of soy sauce, from olive oil soy, to grape juice soy, smoked soy and even a white soy (which surely defies the laws of physics). The best was a sea urchin soy from the port of Shimonoseki, with an almost-but-not-quite intolerably intense uni flavour. It had to be the most umami-ish substance on earth, almost too much umami for any human to handle.

Why, I asked one of the owners, did they ever think to combine champagne and soy sauce? 'Simple,' he smiled. 'Both are fermented. Very nice marriage.'

Soon after, I returned to Flute Flute in the company of Japan's answer to David Hasselhoff and a Japanese TV crew. The idea was that Hasselhoff – in reality, boxer-turned-actor Hidekazu Akai – and I would meet 'by chance' in the street, like old buddies (although I'd never met him before; actually I had never even heard of him), and then hang out in the city and show each other some of our favourite places. This was for a popular weekly food show called *Maki's Magical Restaurant*. I still don't know who Maki is either.

For the same show I had already spent the previous day visiting four restaurants in Kyoto – a 'hidden' ramen bar with no name located in a basement and decorated like a Zen garden; a casual wagyu beef yakiniku place (where you cook the meat over a gas grill on the table); a roll-your-own temaki zushi (sushi roll) restaurant with ridiculously photogenic yet doll-like tiny servings designed purely, I suspected, to look good on Instagram; and a contemporary kaiseki restaurant. That day, my celebrity dates had been Hiroshi Nishidai, a roly-poly comedian in a pork-pie hat, and a well-known actress, Misako Yasuda.

Attempting humour while filming during both of these days was risky. I would essay a Wildean witticism, then have to wait for the young, clean-cut male host – who, with his suit and clipboard looked more like a market researcher – to translate it for the others, then wait even longer for them to decode the humour, and eventually, sometimes, be rewarded with exaggerated laughter.

Akai the boxer lumbered through our day's filming on autopilot, communicating mainly via shrugs and barks, but he seemed to be pretty clued up when it came to the food and had a neat technique for getting his sake glass refilled (which I have now adopted): he would ostentatiously lift the glass up to pretend to see where it was made, thus demonstrating to everyone how empty it was. Nishidai, the stout comedian, turned out to have genuine funny bones, which was obvious despite our language problems, while Yasuda the actress, though stick-thin and prone to covering her mouth coyly when either laughing or eating as all women seem obliged to do on Japanese TV, ate like a stevedore. That woman finished *everything*, and did not spill so much as a drop on her flowing, cream-coloured frock.

During our day together, Akai the boxer took me to an ambitious, upmarket kushikatsu place in Hyogo where we tried some elaborate deep-fried, breaded skewers (aubergine wrapped in minced pork and a perilla leaf was exceptional) and then visited my favourite okonomiyaki place, Onomichi Murakami, in Kita-ku (speciality: mochi and cheese topping), before I led him to Flute Flute.

While filming there, Tsutomu Otsuchihashi, one of the Flute Flute owners, suggested the best way to sample their soy sauces was in donburi – a bowl of steamed rice with toppings. Why didn't I design a special donburi for Akai, suggested the director? Before I could protest, I found myself being shadowed by the camera crew to a nearby grocery story where, on the spot, I had to come up with the perfect combination of ingredients to appeal to the boxer. Whatever I made would not only be subjected to the scrutiny of the Flute Flute chefs and Akai, but then would be shown to the entire nation on television.

In the store, I grabbed some green beans, cherry tomatoes and myoga (a relative of ginger, but sweeter and milder) for a Japanese 'accent', then, just as I was heading for the checkout, I saw some sausages, not a common Japanese grocery item. I plucked them from the shelf of the fridge and returned to Flute Flute to try to create something that might impress Japanese TV viewers. Standing behind the bar with an expectant Akai before me I issued instructions to the Flute Flute kitchen to blanch the green beans as I quartered the tomatoes. I had in mind a dish that would summon the umami powers of Italian food to create something the likes of which the world had never tasted. But it soon became obvious that I had far too many toppings. Unless I toned down my ambition I would end up with an unforgivably cluttered bowl of food. Out went the sausages and the myoga. In the end, I passed a reasonably presentable donburi bowl across the counter to Akai which he ate with almost plausible enthusiasm in the true spirit of Osakan 'kuidaore'.

With my time in Osaka drawing to a close, yet again I was about to leave this amazing city with a lingering regret at the food experiences I knew I had missed. There is just so much good stuff to eat here. I haven't mentioned Kuromon market, for instance, or the Korean quarter, where I go if I am in need of a dose of kimchi. But Osaka's finest restaurant lies far from the city centre in a seemingly random residential suburb north of the Yodogawa River. One evening I took a trip there and spent my customary half-hour or so wandering lost amid the grids of grey houses until finally spotting the entrance to a small Zen garden.

Spiritually, Kashiwaya's private tatami rooms and season-specific, multi-course kaiseki menu place it thirty miles away in Kyoto. 'Yes, we have often thought about moving to Kyoto,' chef Hideaki Matsuo admitted when I brought up the subject of his restaurant's incongruous location. 'Actually, now we have many regulars from Kyoto. We are famous for our location.'

Spring was nudging nature awake when I visited, the first green shoots were appearing, things were un-hibernating. Matsuo-san explained that he had designed the menu that night to lead diners towards the new season, with soft, pillowy, fresh fugu milt dumplings and mustard greens, plum blossom and a dish of tiny, baby conger eel, the latter a visual riff on noodles. There was my favourite Japanese food, yuba – or tofu skin – and plenty of other luxury turns, such as abalone, crab and Matsuo-san's favourite, local shrimp.

'I am trying to make something that satisfies beyond money,' Matsuo said as we sipped green tea after what had been a staggering meal. Kaiseki was a way of telling stories, he added. Every plate had a meaning, but fewer and fewer people either understood what it was, or were interested in learning.

'My regulars understand, but recently people don't seem to care. I have to explain more and more, to try to keep them entertained.' He pointed to the double-ended chopsticks on the table. Did I realise they symbolised that I had shared my meal with God, for instance? 'It takes time to understand this kind of food,' he continued. 'You learn a little each time you visit, but now people come almost by coincidence, or to tick the restaurant off some list.' He said this not with any bitterness or accusingly, more a wistful resignation.

Kashiwaya presented the meal as a Zen meditation on the seasons, culture and the arts. With only the hum of the air conditioning to accompany my sighs of pleasure, the focus was entirely on the food before me, which was transportingly delicious, otherworldly.

My final night in Osaka called for something rather different: Osaka Ryori Asai (formerly Kigawa Asai), another of my favourite kappo restaurants. Here I sat wreathed in my neighbour's rather nostalgic cigarette smoke at the long, black-lacquered counter, enthralled by a set menu which featured crunchy fugu skin, angler fish liver, bracken starch dumplings and fermented sea cucumber entrails (wonderfully briny-slimy), all the while watching the flock of chefs in their white coats dip and dive like swallows behind the counter.

At the end of my meal I turned to the businessman sitting next to me who was sharing a bottle of Mersault with his young lady friend.

'Quite a meal,' I said, puffing out my cheeks.

'Welcome to Osaka!' he replied, raising his glass.

SHIKOKU

Chapter 17

Yuzu

It is rare that a fruit can induce crime but I have routinely committed felonies in the name of the yuzu. I smuggle a dozen in my suitcase back to Europe every time I visit Japan. I swaddle them like precious porcelain, put on my best poker face and stride brazenly through customs, once safely home opening my suitcase to release a fragrance unlike any other. I use their juice to make ponzu, or sorbet, but best of all is yuzu zest infused in cream for the ultimate flavouring for chocolate ganache.

Japan has perhaps the most dazzling range of citrus fruit of any country, many of them unknown beyond its borders. The clementine-ish mikan; the dai dai (a bitter orange); the banpeiyu (a kind of pomelo); and an infinite variety of mandarin-type things. According to Helena Attlee's fantastic book *The Land Where Lemons Grow: The Story of Italy and Its Citrus Fruit*, all citrus originally derive from China, but many Japanese citrus have been cultivated here only in the last few decades while others, like the Sakura-jima komikan which grows on the volcanic island we visited in Kagoshima Bay, evolved here centuries ago. There are komikan trees which are two hundred years old still growing on the slopes of volcanic Sakura-jima. Presumably they are made of asbestos.

All of these fruit are fantastic but the yuzu is The One: I think of it as lemon that has gone to a Swiss finishing school, with a sweeter, more rounded, approachable flavour, more tart than a tangerine, not as bitter as a grapefruit. The closest Europe equivalent is probably the bergamot but that's not really the same at all. When you slice a yuzu in half it is packed with pips; the best part, the heady, floral oils, resides in its zest.

The yuzu has long been familiar to chefs in the West, mostly pastry chefs who use it to give an exotic note to desserts. Joël Robuchon does a stunning yuzu soufflé, for instance. It has recently moved into the food industry mainstream, with yuzu flavourings appearing in everything from Häagen-Dazs ice cream to beer and chewing gum. I even spotted a yuzu-flavoured liquorice pastil on sale in my local supermarket in Denmark the other day – and the Danes haven't a *clue* what a yuzu is. The Japanese don't just use yuzu in desserts, though, they add its frisky zest to soups, to seafood, or red meat, and they even put it in the bath.

The yuzu is thought to have come to Japan from China in around the year 800 where it was originally cultivated as a cross between a mandarin and the hardy, wild ichang lemon. But just you try finding a yuzu in China. I contacted Chinese food expert Fuchsia Dunlop about this and she explained that the Chinese don't use citrus much in cooking other than a bit of dried tangerine peel perhaps. I also asked Adam Leith Gollner, Canadian author of *The Fruit Hunters*, another terrific book about fruit, whether he had ever encountered yuzu in China, but he had not. Keiko Nagae, one of Japan's leading pastry chefs (formerly of Pierre Gagnaire's eponymous three-starred restaurant in Paris), told me she once asked for a yuzu to use in a cooking demonstration she was giving in China and they brought her a pomelo (it turns out the kanji character is the same for both). So it seems China has forgotten about the yuzu altogether.

Japan hasn't. The yuzu is growing more and more popular here. Around half of all Japan's yuzu trees grow on the island of Shikoku, a short trip across the Inland Sea from Osaka, and they are also reputed to be the best, so it is to Shikoku one must go if one is to encounter them in their natural habitat. Plus, I wanted to take my citrus criminal career one step further and not merely smuggle some yuzu home, but grow my own yuzu tree from seed. I thought a visit to a yuzu farmer on Shikoku might furnish me with some useful advice.

So, I went to Shikoku on a yuzu mission (this was on a previous visit to Japan, a few months before the journey with my family), but I did get sidetracked a little. There is *so* much good food on this island, and so much of it is unique to its rocky shores and steep forested valleys. Shikoku has the best udon noodles in Japan, for instance; dazzling seafood; and one of the rarest types of Japanese beef, Tosa beef, which in contrast to the better known, fatty, spoon-tender wagyu beef, is more like European beef: a little tougher, but more flavourful. And Shikoku is the only place in Japan where I have seen octopus beaks vacuum-packed and on sale in a petrol station store alongside the energy drinks and chewing gum. They are very crunchy. And not in a good way.

There is another reason I lost my yuzu focus once or twice. On Shikoku they have a drinking game: 'Bekuhai'. I am no longer entirely sure of the rules, or that there actually *are* any rules to Bekuhai, but the main objective appears to be getting foreigners as drunk as possible in the shortest amount of time. To achieve this they employ sake cups specially designed for the game featuring various booby traps intended to make you drink more, and faster. Some have holes in their bottoms so that the sake runs out if you put them down; others are shaped like faces with grotesque noses so that you can't put them down even if you want to. The people of Shikoku, and in particular its Kochi Prefecture, really like a drink. In fact, if you ask other Japanese people to characterise the locals here, you will receive the simple one-word answer: 'Boozers'.

I first encounter the Bekuhai cups in the smoky chaos of Hirome Ichiba, the main food hall of the island capital, Kochi. On a Saturday lunchtime it was packed with locals intent on having a good time eating the prefecture's signature dish, katsuo no tataki – bonito grilled over rice straw – an addictive, smoky-charred method of cooking this oily, dark-fleshed fish, a relative of the tuna, its skin blackened by the smoke, the flesh still scarlet and raw. The famed 'black current' passes by the coast here carrying with it the bonito along the coast of Japan. Kochi is one of the biggest katsuo ports in Japan, and they eat more of them here than anywhere else in Japan. The katsuo are at their best in the late autumn, and in Kochi they typically eat them with masses of raw garlic and spring onion – unusual in Japan. But the market had much more to offer. There was a stall selling brightly coloured tofu flavoured with tomato, edamame and uni, which I had never seen before; I had never seen Japanese knotweed, that scourge of British gardens, on a menu before either, but its stems have a wonderful crunchy texture and delicate flavour; and, most incongruously of all, there were piles of percebes, or 'goose barnacles', those super-rare shellfish which taste like a cross between an oyster and a clam and look like dinosaurs' toenails. I associate them more with Portugal or Spain, where they cost a small fortune. They are notoriously dangerous to harvest, growing on wave-bashed coastal rocks, but here they were just ¥380 (£2.50) for half a dozen. The highlight for me, though, was Kochi's traditional seafood platter, Sawachi ryori, an elaborate display of shellfish and sashimi with, at its centre, a prehistoric looking, clawless lobster-type thing, like a Morton Bay Bug.

At just 140 miles long, Shikoku is the smallest and least visited of Japan's four main islands. Even many of the Tokyoites I asked had never visited it, and even fewer foreigners make it here. It still has the feel of the remote hideaway it once was, cut off by the ever-churning whirlpools of the Inland Sea, its mountains home to pirates and exiles. The locals consider themselves a bit forgotten, outside of mainstream Japan and are pretty chilled by Japanese standards too judging by the welcome strangers receive in their izakayas. In Kochi I had people offering me drinks and food, which has never happened in Tokyo. (The local dogs are less friendly: Tosa, the old name for Kochi, is famed for its breed of Rottweiler-style fighting dogs. You can still see them fight at special venues in the prefecture.)

There is one other dish in particular which all who visit Shikoku are supposed to try: Sanuki udon, a bowl of thick, soft, white wheat noodles, served with a sauce rather than in a soup, as udon usually is in Tokyo (such distinctions being of great importance to the Japanese). I'd been told there was an 'udon taxi' operating in the town of Kotohira in Kagawa Prefecture in the north-east of the island. If you were lucky enough to hail it, the taxi would supposedly take you to the driver's favourite restaurants. It sounded like one of the more fanciful storylines from the cartoon version of *Sushi and Beyond*, but, one morning, I struck out from Kotohira Kadan, the ryokan where I was staying, with a map of the city on which the receptionist had marked a couple of sanuki udon places. It was before eight o'clock, and there were no other pedestrians about, and few cars, so, imagine my surprise when almost immediately I was passed by the udon taxi. It disappeared out of sight before I had registered the plastic bowl of udon on its roof and so, cursing my slow reflexes, I carried on walking. But there it was, parked around a corner a few hundred yards up the street, as if it had sensed my quest and was waiting like an obedient dog. I climbed in, said the magic word, and a few minutes later I was sitting in Konpira Udon eating the most delicious bowl of udon noodles I have ever had, for less than three quid. The sauce, made from a blend of soy sauce and dashi, was intensely savoury, the noodles thicker than the thick end of my chopsticks, yet super-soft and tender, but the best thing were the bits of crunchy tempura batter scattered on top.

Afterwards, a few yards down the high street, having lingered wistfully for a few moments outside an ice-cream shop selling udon ice cream – the poster of which depicted a soft-serve cone, dripping with soy sauce and sprinkled with chopped spring onion (tragically, it was closed) – I stopped to watch another udon chef at work through the open window of his kitchen. He was standing behind his counter, writhing in a strange manner as if in some silent, serpentine reverie. This was Kiyotaka Iwasaki, and it turned out he was kneading his fresh-out-of-the-overnight-fridge udon dough with his feet to make it more malleable (I should add the dough was in plastic bags and he was wearing socks).

We started chatting. Iwasaki has been making udon for twenty-three years, he told me. Where was I from? he asked. England, I said.

'I play guitar. I love Paul McCartney!' he exclaimed, and sang the opening four notes of the Beatles song 'And I Love Her' with accompanying air guitar: 'Do-do, do-dooo'. I responded with the opening line: 'I give her all my love, that's all I do' which kicked off a kind of Beatles tennis match in which I would sing the first line or two of one of their songs and he replied with another. Now, *that* wouldn't happen in Tokyo.

This would not be a proper Shikoku report if I did not mention the famed 88 Temple Route, a pilgrims' trail upon which many retirees embark once they have finished their careers and which takes up to three months to complete. So, there, I've mentioned it. Not much given to spiritual perambulation, I was more intrigued by Kochi's open-air street market. The largest market of its kind in Japan, it was founded in the 1690s and still runs for almost a mile beneath the palm trees which line the main street through the city centre. It is held each Sunday, with stalls selling local produce and products, fruits and vegetables, several of which I had never encountered before.

Citrus fruits are the star. There are hyuganatsu – the one with the edible pith – and the mellow, lime-like naoshichi, but it is the noble yuzu that I was there for. As this was November and in the midst of the harvest season, there were loads of them at the market as well as a wide range of yuzu products – juices, jellies, dried yuzu and various beauty products, too. The general consensus from the stallholders was that the best place to go to learn more about the fruit was the town of Umaji.

Umaji is the Amalfi of Japan, a one-citrus town. It is home to a thousand people, nearly all of whom are involved in growing or processing yuzu. Like Amalfi, it is one of its nation's Most Beautiful Villages (in Umaji's case this is an official designation, there's a list and a website and everything). It is located up in the hills an hour and a half from Kochi. I followed the road beside the narrow, fast-flowing Yasuda River, every once in a while spotting small yuzu orchards amid the densely forested hills beyond, tiny constellations of intense yellow stars amid the autumnal foliage. (Is there a tree more beautiful than a Japanese maple in autumn, its leaves at once candy-red, lemon-yellow, lime-green and peach?)

The Umaji Yuzu Information Centre was my first stop. Mr Momota Nagano, the manager, introduced me to the myriad products they make from this little fruit. Everything is used, juice, zest, pith and pips, he said. The juice goes into various soft drinks, ice creams and candies, as well as shochu and yuzu liqueur, and there is also a tea made from yuzu juice, honey and sugar. The tea looks like jam but dissolves in hot water and is very popular in Korea. There was actual yuzu jam too, and yuzu-ponzu, yuzu-dashi, yuzu-mirin, yuzu-soy sauce and yuzusco, a yuzu tabasco. The yuzu-miso was amazing, the citrus cutting through the umami-meatiness of the fermented bean paste; and, uniquely, the locals also use yuzu-vinegar to season sushi rice. They put the squeezed hulls of the fruit in their baths to release its heavenly perfume, and they even sell the pips, toasted to be ground to a powder for use in beauty treatments. They pluck the precious blossoms for face cream, and eat the spring leaves in a clear soup (they are said to taste spicy with a faint flavour of yuzu). But my favourite yuzu product, aside from the juice and zest, is yuzu kosho, a pungent condiment which originated on Kyushu only fifty years ago. It is made from salted chunks of yuzu pith and chilli and is perfect with fish or rice, and beef, too. I think it could be the next big thing in terms of Japanese food products internationally. Predictably, in this food-obsessed country, yuzu tourism is also adding income for the villagers of Umaji.

The yuzu trees blossom in the first week of May. From late October for a few weeks the 190 growers in the valley together harvest over 700 tonnes every year, worth around £17m. Pruning starts when the harvest is over, from December to March. As Nagano-san and I stood in the Yuzu Information Centre yard, there was a constant stream of dinky little Daihatsu trucks filled to the brim with little spheres of sunshine arriving and departing. They weigh the trucks as they arrive, he said, and weigh them when they leave having deposited their load.

As a result of the growing demand in Europe, a couple of farmers have started growing yuzu in southern France, but cultivating yuzu trees is a long-term proposition, fraught with challenges, as I discovered when I visited yuzu farmer Hiroyuki Shimota in his orchard a little further up in the foothills above the village.

Now in his sixties, though looking closer to fifty, Shimota turned to yuzu farming when the rice paddies became too strenuous. In recent years Japan Agriculture, a government-funded organisation, has encouraged more and more older Japanese to become yuzu farmers with grants, saplings and advice but the challenges sounded endless.

He explained that, being in a valley, the yuzu don't quite get the ideal amount of light which is why Umaji yuzu are not perhaps as pretty as yuzu grown elsewhere. On the other hand, the chilly climate creates fruit with a more intense flavour. The harder the trees have to fight to survive, the finer the flavour of their fruit, although it is a thin line between that and a dead tree. The wind is also important, as it blows away insects, and so offerings and prayers are regularly made to appease the wind god. Yuzu trees quite like a bit of frost from time to time, which was encouraging as far as my plans to cultivate a tree at home were concerned, but then came the bad news for this particular nascent yuzu farmer.

'It takes fifteen to twenty years before a yuzu tree bears fruit,' Shimota said, casually flicking a large caterpillar from his baseball cap. If I really want to grow my own yuzu tree from seed back home it was clearly going to require an unusual amount of dedication, not to mention a good supply of the chicken manure, old yuzu rinds and cedar sawdust which the trees prefer as feed.

I reached out longingly to fondle a fruit on a nearby tree, and impaled my finger on one of its thorns.

'Watch out for the thorns,' said Shimota as I sucked the blood. The thorns do not deter Shimota's nemesis, the local deer, which outnumber the human inhabitants and chew the bark of the yuzu trees, nor do they trouble the wild rabbits which devour Shimota's saplings.

'I don't make much money from yuzu,' he told me when I asked if he enjoyed farming yuzu. He was now pruning a branch back, part of a regime to control the amount of fruit each tree yields to maintain quality. 'But ninety-six per cent of the land here is forest, and it is very, very satisfying when I look across the valley and see these yellow fruit defeating the forest.'

As usual, after my visit to Shikoku I smuggled some yuzu home. This time I saved their pips after I had squeezed all the flavour out of the fruit and its zest. To myself I made a solemn, two-decade commitment that I would nurture my own yuzu tree from seed. Its fruit will be the best yuzu available in Europe, and they will be all mine.

Following instructions given to me by my new friends in Awaji, I carefully removed the thin outer casing of the pips, planted them in some good soil, and placed the pots on a window sill. Every day, I checked on their progress, watering them only when the soil dried out.

After two weeks, nothing had happened. Not so much as a sprout. I grew nervous as I had read that, if nothing shows after six weeks, then the seeds would never germinate. Six weeks came and went, yet the surface of the soil remained bereft of greenery. But then, a miracle. First one, then six green sprouts broke through, feeble at first but then more robust, and leaves began to form, dark green and glossy, unmistakably yuzu.

Over the next few days, five of the fragile saplings dropped their leaves but today, the remaining yuzu tree is flourishing at around eight inches high. At this rate, if I am lucky, I might have fruit just in time for my retirement.

CHUBU

Chapter 18

The Greatest Restaurant in the World

Humour me for a moment. If we accept that Japan is the greatest food nation on earth, inhabited by the most discerning eaters, and with the most advanced restaurant culture in the world (Michelin certainly agrees, as do virtually all of the chefs I've ever asked), then it seems at least *arguable* that the very best restaurant in the world might also be in Japan, right?

I realise that the various, much-hyped global restaurant rankings, such as the San Pellegrino 50 Best, tend to focus on European and American places, but I don't think anyone takes them very seriously (apart from the restaurant PRs who ensure their chef clients make the list). For many years, the best Japanese restaurant on that list was not even in Japan, for instance. Lima has more ranked restaurants than London. So, the 50 Best list, and its Francophile rival, La Liste (funded by the French government with the specific intention of giving French restaurants a higher ranking), are, I think we can agree, a bit silly.

Perhaps in this day and age it is to the hive mind of user-generated social media restaurant review sites that we should turn if we are to ascertain which are the best and worst restaurants in the world. Ergo, if we agree the best restaurant in the world is in Japan, then it is to Japan's most popular open-source restaurant ranking website, Tabelog, where actual diners review and rate the actual restaurants they actually pay for, that we must look to find the best restaurant in the world.

The most popular online restaurant site in Japan is tabelog.com, with over fifty million visitors every month. Many Japanese use the site's score out of five based on an average of users' ratings as the single most important criterion when choosing where to dine, especially when trying a new place. Almost five million diners have gone to the trouble of placing a review on the site and, interestingly, given the petulance and score-settling that plague user-generated review sites in the UK and USA (and which render them virtually worthless), the Japanese tend to score in the middle zone – a mark in the middle-to-high threes is the norm. Legendary sushi restaurant Sukiyabashi Jiro in Ginza, Tokyo, considered by many to be the best sushi restaurant in the world, scores 3.95, for instance.

At the time of writing, and for some time now, the restaurant with the highest score on tabelog.com, indeed the highest score *of all time* – 4.6 out of 5.0 – is not some temple to French cuisine with a three-hundred-dollar tasting menu, linen tablecloths and a wine cellar worth more than the GDP of a small African nation, nor is it one of those six-seater sushi places in Ginza which hang up if foreigners phone to make a reservation, nor is it even one of the rarefied and venerable kaiseki restaurants in Kyoto where you have to know the CEO of Toyota to get a table. No, the highest ranked restaurant of all time on the most popular open-source restaurant review site in the greatest food country in the world is a, by all accounts fairly rough and ready, restaurant which specialises in grilling game meat over an open flame, located in the remote hills of Gifu Prefecture, north-east of Nagoya.

I first heard about this Valhalla a few years ago when I interviewed Yuko Yamaguchi, the multi-millionaire business genius behind the extraordinary global success of Hello Kitty. I met this striking woman in her early sixties (I'm guessing – her age is a secret) with her copper-coloured pigtails and gothic Lolita garb, in the boardroom of the colossal Sanrio Corp headquarters in western Tokyo. For the first hour or so I sat patiently as she explained the success of her cloyingly cute, mute, pink cartoon cat and Sanrio's latest, somewhat improbable strategy for luring young male Japanese to the brand. But I had heard she was a famous bonne vivante, so what I really wanted to know was, which were her favourite restaurants? Eventually, Yamaguchi-san did give me a few great recommendations in Tokyo (Kohaku, a fabulous contemporary kaiseki place in Kagurazaka, was one), but when it came to naming the absolute best restaurant in Japan, her face softened at the memory, and she whispered the name Yanagiya.

Needless to say, at this point I wanted to dine there more than anything and when, some years later, I found out that my family and I would be passing relatively close by on our way from Kyoto to Nagano, I thought I would try to make a reservation.

I ought to have known that it is never as easy as that with the best restaurants in Japan and, so, of course, Yanagiya turns out to be an 'ichigen-san okotowari' restaurant, meaning 'no first-time customers'. In other words, it does not accept reservations from any old schmuck who has the temerity to ring up out of the blue and offer to pay them money in exchange for food. That would be too simple. No, the message came back from the restaurant that I could only reserve if I had dined there before or had a personal recommendation from someone who had (plus there needed to be four or more of you in the group, although in this instance this was not a problem). Undeterred, I began to put out feelers via food-loving Japanese friends. When that didn't work, I moved on to remote acquaintances and friends of friends. Eventually, I struck lucky through a chain of no less than five people across three cities, the last of which, my actual connection to Yanagiya, I had never met nor even heard of.

I am not especially proud of these tactics but my relentless relay-subterfuge is how the four of us now find ourselves disembarking at a rural bus stop some distance outside Nagoya, clutching a bus timetable kindly printed out by our hotel. For the last hour or so I have diligently ticked off the thirty stops on the list as instructed by my hotel concierge, hoping that, though they were all written in Japanese, I had not made a mistake. All I know is that we must get off at stop number 28 on the list, which, hopefully, is in the town of Mizunami.

Peering at it now in the dark, 'town' appears to be slightly over-stating what is really not much more than a few houses strung out along a mountain road. But where is Yanagiya? I had somehow assumed that the best restaurant in Japan would be easy to spot, perhaps illuminated by a celestial beam. It is not. The only sign of any life in Mizunami is the light from a small supermarket, but the young woman at the checkout knows nothing of 'Yanagiya', nor indeed is she aware of any restaurants nearby.

This is not good. Accusatory glances are shot my way by my family, and frankly hurtful aspersions cast on my ability to count beyond double digits, but to the rescue, as so often happens in Japan, comes an elderly woman bent double by arthritis. She knows exactly where we want to go, and even draws us a map.

We wave a grateful goodbye and, bus timetable now replaced in our clutches by her mystical hand-drawn sketch, head across the supermarket car park. After just a couple of turns we are lost in the dark again but, suddenly, out of nowhere, there she is once more, our guardian angel. She has been following us to make sure we make it to our destination and gestures at some faint lights high up above the village.

A steep climb later and we are welcomed at the entrance to Yanagiya, a sprawling, half-timbered wooden building whose welcoming lights glow softly from behind its paper-screened windows, by a pretty young woman with a baby in a sling on her back. Inside, the restaurant is divided into private rooms by more paper screens. If it wasn't for the bottles of 2004 Romanée Conti at the entrance, one might mistake it for an ordinary country inn. Our shoes deposited in the pigeonholes by the entrance and replaced by tiny slippers, the young woman leads us inside.

Through open doors we can see that each room has its own hearth in the centre. In it is a carefully arranged pyramid of glowing-red charcoal sticks framed by a square counter around which the diners sit on the tatami-covered floor. There is laughter and the chinking of plates and glasses. Our shoulders begin to relax. 'It doesn't seem much like a restaurant, it's more like someone's home,' says Asger. I have that warm, convivial feeling, common to the first few moments in any good restaurant, the sense of relief that we are in capable hands, that we are going to have the loveliest of evenings.

In our room, we meet Masashi Yamada, the restaurant's manager, brother of the head chef and the grandson of the man who founded the restaurant, just after World War II. Yamada is chatty and friendly, and dressed in an indigo samue (like Japanese work pyjamas) with a rock star's quiff and wispy beard. He will be serving us that evening, tending to the charcoal which is already white hot, and cooking our meal in the open hearth 'irori' style.

A challenging note is struck by the appetiser, a small bowl of bee larvae cooked for six hours tsukudani-style and served in a beautifully wonky, wabi-sabi ceramic dish, but thereafter our meal at Yanagiya is an entirely pleasurable tour through a range of freshly caught, fat-cloaked local game meats pierced on wooden skewers, stuck into the ashes angled towards the glowing coals, and grilled to perfection. To begin, there is wild duck skin, chewy and dripping with fat, followed by the bird's tenderloin and breast. And then comes the wild boar.

'Virgins always taste best!' declares Yamada-san as he pushes the skewers of boar – each chunk of meat insulated by a thick parenthesis of glistening, soon-to-be blistering, yellow fat – into the ashes, carefully angling them towards the hot coals. 'Virgin meat is soft, and the fat is sweeter. They eat wild taro and chestnuts. This one was killed two days ago. My dad says that hunters always eat the meat fresh, so that's what we do.'

The taste of that virgin boar – in particular its sweet fat – will linger in my memory for a very long time. It is as if the beast had gorged on Gummy Bears. Almost as good is the next course, venison, with a deep herby flavour that lingers on the palate like a great red wine, and is served with punchy yuzu kosho. Again, the fat of the venison is the real star: its sweet savour literally makes my hair stand on end, an almost primeval frisson of pleasure.

At one point I ask Yamada about the secret of Yanagiya's online popularity. 'I think it is because what we do is so personal, each room with its own chef,' he says as he bastes a skewer of duck leg with the restaurant's seventy-year-old soy / ginger tare. 'It's very rare, this way of cooking. Plus, of course, the meat is all local, everything is from nature. My father was a very strange guy. Even thirty or forty years ago, he insisted on that when everyone else was into farm-raised wagyu. You know the problem with wagyu? It all tastes the same. I like it when every piece of meat has its own taste.'

He talks us through the seasons: duck is good in November and December, as is wild boar and bear. 'After that, the bears are sleeping,' he adds. These were not grizzlies, as found in Hokkaido, but the smaller 'moon bears' – much better eating, apparently. 'I'd really, really love to come back and try the bear,' says Emil, elbowing me intently. In spring come the 'sansai', the slightly bitter, foraged mountain vegetables, like fiddlehead ferns, and freshwater trout. Late spring is the season for the revered ayu – 'sweet river fish' – and the precious unagi. Unusually, at Yanagiya even this is wild, which, as we've heard, is extremely rare. It is expensive too, admits Masashi. These days a kilo will cost him around ¥12,000 (c. £90).

'It is very, very hard to find, we have eight different suppliers, but wild unagi is ten times better than farmed. Have you smelled farmed unagi? Farmed have no muscle, it's all fat. It's a secret, but they feed them with a lot of chemicals and hormones, like lots of farmed salmon. Wild unagi eats natural food.'

After the unagi of summer, come the matsutake mushrooms of autumn. These are the Japanese porcini, as precious as truffles to the French. Later in the year they serve what Masashi coyly calls 'the secret bird', which he hints might be illegal. Was it small, and eaten whole, like the ortolan (beloved of French gourmands and, famously, enjoyed by François Mitterrand as his last meal)? 'Yes, exactly; like the one they eat under a sheet.'

As he talks, one of the paper screens slides open and in toddles a small boy with long, thick, glossy black hair. This is Shu, Yamada's adorable son. 'I hope he will work here one day,' he says as Shu presents me with his business card in the proper, two-handed manner. On it is written his name, 'Shume Yamada', and the title: 'Head Waiter'.

As Asger and Emil play with Shu, I ask his father about this 'ichigen-san okotowari' nonsense, the closed reservation system which seems to me designed to discriminate specifically against foreigners.

'It's not about keeping foreigners out. We want to keep our regulars happy,' he replies mildly. 'We have customers who have been coming here for decades, one of them for thirty-six years in a row, and they need to be able to come every time. That is more important to us than filling every place every night.'

Yanagiya attracts quite a starry array of regulars. One of them is Iron Chef Morimoto, another the Japanese footballer Hidetoshi Nakata, a legend in his home country and to fans of Roma and Bolton, for whom he played until his retirement in 2005.

I met Nakata once, in his sleek, low-lit office in central Tokyo where I went to interview him about a very expensive sake he was launching. He wanted to help brand sake better internationally so that foreigners could understand it, he told me. This is not a bad idea as sake labels are, to my eyes, totally impenetrable. It made sense to try to make the products of individual sake breweries more easily identifiable, to help build loyalty among those, like me, who were relatively ignorant about Japan's national drink. The only real flaw with his sake-branding scheme was that his own sake cost about £800 a bottle. Anyway, Nakata also casually mentioned the fact that he never, *ever* ate vegetables, not so much as a bean sprout – hence, I suppose, his affection for the meat-only Yanagiya.

Our meal ends with a cast-iron nabe pot hung from a hook above the fire. In it is a dashi made with katsuobushi and roasted duck bones into which have been placed more pieces of duck and steamed vegetables. It is served with some rice but, by that stage, we are deliriously full and cannot eat any more.

'I have a difficult time trying to think of a restaurant that is better,' says Lissen while Yamada-san is out of earshot in another room. Emil thinks he knows a few that are better, but Asger strikes a conciliatory chord: 'For what it does, I can imagine it is the best in the world. It is definitely in the lower half of my top ten.'

Instead of an interminable bus ride home, Yamada kindly has the restaurant's driver take us back to the nearest station from where we catch a train to our hotel in Nagoya. There we spend a restless night digesting what might very well be a contender for, if not the most refined cuisine in Japan, certainly one of its best dining experiences.

Chapter 19

Insects

I am lying, prone and embedded in a pile of snow dressed in a neon romper suit, limbs splayed randomly like a figure in a Keith Haring drawing. I have just contrived to poke the end of one of my skis in one of my eyes. Bits of me hurt that I wasn't aware existed, although I have yet to finalise an inventory of precisely which bits. It goes without saying that all dignity has long been surrendered to the slopes.

Lissen has just swooshed by, momentarily shifting into reverse to get a better look at her prostrate husband, before heading on down the mountain. Asger, more slowly, but completely in control, used me as a slalom marker in his measured descent of the Hakuba resort hill, which was rubbing things in somewhat. And that blurry flash of colour? That was Emil, taking the direct route without so much as a glance of concern in the direction of his stricken father.

Our time in Nagano, our next stop following our Yanagiya meal, had begun so very much more enjoyably. As I lie in the snow, I wish we were back in Tsumago eating oyaki – buckwheat dumplings the size of tennis balls. They were nice. Tsumago is an immaculately preserved medieval village up in the hills along the old Kyoto–Edo Nakasendo Highway. It was the first town in Japan to be preserved as an historic site and so its 200-year-old houses and shops, some with the original wooden tiled roofs laden with stones to keep them from blowing away in storms, are now a major tourist attraction. That was also nice.

This is not nice. Something hurts. I think it is my ankle, but the shock of my first skiing accident, which occurred at such a rudely early stage in my first ever skiing lesson, has left me somehow disconnected from my body. I decide to remain lying here in the snow, very still, for a little longer, and think instead about the snow monkeys.

Genuine Japanese icons, the macaques of Jigokudani Wild Monkey Park had been on my must-see list in Japan for years and, despite the crowds of eager photographers surrounding their man-made hot spring pool like paparazzi given access to the Kardashians' jacuzzi, they did not disappoint. I had particularly enjoyed the story of their mysterious disappearance a few months earlier. Nobody had seen a single one of the 200 or so monkeys at their beloved hot pool for ten days until researchers venturing further up into the mountain forests had found the whole lot of them engaged in what could only be described as a gigantic monkey orgy. Concerned about the impact this mass frottage-related absenteeism was having on tourist income, locals had to tempt them back down to the pond with food.

We'd visited Matsumoto Castle, an immense, black, six-storey wooden pagoda, the oldest fortress in Japan, which we had seen on a perfect winter's day with not a cloud in the endless blue sky and crows wheeling on the thermals above its jagged roof. We had posed with locals dressed as samurai in the park and eaten an astonishing meal at a restaurant nearby which served horsemeat, various cuts – belly, artery, heart – as sashimi, all of them delicious apart from the yellowy-white slices of rubbery 'mane fat'. Though none of us had a problem eating horse – 'It's not really a pet like a cat, is it?' as Emil put it – that mane fat was a bit a challenge.

Horsemeat consumption, which has traditionally been high in Nagano, has been cited as one reason for the locals' longevity. The people of Nagano have now overtaken the Okinawans as the longest-lived people in Japan. Nagano's men have an average life expectancy of just over eighty years, women over eighty-seven years. Horsemeat has a third as many calories and an eighth the fat of beef or pork, but the longevity of the Naganoites is more likely attributable to the fact that they also eat more vegetables than the average Japanese. Or was it perhaps another Nagano speciality, the main reason for us coming to Nagano – the local insect cuisine, which we had tried the day before in Ina City, to the south of the prefecture?

We are increasingly being told that the world is going to need to source more of its protein and vitamins from insects. If we are to solve the challenge of feeding seven or eight billion people with something other than methane-producing cows or antibiotic-filled pigs. We are going to have to overcome our squeamishness about eating things with six or more legs, as many others in the rest of the world – South America, Africa, Australia – did millennia ago. After all, really, what's the difference between an insect and a shrimp, or a lobster come to that? Environmentally, there can be little argument. It takes 1,500 litres of water to produce one kilo of beef; you can harvest ten times as many insects for the same and, per kilo, insect meat (insect flesh? We need a word for it, don't we?) has more protein than chicken meat.

'There has been a big increase in people interested in our locusts,' edible insect specialist Yasuharu Tsukuhara had told us when we visited his eighty-year-old, family-run restaurant and shop on the outskirts of this large city on a mountain plain. 'More are buying live locusts to cook themselves at home. Some days we are selling five or six kilos.' Recent appearances by Tsukuhara on TV shows prompted by a United Nations conference on the subject had further boosted awareness of this Nagano speciality in Japan but the prefecture was already famous as the centre of insect eating, or 'entomophagy'. For centuries they have eaten bee larvae, locusts, sanagi (silk worm pupa) and the most expensive insect delicacy, zazamushi (river- or 'Dobson flies', at ¥1,200, £9, for 25g). Insects were never a major food source for Nagano, but during leaner times they have been an important dietary supplement, particularly for the poor.

The insects are usually served as a preserved food, cooked tsukudani-style in soy sauce, salt, mirin and sugar. Judging by the display in the cabinet in Tsukuhara's shop, they look like weird caramelised snacks, apart from the bee larvae which resemble plump grains of wild rice, some light brown, some dark. But then I caught sight of some gruesome, maggoty-type things with lots of legs and fangs. They were not so appealing; in fact, his cabinet was beginning to bring back an unwelcome memory of an insect restaurant I once visited in Hanoi. The bee larvae there were not at all nice but I had been properly traumatised by a plate of bitter, black scorpions. They were like eating plastic egg boxes filled with soggy sawdust. There's your 'difference between lobster' right there.

Tsukuhara, a straight-backed, broad-faced man, is something of a celebrity in international entomophagy circles. On a recent appearance at an insect eaters' conference in Holland he sold all the insects he had brought within minutes. (Improbably, Holland is the biggest insect consumer in Europe: I've actually seen insect 'meatballs' in its supermarket chains there.) He regularly travels to other countries with similar insect-eating traditions, visiting Laos often. 'Children there can gather three to five kilos a day!' he marvelled.

He harvests the insects from the rice paddies, as people have done in this part of Japan for centuries. In Kyushu, too, they have a tradition of eating bee larvae, while further north in Tohoku they prefer locusts. In Nagano during the Edo period, the cry of the door-to-door insect vendor was apparently as common as the tofu seller's.

'Elementary school children and grandparents used to gather a lot of locusts in the rice fields in Miyagi [whose coast was struck by the tsunami in 2011], sometimes seven or eight tons a day,' he added. 'But since the nuclear disaster their parents won't let them. Now we get them from the wild in Yamagata Prefecture instead.' The bee larvae harvest has also had its challenges recently. He had noticed that the bees were moving north, perhaps nudged by rising temperatures in their usual habits. 'We used to get the larvae from Hiroshima, but not any more. Now we are seeing them in Hokkaido more and more.' Pesticides are yet another enemy of the insect gourmet, for obvious reasons.

We had been brought to Ina City by a kind contact at the local tourist board. As Tsukuhara and I chatted over a cup of Laotian silkworm shit tea – made from the excreta of silkworms fed exclusively on mulberry leaves – I looked up from my notebook to see that two photographers, a cable TV cameraman and two journalists, apparently invited by the tourist board man to observe the cartoon family eat insects, had silently sidled into the café and were now recording everything intently. Discussing the nuances of infused silkworm excrement (it has a light, acidic flavour, not bad at all; as Tsukuhara puts it, 'You would never think it was shit') while being scrutinised by a room full of strangers seemed to me the very definition of awkward.

I ploughed on with my questions and we all tried some silkworm larvae. The larvae looked like toasted maggots and had a plasticky carapace which, once broken, revealed a soft, mealy interior tasting not unpleasantly of peanuts. The locusts, our next sample, had a mild prawn flavour. Their bellies were soft but I struggled with their spiky limbs. We adjourned to Tsukuhara's kitchen where, alongside two deep, broad cooking pots the size of christening fonts in which he stews insects in soy sauce and mirin, he took a smaller pan and fried up some bee larvae in margarine, with salt and pepper. Though Lissen was troubled by the threat eating the eggs of bees poses to their already beleaguered population, they had a not unpleasant delicate nutty-chickeny aftertaste.

And there could hardly be a better advert for entomophagy than Tsukuhara and his family. He told me he was seventy-one years old, but if he had said fifty-one I would have believed him. His son, Shinya, forty-one, has taken over the day-to-day running of the company. His mother, Harumi, now ninety-nine, was until recently very much involved too.

'She is the most important part of this family,' he said, showing us a newspaper cutting with her photograph. Her cherubic face radiated good health. 'She is like our god.'

Tsukuhara, in a back-to-front baseball cap and sleeveless puffa jacket, clearly had no intention of retiring; he is still researching, making new discoveries, new insect innovations. 'We are working hard to spread insect cuisine, working with universities to explain the benefits of eating them, healthwise and for the environment, and to get people to be more mindful that insects are an important part of nature, not just a pest to be killed with chemicals.'

He had plans to introduce new insects to the Japanese food chain: 'I am thinking about trying to sell stinkbugs. In South Africa they sometimes put them in bread. I know that they don't sound that good and they have that unique smell, but that's what gives them a special flavour. I cannot explain how delicious they are.'

I wondered if he had heard about some of the more avant-garde restaurants in Europe, Australia and South America which have recently been putting insects on the menu. A few years ago in Copenhagen, at restaurant Noma's first MAD FoodCamp Symposium, onstage I introduced the Brazilian chef Alex Atala of restaurant DOM in São Paulo, who finished his talk by offering tastings of live ants. We were invited to squish them and then taste them: they had a wonderful flavour of ginger and lime. Afterwards, Noma began serving ants on a raw prawn as a kind of seasoning and, since then, the restaurant's experimental laboratory has also created a kind of fish sauce made from fermented locusts.

Tsukuhara knew about all of this, of course. And, after Noma served its ants-on-prawns dish at its pop-up in Tokyo in 2015, he had heard of other chefs in the Tokyo area putting them on pizzas and curry rice. He was working on insect fermentation as well as an alcoholic drink infused with bee larvae and bees' nests, which are rich in sixteen types of amino acid (from the bee spit used as its glue). He had even recently sent some bee larvae butter to Cambridge University for research.

After thanking Tsukuhara for his many gifts of plastic-packed insects to take away, we left his restaurant, still not entirely convinced that we would be adding insects to our diet but definitely certain that everyone else should.

Back on the ski slopes the next day, I disentangle my legs from my skis, and slowly make my way down the rest of the nursery slope, sliding all the way on my bottom. I return to our hotel room. Waiting for me in an email attachment is a press cutting, kindly sent by our friend at the tourist board. It is a report on the previous day's visit to the insect restaurant.

Above a photograph of me sipping from a tea cup is the headline: 'British Journalist Drinks Shit Tea'.

Chapter 20

Wine

In Koshu City, Yamanashi Prefecture, there is a statue of Buddha which is said to be over 1,200 years old. This is remarkable, though not unique. What is special about this statue at the Daizenji temple is that in his left hand the Koshu Buddha is holding a bunch of grapes.

The story goes that the Buddha depicted in the statue, Yakushi Nyorai, the Buddha of Healing and Medicine, appeared to Gyoki, the priest who founded the Daizenji temple, in 718, and presented him with a bunch of grapes. Gyoki took this as a sign that grapes were of medicinal and spiritual significance and, as well as carving this likeness of Yakushi Nyorai holding the grapes from a single piece of cherry wood – now rather fragile, the statue is only shown once every five years (the next showing is from 1 to 8 October 2018, if you're interested) – he also planted the first ever grapevines in Japan in the grounds of the temple.

This may or may not be historically accurate but it is true that grapes first came to Japan around the time of Gyoki. DNA analysis of Japanese grapes has proven that they came originally from the Caucusus, so they probably arrived via China and the Silk Road, with Buddhist monks. The grapes were most likely of the Koshu variety (after which Koshu City is named), which have been cultivated in Japan as table grapes ever since.

Grapes are all very well but it is wine that has brought me to Yamanashi Prefecture today. My family and I have travelled on from Nagoya to Tokyo where I have left them for the day to rediscover their favourite city while I go on a hunt for the best wine in Japan.

Wine was not made in Japan for some centuries after Gyoki's grape revelation, not until the Portuguese Jesuits arrived in the sixteenth century. They probably also used Koshu grapes but their nascent wine production was purged along with all the other accoutrements of Christianity, and it wasn't until the late nineteenth century, when Japan reopened for business to the Western world, that the Japanese wine industry began its long, slow fermentation.

Around that time, two young men, Masanari Takano and Sukejiro Tsuchiya, left their home town of Katsunuma in Yamanashi Prefecture for France to learn how to make wine the French way. They returned to run the Mercian wine company which remains one of the biggest in Japan. But *still* wine did not really take off in Japan. The industry bumbled along for a few decades more trying to make something drinkable out of this humdrum table grape variety, but was mostly eclipsed by the emergence of domestic beers like Kirin and Sapporo, and in particular whisky, almost being wiped out entirely by cheap wine imports after World War II. But then came the golden years of the 1970s and 1980s when a more prosperous Japan opened up to even greater Western influence, particularly in terms of its food. Foreign wine imports grew and domestic wine also began to find a market, although the interest in Japanese wine still stemmed primarily from its novelty value, or from some kind of misguided jingoism.

In my experience, Japanese wine remained borderline undrinkable. Much of it was an industrial product made from imported frozen grape juice concentrate, often these were flowery, soapy-flavoured whites which left a taste in your mouth as if you had walked briskly through Harrods perfume department.

So why bother? After all, sake, which is obviously so much easier to make in Japan, not only rivals wine for complexity and deliciousness and uses an ingredient which is more easily cultivated in Japan, but it pairs even better with food (there, I said it).

Generally in life I prefer to cling to my ingrained, ill-informed prejudices. It just makes things simpler. Thus, I had told myself that

Japanese wines were really only worth drinking once, and to be fair, in this I was not alone: a typical headline on the subject was 'Japanese Wine: Not As Bad As You Think', which I once saw in the *Japan Times*. The typhoons, humidity, rain and relatively low level of sunlight, combined with unsuitable, meagre soils, meant that Japan was never going to be a wine country to rival France or, these days, even England. And life was just too short to drink bad wine. This certainly simplified the drinks choice when in Japan: I stuck resolutely to sake.

But, slowly, news began to reach me that something was afoot in Japanese wine. Sales increased 35 per cent between 2009 and 2014, breaking all records. It had become normal to see Japanese wine for sale at convenience stores; in fact, these days there is often as much wine on offer as there is sake, but I began also to see Koshu wines on menus at decent restaurants, like the Michelin-starred Les Créations des Narisawa in Tokyo. In the UK, Marks & Spencer began selling Japanese wines made from Koshu grapes for £12.99 a bottle.

This recent success has been driven in large part by female drinkers, but the Japanese were also learning to drink wine at home, not just at European restaurants. My own Damascene moment came when I was offered a glass of an excellent Japanese Pinot Noir by chef Ikegawa at my favourite yakitori place, Torishiki, in Meguro, Tokyo. It tasted every bit as sophisticated as a decent, dry Alsatian Pinot Noir – it was a wine you would want to spend some time with.

I started to read up a little more on the state of the Japanese wine industry and to taste more Japanese wines too (such are the flimsy excuses upon which I justify my alcohol intake). Here is what I learned: there are a growing number of natural wine producers in Japan, particularly in Hokkaido; the number of wine bars was rapidly increasing in major cities. They make wine in Nagano and on Kyushu and, recently, efforts have been made to turn the disaster-struck Miyagi Prefecture into a wine tourism destination, but the main wine-growing region in Japan is still

Yamanashi Prefecture, where the industry is focused on the Kofu Basin a couple of hours west of Tokyo, just the other side of Mount Fuji.

My train from Tokyo climbs through forested mountains and river valleys, the frequent tunnels turning the landscape into a real-life zoetrope. There is darkness, then a flash of outrageously slanting scenery, then darkness again, a glimpse of Fuji, and then finally, as we emerge onto the Yamanashi Plain, landscape covered with massive canopies of vines trained in pergolas two metres from the ground, squares of white paper carefully placed over the bunches of grapes to protect them from the elements.

I get off at Katsunuma Station, a semi-rural farming area in the heart of the Kofu Basin. There are forty wineries in this town alone. A short taxi ride takes me to the ivy-covered entrance to the Grace Winery main building where Ayana Misawa is waiting to show me around. Grace was founded in 1923 by Chotaro Misawa, Ayana's great-grandfather. She is the first woman to run the winery.

'When I was a child, I thought wine-making was a man's job,' Ayana says as we look around one of the original barns which now has a tree, planted in 1923, growing right through the roof in the middle of it. There is something of that tree's determination in Ayana. Though friendly and welcoming, she also has an evident steeliness. She is a woman on a mission.

'People used to say you can't make great wines from Koshu grapes, but my grandfather and father believed it was possible,' she tells me as we stand by the vast stainless steel tanks in which they make Grace wine. 'I want to continue what they started. It takes several generations to make a great wine.'

Grace produces 200,000 bottles a year, a comparatively tiny yield, only 10 per cent of which is exported. 'I'd love to export more, but we could sell all of it just in Tokyo if we wanted to,' she says. A decent bottle of Grace wine costs around ¥5,000 (£35), expensive for Koshu, although some of their wines can cost double that, virtually unheard of in the world of Japanese wine.

There is no track record of making really good wine from Koshu grapes, certainly not wines to challenge the best of the New World, or even Europe. 'Every year is challenging,' admits Ayana. 'There are huge vintage variations: once every ten years we get a great year.' As well as the many meteorological challenges, labour costs are high and so are land prices. There are so many more lucrative things you can do with a patch of soil within two hours of Tokyo, plus, there are poisonous snakes at large. Ayana insists that no pesticides or insecticides are used on Grace's wines, and they only use organic fertiliser.

To grow Koshu grapes for eating, the Japanese use a highly productive style of vine training – those vast canopies, sometimes fifty metres wide, which I had seen from the train. That, and the grape's unusually thick, pinkish skin, helps protect it from the humidity which can cause fungus to develop and also helps the plants get as much sun as possible to produce a maximum yield. A single vine grown this way can give as many as 500 bunches of grapes – good news if you are growing table grapes – but that kind of yield means it is impossible to achieve the sugar levels needed for decent wine making, as Ayana explains. 'I really wanted to change from those huge yields. They are fine for fresh, fruity wines, but not so good for the serious Koshu that I wanted to make. I wanted to make a super-Koshu.'

A few years ago Ayana began experimenting with conventional vertical vines which, though they yield as few as twenty bunches per vine, produce a far better quality, more flavourful grape. It was a technique she had learned during three years studying wine making in Burgundy and Bordeaux, where she was the first of her family to undergo such an education.

'At some of the vineyards in France they had never seen a Japanese person before, let alone worked with a Japanese woman,' she recalls. But Yamanashi people are mountain people. The women in particular are very strong. We are used to a tough life.

'I want to prove Koshu is a wonderful variety,' she emphasises once more. We have now driven to a viewpoint high above the misty, fruit-filled valley. 'My father and grandfather dedicated their lives to it.' Ayana is quietly spoken, serious, intense, but I notice that whenever she speaks about these two men her voice grows quieter still. She explains that her father spent years trying to grow superior Koshu grapes for wine production from seed but eventually gave up. Her vertical shoot method has enabled them to achieve that, and turn Koshu into a proper wine grape.

'Your father must be very proud of you,' I suggest. She pauses and, for a moment I sense she is about to well up, but the steely look returns. 'I need to prove he was right.'

According to Ayana, London is the most important wine market in the world, so the awards lining the Grace showroom from the likes of *Decanter* magazine (a gold medal from its World Wine Awards – the first ever for a Japanese vineyard), and praise from English wine writer Jancis Robinson – who called Yamanashi 'the Bordeaux of Japan' – are clearly important. But there is one man whose opinion, for better or worse, still counts above everyone else's in the wine world: Robert Parker, whose rudimentary percentage ranking system for wines has transformed the global wine industry. So what did Parker make of Ayana's Grace Wine revolution? Parker has actually visited Grace Wine, and I have seen what he wrote in their visitors' book.

We return to the main building for a tasting. Ayana is called away to the telephone and in walks an elderly man who introduces himself. This is her father, Shigekazu Misawa, now in his seventies. We talk a little about the wines on the table in front of us, and it is then that I mention Parker.

Misawa-san abruptly rises from the table and leaves the room. What have I said? Had Parker given them a bad review? Did they despise the American's fixation on heavy, fruity wines, and the homogenising effect he had had on the New World wine industry?

Misawa-san returns a few moments later, carrying their visitors' book. He opens it proudly at the page signed by Parker during his visit in 2004 on which is written:

'To Grace Wine,
Congratulations on a very fine 2004 Koshu. I was very impressed with this wine and wish you great success.'
Thank you for the visit –
Robert Parker

(Parker later gave the wine 87/88 out of 100, a decent score from him for a light wine with low alcohol – 10.5 per cent.)

Ayana returns and her father ambles off. She has generously arranged for me to taste some of their wines, but the tasting begins awkwardly. Their entry level wine, Gris de Koshu, is rather acidic and perfumey, confirming my prejudices about Japanese whites. The more expensive Grace Koshu white wine is better, more subtle, though perhaps still too delicate for me. Ayana says that its clarity works well with sushi, and I think its dry, fruity tartness would also be a match for yakitori and tempura. Next up is a Cuvée Misawa Akeno Koshu, made with grapes grown on Ayana's innovative vertical vine system. This is better still. I can taste the minerality of the volcanic soil and it has a strong umami 'length'. The rosé is OK too, with a friendly caramel flavour. But then comes another, different, problem: the fifth wine Ayana offers me, a red Cabernet Sauvignon/ Merlot blend, is stunning: elegant, complex, and nicely tannic – genuine echoes of Bordeaux. Though this is only supposed to be a tasting and there is a spittoon on the table, I can't stop drinking it. I find myself hoping another phone call will take Ayana away for a few moments, so I can guzzle some more of this fantastic wine.

'Koshu is my passion, my great love,' Ayana says, looking out of the window at the vines beyond. I take another large slurp of this wonderful red wine and, by the time her eyes return to the table, am nodding sympathetically.

TOKYO

Chapter 21

Ramen

You're bored of ramen, aren't you? Sick and tired of food nerds raving about the latest yuzu-infused broth, or this 'amazing place' they know where they 'make their own noodles from scratch'. You're exhausted from reading endless magazine stories about the ramen revolution, ramen burgers, ramen burritos, ramen wars; tired of ramen Nazis telling you that you don't understand what makes a good bowl, assuring you that you will never taste a bowl as good as the one they once had in a back street in Takadanobaba, that you can never properly appreciate Hakata ramen without going to Kyushu, or butter corn ramen without a visit to Sapporo.

I love eating ramen, good ramen, but my patience with all this bullshit has run out. My breaking point came one evening in Tokyo. I had heard of a ramen restaurant which was attempting to take noodle soup upscale, a self-proclaimed 'kaiseki ramen' joint in Ebisu.

A traditional kaiseki meal consists of a fixed template of courses showcasing seasonal ingredients, presented simply but artfully on carefully chosen tableware. As I took my place at the restaurant's black lacquered bar with gold-leaf table mats, having left my family for the evening to dine solo, I was genuinely interested to see how this would translate into ramen.

Innovation number one: this is the first restaurant I have ever eaten in where the staff offer to provide special lighting so that I can photograph my food better. I decline but everyone else seated in this inhospitable concrete bunker is clicking away noisily. (In Japan, all mobile phone cameras must make a shutter noise when you take a photograph as a result of legislation introduced to combat the unfortunately high incidence of sex pests shooting up women's skirts on escalators.)

The hors d'oeuvres serve as more of a warning than a welcome: a charmless paste of pumpkin and gorgonzola still lingers like a stubborn stain on my memory, and I also shudder-remember a thick, overly salty mushroom soup. The traditional slice of pork, the chashu, which usually adorns the bowl of ramen is served separately and for some reason has been poached in jasmine tea then blow-torched for good measure. That'll teach it. When the actual soup arrives it is nice enough, but rather thin, as are the noodles (I detest thin ramen noodles. Ramen is no place for somen: thin noodles overcook in the residual heat from the soup).

Towards the end of the meal, the owner enters wearing a t-shirt sporting the logo of the industrial pasta company Barilla. He spends most of his time showing off his very large watch to some of the other diners. I leave desolate, despairing and also hungry.

My kaiseki ramen experience sparks something of a crisis in me. The restaurant's fancification of something which ought to be quick, cheap and delicious seems to suck all that is great from a bowl of ramen. The only two things that really matter with ramen are the noodles and the soup, yet like so many in the world of ramen these days they had seemed much more interested in 'the concept' and the fripperies. But I don't want a concept, or a deconstruction, or a poshed-up bowl, I want thick, slightly chewy noodles, a soft-boiled, soy-soaked egg, a slice of tender chashu and a deep, rich soup that forces me to let my belt out a notch, all for under a thousand yen. Is that too much to ask?

I thought not, but my faith had been shaken. I needed ramen reassurance; I needed to know that all was still right with the ramen world, that a good, solid, simple, cheap, sustaining bowl was still an attainable dream.

The windswept concrete plain beside the old Tokyo Olympics athletics stadium in Komaba Park on a chilly Wednesday afternoon might not seem the most obvious place to seek solace, but for a few days every year this is home to the Ramen Show featuring twenty temporary outdoor ramen restaurants and some of the best ramen chefs in the land. After lengthy queuing with a mixed demographic of ramen nerds (there were even some females), I try three disappointing bowls. The first, from a restaurant from Akita, is way too salty; another is made by a seventy-year-old female chef. This initially offers hope, but it has a distressing aftertaste of grease; a third bowl, which uses whole 'tai', or sea bream, as a soup base is a waste of that most elegant of fish. I feel a strange affinity with Goldilocks.

I talk to the chef responsible for the first of these. He wants 'to translate Japanese culture into a bowl of ramen,' he says. Inspired by soba noodle traditions, he makes his ramen noodles to order in front of the customers in his restaurant.

'I'm interested more in culture than tastes of fashion,' he continues earnestly. 'I want to keep my restaurant going for a hundred years, and pass on my techniques to other generations.' The chef, who has bleached blond hair, white-framed sunglasses and a CND earring, dismisses all the ramen he has tasted outside of Japan as 'wrong'.

I had by this stage grown used to the grandiloquent pontificating of ramen chefs. 'Ramen is like the American Dream: you can make your fortune by expressing yourself freely,' one chef had told me. Another once claimed that ramen was 'the perfect food'. This kind of guff has long historical roots in the ramen world. Another ramen chef, Yokohama's so-called 'Ramen Nazi', Sano Minoru, famously forbade his paying guests from talking, or wearing perfume, so that they might better appreciate his soup and, as far back as the 1960s, the 'legendary' ramen joint, Ramen Jiro (no relation to the sushi chef Jiro Ono), close to Keio University in western Tokyo and famed for its gut-busting bowls of oily, garlicky tonkotsu, published its six ramen commandments. The first three were:

1. Live purely, truthfully and beautifully. Go for walks, read books and smile when saving money. On the weekends, fish and practise copying sutras.
2. For the world, for people, for society.
3. Love & peace & togetherness.

I mean, seriously.

In my time writing about food, I have had to endure a good many pretentious lectures on life and creativity from chefs – Italians with Michelin stars are by far the worst offenders – but ramen chefs do seem even more prone to philosophising than the norm. Perhaps it is an insecurity born from a life spent cooking a so-called 'B-grade' food, as fast foods like ramen are categorised in Japan; or that they feel a need to compete with other more highfalutin' forms of Japanese dining, like kaiseki ryori, or sushi. Maybe the relatively restricted framework of ramen – everything in one bowl – makes them just more frustrated generally and this vacuous preaching serves as some kind of safety valve. But my experiences at the kaiseki ramen place and the ramen festival have left me questioning everything. A fundamental truth which I had held dear for many years – my carefully formed and cherished ramen world view – have been, if not shattered, then at least fractured. I had spent years assuring those who had never been to Japan that the ramen was unimpeachable here, by far the best anywhere in the world, and that it was *literally impossible* to eat a bad bowl in Tokyo. 'If you take the very best bowl of ramen you can find in London or New York,' I would tell well-intentioned people who foolishly recommended ramen restaurants in either city to me, 'it will only be as good as an average bowl in Japan.' It was an insufferably smug, superior attitude. I realised this at the time, but I felt it was my responsibility to put people straight on just how great ramen in Japan was. It was my duty to inform these poor, misguided ramen ingenues that only by travelling to the other side of the world could they properly appreciate the greatness of noodle soup and understand that there were no bad bowls in Japan. But here was proof that it *was* possible to find poor-quality ramen in Tokyo after all – a new and troubling development which gnawed at the very essence of all I held dear and true in the world.

If ramen could be this bad – IN JAPAN! – what else might have I misunderstood about this country and its food culture? What if all the years that had passed since I was first introduced to Japanese cuisine had been spent in some kind of mirage, clouded by delusional wish-fulfilment? I'd invested so much of my energy and reputation telling people how great Japanese food was, perhaps I had become blind to its faults and failures, or, even worse, was in denial. What if I had become so brainwashed by the imagined unimpeachable greatness of Japanese cuisine that I had become corrupted, oblivious to its frailties, a mealtime mythomane?

I needed an antidote, I needed it quickly, and I found it in tsukemen. Tsukemen is ramen but not as we know it. Think of tsukemen (pronounced 'sook-men') as being ramen's fatter, slightly retarded younger brother. Tsukemen is not noodles *in* soup, tsukemen is noodles *and* soup. This is dipping ramen: two bowls, one containing chunky wheat noodles with not quite the comely girth and softness of udon but almost, served alongside a thicker, more intense, reduced liquid poised in its savoury viscosity between a dip and a soup, not thick enough to be described as the former, not thin enough to be the latter. Tsukemen is more filling (you get almost double the noodles, c. 350g compared to around 180g in a standard bowl of ramen), arguably more satisfying, and definitely more messy.

Though it has been around since the 1950s, tsukemen's time has come. Its popularity has been rising over recent years, as evidenced by the fact that there are now tsukemen restaurants specifically targeting women – usually a sign that a type of food has reached critical mass in Japan. And now, having spoken to a few chefs from each camp, I also suspect tsukemen chefs are less prone to the absurd pseudo-intellectualism that has characterised ramen chefs in recent years, and more prone just to giving their customers something hearty and delicious to eat.

At the same time as the Ramen Show was taking place at the old Olympic Park, there was another ramen festival, Tsukemen-Haku, a ramen vs tsukemen showdown, in full swing closer to Shinjuku.

Kabukicho is Tokyo's red-light district, home of the notorious 'soaplands', love hotels and massage parlours, as well as sleazy hostess bars, pachinko parlours and nefarious drinking dens. Venture there or the adjacent warren of the Golden Gai as a lone foreigner and you will be fleeced by exorbitant 'cover charges', your drink might be spiked, you'll get beaten up, or maybe end up with a particularly tenacious STD. The other day, there was a full-on yakuza riot there. The boss of the Matsuba-kai gang had an argument with a taxi driver. A rival boss, Chikahiro Ito of the Sumiyoshi-kai, happened to be passing and made some or other snide reference to his enemy's character. Punches were thrown which soon escalated to the point at which fifty or so gangsters were observed brawling in the street. Over a hundred police were called. Just another night in Kabukicho.

With all its sleaze and the apparent disregard for the basic principles of Japanese hospitality, Kabukicho is so very not typical of Japan, but somehow it is also just as much a Tokyo icon as the Imperial Palace or the Hama Rikyu Garden. I am strangely drawn to it, as others are drawn to sewer safaris. It has *texture*. Certainly Kabukicho is not the kind of place any responsible parent would bring impressionable young children but I had last been there with my offspring a couple of days earlier to visit the hilarious Robot Restaurant, and we had had a ball.

You might have seen footage of the Robot Restaurant on one of those TV travelogue series, the kind usually filmed over a couple of days due to budget restrictions and fronted by some wide-eyed, borderline racist comedian. Typically they will visit the Robot Restaurant, hook up with a 'geisha', do an onsen and eat some kind of wriggly seafood, before moving on to shoot the South Korea episode.

The Robot Restaurant is less a restaurant and more an orgy of liquid crystal, neon, lasers and mirrors, featuring bikini-clad J-Pop dancers on trapezes, five-metre-high remote-controlled pneumatic-breasted cyborgs, mock dinosaur vs robot battles and, at one point towards the end, a full-sized, neon-trimmed tank. It's part coked-up carnival parade, part sci-fi sex show, and the food is terrible. The bar/waiting room is almost as entertaining: a kaleidoscope of liquid crystal screens, crazy gilding, crystal chandeliers, disco lights and mirrored walls. It must be an epileptic's nightmare; like being inside

Liberace's head after he's taken too many of his diet pills. Everyone should go. Once.

When we visited, the ushers invited Asger and Emil to take part in the show and 'battle' a robot. Audience participation tends to throw my children's contrasting characters into even sharper relief: on this occasion, Emil, too cool to be manipulated for others' entertainment, declined. Asger, always happy to be the centre of attention no matter the context, readily agreed, and so, as the show approached its climax, he left his seat and joined the battle on the floor, administering thumps to a giant robot with preposterous oversized boxing gloves as we cheered him on, waving our glow sticks enthusiastically.

Now I think of it, whoever is behind the Robot Restaurant really should be put in charge of the opening ceremony of the 2020 Olympics.

On that occasion, at night, all of Kabukicho's rich tapestry of ne'er-do-wells and low-lifes were present on the streets: the yakuza bruisers, the pimps and the bouncers, but during the day it just looks shabby. I pass by Tokyo's pungent Korean quarter, Shin Okubo Koreatown, and continue on to the tsukemen festival, which is taking place in a small urban park surrounded by high-rise blocks.

Two rows of Portakabins at either end of the park have been turned into ramen kitchens for ten of Japan's top ramen/tsukemen restaurants to set up temporary stall (five making ramen, five making tsukemen), with a large, open-sided marquee in the centre of the park with trestle tables for the slurping aficionados. There are some unusual types of soup on offer – one restaurant is using a lamb bone broth, which I have never heard of before, another has based its soup on mushrooms.

My guide to all of this is Takamune Yano, executive chief editor of the best ramen magazine in Japan, *Ramen Walker*, whom I had met a couple of times before at the magazine's publisher, Kadokawa (which also happens to be my Japanese publisher).

I spot Yano-san, dressed in his customary salaryman uniform of navy blue jacket and grey slacks and carrying his black rucksack, at

the entrance to the festival, and we begin to peruse the various
offerings. Yano-san commands an incredible level of detailed knowledge about each ramen shop and its chef, from the length of time
you have to queue, to where they trained, for how long, and the
intricacies of how their broth differs from their master's. He is
similarly clued up on the economics of running a ramen joint. 'If
you own four or five decent ramen restaurants, then it's a Benz for
every member of your family,' he tells me as we walk around the
festival.

I had come to think of Yano-san as 'Ramen Man', a Clark Kent
figure with ramen superpowers. Merely being in his presence means
I am granted not only queue-jumping ability, but backstage access.
That is how I come to meet, Masaaki Hayasaka, the owner-chef of
Ufushin in Sendai, eastern Honshu, who is also director of the
Ramen Union.

I am introduced to him behind his temporary kitchen and begin
with the obligatory discussion about ingredients and technique.
Hayasaka-san's noodles feature 'silk gel' (whatever that is) and, for
this event, he is blending two broths, one tonkotsu (boiled pork
bones) and the other made from konbu and various dried fish
(sardine, bonito and squid). This was a very good thing as far as I
am concerned. Though I like it from time to time, tonkotsu, with
its milky soup of endlessly boiled pork bones, is not my favourite
type of ramen. For me, a soup made at least in part from some
kinds of dried fish is a prerequisite for great tasting ramen.

Hayasaka is a large man with a cube-shaped, closely shaved head.
He is wearing a pink and white swirly-patterned shirt, stretch pants
and a silver earring with a blue stone in one ear, and sporting a
goatee. He has one other distinguishing physical feature which we
shall address in a moment.

He started his career in a Western-style kitchen aged sixteen,
turning to the path of ramen aged twenty-three because, as he puts
it, 'You can make more people happier more easily with ramen, and
when you are a ramen chef you get to see their faces when they
eat.' Now in his forties, Hayasaka has come to the conclusion that

money and possessions did not make him happy. 'I always tell my apprentices: up until forty, you can think about what I call "primary success": money, women, cars, but any longer and you need to think about other things. Then it is time to start giving, the "secondary level" of success, and if you only ever achieve the primary success, then you should be ashamed of yourself.'

He tells me all this, not in a preaching or pompous manner, but speaking softly, from the heart. We sit at a makeshift workstation in a tent behind the Portakabin kitchen where his restaurant has set up temporary shop. We are surrounded by catering packs of soft drinks, ashtrays, rice cookers and, oddly, a Mexican wrestler's mask hanging on the side of the tent. 'No matter how rich you are, it doesn't mean you can make people happy,' he continues. 'And if you can't make someone happy, you are nothing. Ramen is my chosen medium of happiness.'

As we talk, Hayasaka makes gyoza with one hand. This is his only hand. He used to have two hands, but six years ago he lost his entire right arm in a grisly ramen accident. It happened one summer afternoon six years ago when Hayasaka had been making noodles in the back room of his restaurant.

'My noodles have a high hydrolysis rate,' he begins the tale. 'They use lots of water because I want them to be easy for my customers to digest. Lower water content makes them difficult to digest, especially for children and the elderly. But in summer, it is harder to make noodles with a higher water content because the dough gets so sticky.'

To mix the dough, Hayasaka-san uses an industrial mixer. He shows me a photograph of one on his phone. It looks like something almost agricultural, a fearsome metal bathtub with whirring blades capable of handling thirty kilos of flour at a time. Like many chefs, Hayasaka-san has no inhibitions about placing his hands in kitchen machinery while it is in motion. In professional kitchens, safety guards are for amateurs. But this time, reaching in to adjust the dough while the machine was still running his hand had become jammed in the super-sticky wet mixture. His entire right arm was damaged beyond saving and eventually had to be amputated at the shoulder.

'I thought about what I can do, not what I can't do,' the chef tells me when I ask him how he faced up to life after the accident. 'When chefs make food, they have to make do with what they have in the fridge, and it is the same with life. People may think I have lost my arm, lost fifty per cent of what I can do, but no. I live life, not fifty per cent of life. The only thing I can't do is put my hands together and pray, so I had to find out how I could give thanks in a different way.'

He was right-handed so started training his left hand while still in hospital. Within a month he was writing again. He left hospital after two and a half months, and was back at work in his kitchen the next day.

Hayasaka believes that his personal tragedy helped him empathise with the victims of the earthquake and tsunami which struck the coast by his home town of Sendai to such devastating effect in March 2011. His restaurant was not directly affected, but Hayasaka-san immediately sprung into action and headed off to the epicentre of the disaster around three hours' drive away with a mobile kitchen which he had already prepared for use in educating elementary school children in ramen-making. He ended up driving to the disaster zone every day for eight months, calling in favours from suppliers to source produce, gas canisters and water, serving more than 100,000 bowls of ramen during the course of that first year. But he did more than feed people. 'I think that those who had lost their houses and relatives saw me, a chef who had lost one arm, and I think it maybe inspired them to keep going.'

Hayasaka invites me into his kitchen where his team, dressed all in black, one of them wearing a Mexican wrestling mask, are in full flow serving bowl after bowl of ramen (not, today, their usual tsukemen) to a long queue which has formed out front. And that is how, after a brief initiation, I find myself part of a crack ramen kitchen brigade.

I have never enjoyed the heat of service in a professional kitchen, though I do understand why some get a kick out of it, and my experience in a ramen kitchen is as stressful as my other kitchen experiences. Hayasaka shows me how to cook the noodles and his technique for shaking the water off once they are ready, before gently sliding them into the bowl without splashing a single drop of soup. I manage to assemble a dozen or so bowls, cooking the noodles, draining them, first ladling in the tare – which in the case of ramen is a kind of essence, or flavouring – then the soup, adding the toppings of chashu, meatballs, wakame and spring onion, before passing them over the counter to the bewildered diners, before I give up and leave the kitchen to the professionals (to their obvious relief).

After the stress of the kitchen, Hayasaka and I chat a little about the difference between ramen fans and tsukemen fans. Mostly, people like both, he says, but there was a key difference with the way you eat the latter. Tsukemen doesn't stay hot for long (hence the practice of one tsukemen restaurant in Tokyo I once visited where they reheated half-finished bowls by placing a super-hot pebble in the soup), so you have to eat it quickly, and you mix the ingredients yourself, in your mouth. 'In Western food, you take a piece of potato and eat that, then you take a piece of meat and eat that, but in Japan we eat small pieces of different elements of a dish and combine them in our mouths to control a complex and changing flavour – that's the Japanese way, and also the tsukemen way,' he explains. Tsukemen was simpler, cruder, and usually more salty than ramen, but it always provoked a stronger reaction from his diners.

Where did he stand on the age-old ramen conundrum: which is more important, the noodle or the soup? Most chefs I have spoken to say 'both', but Hayasaka is firmly in the noodle camp. 'Because of the shape of Japan, long and thin from north to south with wide variation of humidity and seasons, local types of ramen have evolved with different noodles. In the south, you have a low hydrolysis rate because of the humidity. They don't use too much water, so the noodles will be al dente, and so then the broth must be thicker, like tonkotsu in Fukuoka. In the north, you can put more water into the noodles, so the broth can be thinner and the noodles don't overcook in the broth. So, you see, the noodle dictates everything.'

When it came to finally trying his ramen, rather awkwardly, Hayasaka's soup that day is not especially to my taste: it's a bit watery, and the chashu is an unappealing grey colour. He has, though, done a great deal to rehabilitate the nobility of the ramen chef in my eyes and there are plenty of other wonderful bowls on offer at the festival. The best is the tsukemen by the restaurant Tomita, from Matsudo in Chiba just outside of Tokyo – noodles as thick as rope, dipping sauce the colour of oxtail soup and a massive chunk of tender chashu (as well the chef tells me quite happily, as a dash of MSG).

I wish you could taste it because I yearn like Heathcliff yearned for Cathy, like Hachiko, the dog immortalised in a statue outside Shibuya Station yearned for his master, to taste Tomita's tsukemen again. And that is the real power of great ramen.

Chapter 22

Tea

The man in the white lab coat removes the bamboo ladle from the top of the brown earthenware water pot where it has been resting, carefully lifting the handle first, then the bowl in two separate, measured, tai-chi-like movements. He scoops some hot water and pours it over the dark green leaves in the broad, flat stoneware bowl. An infusion is permitted for just a few seconds before he covers the bowl with a lid, swirls the leaves and water, pours, and vigorously shakes the last drops, not much more than a thimble-full in all, of a luminescent golden liquid out into the small white bowl in front of me.

I lift the bowl to my lips and sip. It is the most intensely delicious tea I have ever tasted. Rich and grassy, toasted, bitter, fresh and mildly sweet, it is like a distillation of the entire plant world.

The second cup from the same leaves is infused for slightly longer with a greater yield. If anything, it is better than the first, deeper, richer with a pleasing bitter aftertaste. After the third serving, poured over ice and served in a tall-stemmed wine glass, I am buzzing. As a non-coffee drinker I am not used to this much caffeine and in my giddy state accept as perfectly reasonable the tea master's invitation to now *eat* the leaves themselves with a drizzle of ponzu. They are delicious.

Though I haven't lived in England for over a decade and a half I still think I make a passable Englishman. I appreciate a good queue. I apologise if someone treads on my foot. I know how to pronounce 'Magdalene College' and 'Holborn'. I eat my main meal of the day in the evening and cry during the opening titles of *Dad's Army* – sometimes simultaneously. I feel at home in a pub, and still calculate currency transactions via sterling, which makes no sense whatsoever. I can deploy passive-aggressive politeness with Exocet precision; I still learn most of what's happening in the world from the BBC; and I even own a pinstripe suit. But there is one aspect of Englishness in which I have always felt inadequate, a failure: in all the years I lived in England, and for many thereafter, I never drank a single cup of tea. Not so much as a sip. It wasn't a religious thing, the rest of my family all drank tea, as did friends, I just never got round to it somehow. Lukewarm, milky-brown, sugary liquid just didn't really hold that much appeal.

This was often inconvenient. If you've just heard you have got the job, or you have lost your dog; if your aunt has died in a ballooning accident, or you're feeling at a loose end; if it's late morning, or mid-afternoon; if there is an ad break on television, or if it's raining – for English people everywhere, whatever the situation, the universal solution is: 'Would you like a cup of tea?' If you decline the offer, they literally have no idea what to do next. It hardly helped that I didn't drink coffee either. I might as well have been Belgian.

And then I came to Japan for the first time. I went to a sushi restaurant and, after I had finished my meal, was given a thick, ceramic beaker of a hot, clear, jade-coloured liquid. I waited for it to cool down, having by then already learned from painful experience that the Japanese have a far, far greater tolerance of high-temperature foods than other humans, and sipped tentatively. It tasted lovely: grassy and fresh with an arresting bitterness, a flavour I had never experienced before. This was bancha, Japanese green tea. Here I was, drinking tea! All grown up at last. And I liked it.

Over the years since that first visit, I began to explore the world of Japan's teas. Broadly speaking, at the bottom is bancha, which is a green tea made with the third or fourth harvest leaves. There are twenty-two grades of bancha alone, along with bancha hojicha, which is roasted, ideally over charcoal, and whose burnt-toast flavour is the closest I ever get to drinking coffee (although it actually has less caffeine than the other green teas). Kukicha is also considered a lower grade tea because it is made from the stalks of the leaves, although I sometimes prefer its punchier flavour; you can also get roasted kukicha – the wonderfully named kukicha hojicha. Higher up the price range you have the shincha teas, sencha and gyokuro, made from the first and second flush leaves. Sencha is the most common Japanese green tea but, depending on aspects of *terroir*, farming techniques, blending, ageing and processing, a top-notch sencha can be every bit as good as the supposedly more aristocratic gyokuro (which means 'Jade Dew'). Gyokuro is the valetudinarian spinster of the tea world, grown beneath shade to protect it from direct sunlight, thus boosting its amino acid-rich chlorophyll levels.

There are many more types of Japanese tea besides these – mugicha (made from barley), sobacha (as the name suggests, buck-wheat tea), some rare black teas and, in terms of green teas, there is also the cheap konacha, made from the leftovers from sencha and gyokuro; kamairicha; kabusecha; koicha made with leaves from bushes over thirty years old, and some that don't even start with 'K', like matcha, the type usually used in the tea ceremony. Matcha is made from gyokuro or sometimes sencha leaves that have been steamed and then stone ground to a powder, and is further divided into culinary grade, which is what we mostly get in the West, and the good, drinkable stuff.

Each and every one of these teas are made from precisely the same plant (*Camellia sinensis*), which is also used to make the cloying, builder's teas from which I had recoiled as a child, the only differ-ence being that, for the most part, Japanese tea leaves are not fermented. As well as making green tea taste less musty and dusty than black tea, this has the added benefit of preserving their poly-phenols, the powerful antioxidants which supposedly help in the reduction of cholesterol and fat in the body.

Looking back, at the beginning of my belated tea education I should have started with a few more cups of bancha, gradually acclimatising my palate to the grassy bitterness of green tea, perhaps progressing to a sencha and then the more full-on flavours of kukicha with perhaps a little detour to the hojichas and genmaichas (forgot to mention these – they are green tea combined with toasted rice, originally to bulk them out and make them more affordable and, in the case of matcha genmaicha, with some matcha powder in the mix). Only then should I have ventured to the uplands of high-grade, first-flush gyokuro, perhaps then risking a full-on, proper grown-up cup of high-quality, stone-ground matcha. But I didn't. My big mistake was to jump in the deep end with a cup of super-thick koicha matcha at a traditional café in Asakusa. Bitter, thick and frothy, it was like drinking toad bile and it set my tea adventure back by some months.

Yet, slowly, like a rescue animal nervously nosing its way from its cage into the wild, I dipped a toe back into bancha after meals at restaurants before slowly scaling the ladder to the highlands of gyokuro.

These days I drink some form of Japanese green tea every morning at home but I can never quite replicate the clarity of flavour of good-quality tea in Japan. I wanted to find out why, which is what has brought me to Souen, a super-sleek contemporary tea house in a gallery complex in Nishi Azabu, in central Tokyo. Here, having studied his craft for twelve years at traditional tea houses and restaurants in the city, tea master Shinya Sakurai is, in his quiet, intense way, revolutionising the traditional Japanese tea ceremony.

And not before time. I realise that, as a chronic Japanophile clearly guilty of fetishising many aspects of Japanese food and culture, I should love the tea ceremony, revere the Way of Tea, but, as we saw in Matsue, I don't. Part religious ceremony, part meditation, part performance art, the tea ceremony supposedly embodies notions of aesthetics and good character which are, I'm afraid, beyond me. There is no disputing that I could do with more 'harmony', 'respect', 'purity' and 'tranquillity' in my life (these are the four tenets of the ceremony), but I just can't quite see how watching a pedantic elderly woman take two hours to make a cup of matcha will enhance any of these things in my life.

Sakurai-san's tea experience is very different, although it still proceeds at a dignified pace. Starbucks it ain't. I arrive stressed and rushed, having left Lissen, Asger and Emil exploring the many wonders of the nearby Tokyo Midtown complex – the three of them being more coffee people – and experience my usual difficulty finding the place in this quiet backstreet close to Roppongi but, as he begins to make what will be the first of several courses from his 'tea menu', Sakurai's measured pace and 'in-the-moment' focus serves notice that I must readjust my mood to match his. Slow down. Focus. Enjoy.

And enjoy I do, through servings of the thrice-infused gyokuro and then hojicha (with its aroma like a wealthy spinster's mullion-windowed home) accompanied by some jewel-like seasonal wagashi and exceptional pickles for the roasted tea. The latter is a reminder that the kaiseki meal itself originally evolved from the tea ceremony, with small courses of savoury food being served between the teas to combat the effects of their bitterness on the stomach.

To finish, Sakurai-san sieves some matcha powder (it has a tendency to clump together due, bizarrely, to static electricity) and whisks up a thick, frothy bowl of matcha, the caffeine levels of which leave me virtually seeing stars as, in the case of matcha, you actually consume the leaves in powder form rather than merely infusing their flavour into water. 'This must be how Pete Doherty feels most of the time,' I think to myself as I bounce giddily out onto the street.

My one major takeaway from the tea menu at Souen is that, aside from sourcing tea from the best growers (in this case, the gyokuro was from Shizuoka, the roasted tea from Yame, close to Fukuoka), water is the key. Sakurai-san goes as far as importing super-soft water from Kagoshima in southern Kyushu. The temperature of the water you infuse the leaves in is also critical. He transferred the water from pot to pot to cool it to less than 50°Celsius in the case of the gyokuro, and 80°Celsius for the matcha.

In Japan, tea is grown from Kyushu in the south-west, to as far north as Niigata, beyond which the climate gets too cold, but Shizuoka, an hour by Shinkansen south of Tokyo, is the country's largest tea region and one of the most highly regarded in terms of quality.

My tea education continued a few days later with a visit to a grower there, Yoshio Moriuchi, a multi-award-winning, legendary tea master, the ninth generation of a family which has been cultivating tea in Honyama, Shizuoka Prefecture, for almost two centuries. He even supplies the royal family.

'Tea came to this part of Japan in 1214,' Moriuchi told me proudly. 'The climate here suits the plants so well,' he continued. There are four very distinct seasons, with good rainfall and lots of fog which helps protect the leaves from the sun, making the tea sweeter – although a good cup should feature astringent, sweet, bitter and umami flavours all in one. Moriuchi also insisted I eat the leaves after they had been steeped, which by this point seemed perfectly normal.

Moriuchi's verdant, buxom bushes grow without pesticides (I notice that some of them are home to very alarming looking spiders), right next to the shops, houses and shrines of the town. He showed me how he and his wife steamed the tips of young leaves (for just twenty seconds at 70°C) and rolled them on something resembling a kind of metal-topped pool table in their shed overlooking a car park and convenience store. Tea-rolling is a highly skilled job – you have to keep the leaves moving constantly until each forms a perfect needle shape otherwise they get overheated and ruined, and during the process they lose about 60 per cent of their weight.

Moriuchi-san is famous for his high-quality sencha, which sells for ¥5,000 (£35) for 40g. It has a refreshing, almost briny flavour – perhaps because it is grown quite close to the sea, but that cost may be one reason why fewer and fewer Japanese are drinking high-quality green teas. Even though every vending machine in the country sells cheap bottles of green tea (cold or, somehow, miraculously, also hot, depending on the season), consumption of green tea for home-brewing is down by 20 per cent from its peak. High-quality green tea is typically drunk to accompany a traditional Japanese meal, Moriuchi explained, and, as people eat less traditional food, they are drinking less green tea.

Moriuchi's teas are perhaps the best I have ever tasted, but during my travels in Japan I have occasionally stumbled upon the more obscure, local types of tea grown in tiny quantities and which rarely make it beyond their prefectural boundaries. My favourite is from southern Shikoku.

When I was visiting the huge Sunday produce market in Kochi (the best market in Japan, at least that I have seen), the capital of the island, on my yuzu quest, I had chanced upon a stall selling a tea which looked like cannabis resin – small, brown blocks. A Western man was busy buying literally every single bag of it that they had, hastily thrusting handfuls of notes into the hands of the bewildered owner. I asked him what he was doing.

'This is amazing tea, the *most* amazing tea,' he said, breathlessly filling his holdall. 'If you can find it in Europe, you will pay a hundred euros for fifty grams.' The man, who was Spanish, was planning to open a museum dedicated to smells outside of Barcelona, he said, and he wanted the tea as an exhibit.

The stallholder offered me a taste of what turned out to be a wonderfully sharp-sour, golden-brown brew. It was called goishicha, a rare tea made from leaves which were fermented, twice in fact; once with a mould called kabi and another time with a lactic acid bacteria, in large cedar barrels for up to thirty days. This turns the leaves into something that looks like peat, which is dried in the sun. The 'peat' is then cut into small squares, from which the tea's name derives – the squares look like the black counters used in the board game Go. It was rich in umami but also had a gentle, tangy lactic aftertaste. I managed to grab the last bag before the Spaniard snaffled it up.

There was one final stop on my Japanese tea odyssey: the place where it all began, which I was able to visit during this most recent journey with my family.

Like much of its food and drink culture, tea came to Japan from China in the ninth century, albeit in very limited quantities and for medicinal use. But the widespread cultivation of tea bushes in Japan began a couple of hundred years later with a Buddhist monk.

This was Myoan Eisai (sometimes known as Yosai Zenji), the Okayama-born founder of Japanese Zen Buddhism. He visited the home of Zen, Mount Tiantai in China, in 1191 and became infatuated with matcha and a firm believer in its medicinal properties, as well as its practical effects in helping monks stay awake during meditation. After his second visit he returned from China bearing tea seeds, or actual plants (no one is sure), with which he planned to begin its cultivation in Japan. In their book *Tea in Japan*, H. Paul Varley and Isao Kumakura call this 'the most important event in the history of tea drinking in Japan'.

The first place Eisai landed on his return from China was Hirado, on the north-east tip of Kyushu. You'll remember Asger and I had visited Hirado and spent some time stuffing our faces with Casdous – the super-light, eggy spongecake introduced by the Portuguese in the seventeenth century – but, afterwards, we also paid a visit to Senkoji, the temple Eisai founded when he returned to Japan in 1191.

When I had first read about Eisai bringing tea to Hirado I had idly wondered if there were any remnants of this historic moment. A plaque or statue perhaps, or a tea shop. What I didn't expect to find was a living monument to the birth of green tea in Japan.

'I feel a connection with Eisai every morning when I pray for him,' retired policeman, now Buddhist monk, Sokan Tanaka told us, as we sat on the floor of the Senkoji Temple in the hills above Hirado.

Tanaka still used matcha in the way Eisai had: 'Our longest meditation is in early December when we meditate for twenty-five hours over the course of a week. Sometimes we sleep sitting here. While we are meditating we drink green tea twice a day to help us stay awake.'

When Asger and I visited it was freezing. I could only imagine how intolerably cold this wooden building with no central heating must be in December. But Tanaka had a solution: 'If you fall asleep, the other monks will hit you with this.' He pulled out a large stick.

'Show me,' I said. 'On him.' I gestured towards Asger who was kneeling on the tatami mat, looking idly in the other direction out of the window.

Tanaka wore indigo-dyed monk's robes tied with a neat bow across his chest. His head was shaved, revealing cauliflower ears – evidence of the fact that he had once been a judo champion. He brought the stick gently but firmly down on Asger's back. My eldest son gave me a look which indicated that, between this and the bakery, he preferred the bakery visit. Why, Asger asked Tanaka levelly, was this something people chose to do voluntarily?

'There is no answer to "Why do you do this?" It is *satori* [the Japanese for "enlightenment"]. It is a realisation of being alive,' said Tanaka.

Tanaka invited us into his home adjacent to the temple, where he told us a little more about his life. He first came to this part of Nagasaki Prefecture when he was working as a policeman. He was sent to police an anti-America demonstration when the USS *Enterprise* (the aircraft carrier) docked in Sasebo harbour, and he fell in love with the region. He returned years later as a monk with a mission to revive Eisai's temple, the place where Zen Buddhism was first practised on Japanese soil, and where he now lives with his wife, Hiromi, tending the temple and teaching pottery-making to locals.

As we sat around an open fire in the middle of the room, Hiromi offered us a cup of matcha, electric-green and frothy. I tasted it, expecting the usual bracing bitterness, but the drink was smooth and mildly grassy. I wondered aloud where it came from.

'The tea we grow is mild, maybe because of the cool temperatures up here,' said Tanaka.

I paused, mid-sip. 'What do you mean?'

'It is made from tea grown from Eisai's tea plants. We have plants which are descended from Eisai's growing just across the road. Fifteen years ago, there was a big tea ceremony here and some scientists took a DNA sample from the tea bushes we grow and compared them to the tea bushes from Mount Tiantai. They are

the same, so I do believe our tea bushes are descended from the
ones Eisai planted.'

He led us across the small country road in front of the temple
to a group of forty or so tea bushes growing on a gently sloping
patch of land surrounded by trees. This was the actual tea plan-
tation founded by Eisai. From here, the monk had travelled through
Japan with more seeds and planted more tea bushes on his way to
Kyoto, including at Shizuoka. Afterwards, Eisai wrote his own book,
The Book of Tea, to instruct the Japanese on how to grow the plant
and process the leaves into matcha via steaming and drying, and
then how to brew and drink the tea in the Chinese manner. Over
time, tea drinking became associated with the temples, both as an
offering to the gods and to keep monks awake during meditation,
before becoming an integral part of the tea ceremony so beloved
of the idle samurai class.

And it all started here on this hillside above Hirado. 'Not many
Japanese people know about this,' said the monk as we thanked him
and prepared to leave. 'Not even locals here know the story but this
is where green tea started in Japan.'

Chapter 23

Soba

Let us linger in the past for a little longer, although not quite as far back as Eisai's time. Let me take you back to a more recent era defined for some reason almost entirely by those words beginning with 'D': the shokunin words like discipline, dedication, decency, diligence, discernment and determination; back to a time when people took pride in their work, whether they were craftsmen, artisans, butchers, bakers or Bakelite makers. In the good old days, from what I understand because this is a little before my time, everyone made an unspoken commitment to doing their job as well as they could, to serving their customers to the utmost of their ability, and they did so in order not to display their achievements on Instagram or showcase their successes on Facebook, but simply because it was the right thing to do for their customers and, by extension, for society. They did it out of a sense of another 'D' word, duty.

This, I suppose, is how many people imagine Britain to have been in the first half of the twentieth century. It is certainly true that, back then, there still existed a strong tradition of craftsmanship, things were still *made* in Britain, and they were made to last. Shops wrapped things in waxed paper and string, milk was still delivered to your door, and if you bought one of those new-fangled vacuum cleaners, you expected it to outlast you. Made in Britain stood for quality and durability. Yes, the *Titanic* sank, but look how well it has survived down there on the ocean floor!

Read certain newspapers and you might think that such principles no longer exist in Britain. I don't know whether that's true but I do know that the 'D' words do endure in Japan. Over the years I have lost count of the Japanese people I have met working in the food industry who embodied what is, to British eyes, a perhaps old-fashioned dedication to their craft, people who work every single day towards achieving a probably ultimately unachievable perfection with humility and resolve. I want to introduce you to a couple of these people.

The first thing I try to eat when I get off the twelve-hour flight to Tokyo is soba. Particularly 'zaru soba', which is served not just cold but chilled, with a dashi- and soy-based dipping sauce, garnished with spring onions and wasabi. Cold soba took some adjusting to, but I now think it is the best way to eat soba, and after a flight it always just feels like that's what my body needs most: something pure, ascetic and tasting of health-giving minerals.

The best soba I ever had was not at one of the classic, big-name soba restaurants, like Kanda Matsuya or Daikokuya; it was not even the incredible uni-soba at Honmura An in Roppongi (although, boy, was that great); it was at the humble two-up, two-down home of Yoshihiro Hibiya in Nakanoku, Tokyo.

I was first taken to this anonymous little backstreet house, its exterior a mess of corrugated iron, air-conditioning units, gas pipes and shutters by some Japanese friends who knew I'd get a kick out of a multi-course meal based on buckwheat. And I did. Much as I liked soba, I never imagined it could be capable of holding my interest over six courses, but as my friends and I sat on the floor in Hibiya-san's front room he worked alone in the open kitchen to the rear of the room, calmly creating buckwheat porridge, warm soba, cold soba, and other buckwheat-based dishes, serving us with a dazzling array of rare and delicious sakes to match. The purest of the buckwheat dishes Hibiya makes is the simple, unadorned porridge made with soba flour ground from three-year-old grains. It has a delicate, nutty, metallic flavour. It was the first soba dish he ever served me: an audacious way to start a meal, I thought at the time.

So, when I wanted to learn more about soba and how to make it, it was natural that I should return to La Strada, the incongruous

Italian name Hibiya-san has given his restaurant. (I once asked him about this but he said there was no great meaning behind it. He just liked Italy.)

I was also intrigued by Hibiya himself, the soba loner, this buckwheat monk, who has dedicated his life to this hardiest of grains which can grow even in the most meagre of soils (hence soba's traditional popularity in the Tokyo region where the soil is not so rich). Though friendly, he was a shy, intense man with long, centre-parted hair fringing black-rimmed glasses. When I turned up for my soba lesson he was wearing grey combat trousers, green crocs and a yellow t-shirt.

'The most interesting thing is, if you want to make really good soba, then it gets more simple,' Hibiya-san explained to me as he tidied his kitchen, not much larger than a standard Japanese domestic kitchen. He offered me a glass of water. I had arrived earlier than we'd arranged, just before midday, and had clearly roused him from his bed. Every surface of his kitchen and front room was covered in dirty crockery and sake cups from the previous evening's guests.

We stepped over the empty sake bottles by the door and moved to another kitchen upstairs. This is where he makes the noodles fresh every day for his guests, five days a week for lunch and dinner. In one corner of the room was a stone mill. He sat beside it and began by grinding some buckwheat grains, turning the top stone by hand to transform the buckwheat grains to flour. It was a painstaking operation. Ten or so of the pyramidal, pistachio-coloured grains would be nudged down the hole into the space between the two stones; he would give the heavy stone four laborious, slow rotations, then push a few more grains down the shaft. He used a flour-encrusted paintbrush to carefully assemble every speck of flour. I stood watching him, a sharp buckwheat grain on the floor sticking up through my sock into the sole of my foot.

'My soba's taste is the taste of this mill,' Hibiya said, straining to push the grey, granite millstone. I assumed grinding by hand was better because it didn't heat the flour as much as an electric mill, but Hibiya wasn't bothered by that. I got the sense that he just enjoyed the sheer bloody-mindedness of the physical graft; he relished having to transform the grains into flour through his own labour.

He took the fresh-ground flour and mixed it with a little wheat flour at a ratio of 10:1 in a shallow, very wide red-lacquered bowl, (called a *konebachi*), then began to add a little chilled water, mixing with the fingers of one hand slightly splayed. The amount of water he uses changes depending on the humidity and the flour, he explained. Buckwheat is gluten-free so the wheat flour helps hold the dough together: without it, the noodles become very brittle and have a tendency to partially dissolve when you cook them. Now using two hands in a ying-yang motion he mixed together the flour and water to a crumb-like texture, added more water before, in a split second, bringing it all together to form a dough, dabbing it around the bowl to gather up the remaining crumbs so that not a speck was wasted. He now repeatedly smeared the dough on the bowl, as if preparing *pâté brisée*, until finally he was ready to make the noodles. He covered the lacquered bowl with a large wooden board, whipped out a thin, metre-long rolling pin, and swiftly began to roll the dough out to an even thickness of a little less than a millimetre. He had a very specific technique for rolling, curling his fingertips under his knuckles, and shuffling the hands out to the ends of the pin and then back into the middle until the knuckles of his thumbs met, then back out again.

Next he bought out a smaller, heavier board on which to chop the noodles using a large, deep, oblong blade. I noticed the blade was strangely mottled, a result, he said, of the strong (and good) bacteria that live in buckwheat. He dusted the board with a special, coarser flour, called *uchiko*, then folded the flattened dough into thirds and chopped it with machine precision into slender shoelaces. He invited me to try but I ended up with something more resembling tagliatelle (this was not a complete catastrophe as it could be used in another of the dishes Hibiya serves, atsukezuri soba, made from broader noodles).

The most recent trend in soba has been the ageing of the grains, vacuum-packed and frozen, sometimes for up to eight years. It made for a stronger, richer flavour and darker colour. This was necessary to counter the fact that the flavour of buckwheat has been getting weaker over the years because of climate change and soil depletion. 'Japan is getting warmer, the soil is exhausted,' Hibiya sighed. As a result, Chinese imports had increased, rendering domestic production less economically sustainable.

I wondered how he had ended up as a soba chef. In his early twenties everyone had been telling Hibiya to settle for life as a salaryman, he said, and he had done so, at least mentally. But he took a last chance to travel in Europe before starting his working career, and it proved to be a life-changing decision.

'Young people in Europe seemed to appreciate their own culture much more than I did mine. And worse was, they knew more about my culture than I knew about theirs.' He returned to Japan, which was in the midst of a soba boom and became particularly taken by the way in which soba restaurateurs integrated so many other aspects of Japanese crafts into the work – the ceramics, sake-making, glassware and so on. There was another benefit: 'They don't drink sake in the afternoon in udon or ramen restaurants.'

He allowed himself until the age of thirty to secure a career as a soba chef, training for seven years at four different, traditional restaurants in Tokyo. He is now thirty-nine. He opened La Strada four years ago, and quickly became a revered figure among the capital's soba aficionados for his single-mindedness and the purity of his soba.

Hibiya has much in common with the second food shokunin I would like you to meet, Tomokazu Horiguchi, of the Gekko mochi café in Minowa, in north-eastern Tokyo. To me, Hibiya and Horiguchi are twin spirits.

I went to Minowa on a tip-off from a mochi connoisseur who, knowing how much I love these chewy-doughy rice dumplings with their 'nodogoshi' ('good throat feel'), insisted that I experience them in what she said was their most Platonically perfect state. Horiguchi was doing something very special, my friend told me: he had perfected the increasingly rare art of handmade mochi.

Gekko is in another of those slightly shabby, local shopping arcades or *shotengai*, the 'Joyful Minowa Shopping Street' to give it its proper name. Its neighbours include a fishmonger, a butcher's, a grocer's, tea shop, pickle store and one of those time-warp old men's clothing stores for which I have a strange affection, selling patterned pullovers and sharp-creased slacks.

In the tiny backroom kitchen, bending my head beneath clothes drying on a line, I watched Horiguchi-san, tall and slender with a long neck and receding, spiky hair, pound the mochi the old-fashioned way with a hefty wooden mallet.

'Hand-made is better,' he grunted as, having tipped out a large ball of steaming hot, just-cooked mochigome (glutinous rice, actually gluten-free) into a cedar tree trunk with a bowl hollowed out of its top half, he began pounding it into a single, smooth, homogenous pillow of rice. I watched, hypnotised, as the individual grains of rice were consumed within a dense, sticky singularity. He added nothing to the rice either before or after steaming it – no salt, no sugar, no flavourings. Wearing his white lab coat, he swung the croquet mallet up and over his shoulder and back down onto the rice with brutal yet controlled violence, in a kitchen so tiny it would not have been possible to do the same with a cat. A small fleck of rice flew from the bowl and stuck beneath the calendar pinned to the wall.

After twenty minutes' pounding, now satisfied that every single grain was beaten into submission, he gave the smooth white ball of ricey ectoplasm a loving pat, sprinkled some potato starch on a chopping board and, within a few minutes, had moulded by hand sixty-six bite-sized pieces of mochi and set them out in military ranks in front of him, each of them weighing precisely forty-five grams.

Now forty-four, Horiguchi has been making mochi six days a week for over thirteen years. Reading between the lines, I think he might have had something of an early mid-life crisis around the age of thirty; that was when he quit his job in an electronics store and set out on his path to learn the traditional ways of the mochi maker. Out front, in the tiny, ramshackle café cluttered with mementos, stacks of old newspapers, mismatched wooden chairs and formica tables, there was a yellowing photo on the wall taken the day the Gekko café opened with Horiguchi outside the shop. In the photo he is wearing a *samue* and posing with his then new mallet and pristine cedar tub amid a display of floral bouquets traditionally given to newly opened enterprises in Japan. I don't know why, but I found this photograph quite poignant. Horiguchi is not smiling broadly, as you might expect of someone about to embark on a new business venture. He looks humble, but confident. He is flanked by what I presume are four companions (co-owners and waitresses?) yet he still looks lonely somehow, as if he knows his will be a solo journey.

Perhaps I am projecting. We actually said very little, he and I, during the morning I spent watching him work in his shop, but Horiguchi kindly followed up on some questions via email, which I had translated. One only achieved the soft, smooth, stretchy texture of his mochi through pounding the rice by hand, he wrote, it could never be achieved by machine. He uses rice from Aomori. It was tasty and sweet, better than any other he tried. Every day he takes 2.5kg of rice and turns it into 3.8kg of mochi, the steaming time varying according to the humidity of the day. In the summer, the rice contains less water, so it takes more time to cook.

As I was watching him work in the cupboard-sized kitchen, the only sounds the gentle shuffle of mochi dough on floured board and the hum of the extractor fan, it had occurred to me that across this city, across this country, right at that very moment, there were thousands of men and women like Horiguchi-san; humble, unassuming, dedicated craftspeople carrying out their various tasks with precise rigour, doing what they do, making what they make, with no thought or hope of riches, fame or acclaim, just the goal of making noodles, or tofu, or patisserie, or sake, or wine, or wagashi, or whatever it was, as excellently as they possibly could, working with the simple but, I think, noble aim of bringing a transitory moment of sensual pleasure or nutritional sustenance to their customers. There seems to me to be a profound dignity in that. I am sure there are mornings when all of them, Horiguchi included, wake up and have no desire to continue, occasions when the relentless grind of the repetitive slog wears them down, when bones are aching, wounds are fresh and the motivation for their drudgery is obscured by the dreary fog of tedium and tiredness, but still they forge on, the culinary shokunin of Japan, improving their craft by tiny increments, refining and honing, aiming higher for no other reason than that is their path.

A few minutes later, Horiguchi had finished making the mochi and I was sitting at a table in the front room of his café, the only guest. He set three dishes before me, his entire menu: a savoury dish of mochi with grated daikon, a smattering of spring onion and a soy / dashi sauce; two mochi balls, one covered with kinako powder (toasted, ground soy beans) the other with ground black sesame seeds; and, the third dish, a ceramic matcha bowl with smaller, twice-steamed, gnocchi-sized mochi, with adzuki paste and matcha ice cream. This last dish in particular offered a combination of complex, bitter, sweet and umami flavours that was worthy of any Michelin star table.

In truth, Horiguchi's mochi needed no accompaniment: I would happily have scarfed them down on their own. Alone, they tasted ravishingly of fresh-cooked rice. And *what* rice: so sweet and nutty, so intensely pure and clean. I could never have imagined rice could taste this good, and then, of course, there was the mochi's deeply satisfying, comforting, soft-chewy texture.

For sure, I thought to myself, this was *a* meaning of rice. For Horiguchi it was the meaning of everything.

Chapter 24

Sushi

My first thought on being asked to be a judge at the British round of the Global Sushi Challenge, an international competition to find the world's best sushi chef, was about the quantity of sushi I would be able to eat during the course of the day.

I spent some time thinking about this because I really love sushi and am capable of putting away a quite frightening quantity. I do this by eating it quickly so that my digestive system is caught unawares and then lying very still for about ten hours nursing a stomach bloated like a hippo's corpse.

My fellow judges at the British round of the competition will be from the Tokyo-based World Sushi Skills Institute (WSSI), along with Hideki Maeda, head chef of Nobu, the London restaurant where the round will be held, and Jack-Robert Møller, the UK director of the Norwegian Seafood Council which is sponsoring the competition worldwide, presumably with the intention of getting more of us to eat their farmed salmon.

I arrive at Nobu, London – this was a November morning some few months before I and my family left for Japan – having not had breakfast in preparation for the vast amounts of high-quality sushi I will put away. The competition is to take place in the restaurant's windowless private function room. Here, two rows of workstations extend from either end of a judges' table. Gathered restlessly outside the room like racehorses about to enter the gates are the nine contestants, all professional sushi chefs from across Britain, all wearing chefs' whites.

Before they start, Hirotoshi Ogawa, the chief examiner of the WSSI, a short, intense-looking Japanese man wearing a white lab coat and carrying a clipboard, gives a pep talk about keeping work-stations clean and tidy, and not wasting any raw ingredients.

'The most important thing is not to cut your fingers. In every country so far, someone has cut their fingers,' he says, adding that, according to the rules, ten points will be deducted for cuts.

One contestant raises her hand: 'Can we use a strip of nori to tie the tamago to the rice?' Ogawa-san crosses his index fingers in the Japanese manner.

'Egg is the hardest to make as nigiri. If you use nori to hold it on then we can't judge it. If you can't do the egg nigiri without nori, then you are not a professional sushi chef!' The contestants exchange nervous glances.

They will face three challenges: the first is to make two plates of classic Edo-mae sushi in ten minutes. Edo-mae is the sushi style we are most familiar with in the West – nigiri and maki, traditionally made with a specific range of fish caught in and around Tokyo Bay – but to make the fourteen pieces of nigiri and two cucumber rolls cut into six pieces each required, and to do it according to the WSSI's exacting standards in such a short period of time, is going to be tough. The second 'creative' round requires them to make forty pieces of sushi in their own style, for which they have an hour. The third challenge will be to make a single piece of their signature nigiri ushi for the judges to taste.

As this last part is announced, there comes the awful, dawning realisation that these nine pieces are the only sushi I will get to eat during the entire day. As soon as Ogawa-san finishes his address, I take him aside.

'Yes, that's right,' he explains. 'It is not so good to eat the sushi from the other rounds. Perhaps there is a hygiene risk and so on.'

My stomach rumbles and I hastily downgrade my expectations for the day. He hands me a marking sheet with categories including 'Visual', 'Hygiene', 'Taste' and 'Creativity', and then turns away to test the sharpness of one contender's knives. We are to keep a special eye on whether they rinse their hands in the bowl of vinegared water provided, he adds. They must do this between each and every piece they make, as it is essential for killing bacteria. In other food preparation situations, you might expect the chefs to wear disposable rubber gloves but these are firmly shunned by the sushi crowd. A sushi chef needs to be able to feel the grains of rice and handle the fish with extreme care. Following some unfortunate food poisoning incidents, New York City's Department of Health has recently begun insisting that sushi chefs use them, which has made them a laughing stock in Tokyo: 'Can't make sushi with gloves!' one of the city's leading sushi chefs barked dismissively when I asked him about this.

The air is fragrant with the nutty aroma of cooked rice as the ten-minute challenge begins in complete silence. 'In Japan, the chefs are perhaps not so creative, but they are much faster. There, we only give them two minutes,' Ogawa confides. But still, ten minutes is not enough for the contestants today. It is incredibly stressful to watch them; the round has the frantic feel of a *Generation Game* challenge. At one point, I try to lighten the mood and make a comment to one of the contestants, Poppy Sherwood, from a restaurant called Wabi in Horsham, Sussex. Ogawa-san takes me aside: 'No talking to the contestants during the ten-minute round!' At the end of the round the contestants stand back from their hideous, ramshackle plates of sushi, spattered with random grains of rice and slices of fish which look like they've gone a few rounds with Edward Scissorhands. All but one of them fails this round completely.

While the contestants work on the second round – two plates of twenty pieces each, in their own style – I chat with the Norwegian Seafood Council guy. He is open about the fact that the competition is devised to promote Norwegian salmon. Salmon is nowhere near as ubiquitous in Japanese sushi restaurants as it is in the UK. In fact, up until the mid-nineties its use in sushi was virtually unheard of there. The Norwegians have spent about a million pounds on the Global Sushi Challenge, holding rounds like this in fourteen countries including Japan, France and the US, and the final to come in Tokyo. It is far more ambitious than any previous sushi competitions (with which the WSSI has also been involved) and Møller and others involved expressed to me their desire to see the Global Challenge become a kind of Bocuse d'Or for sushi, although Møller admits that this inaugural competition has not quite attracted the talent they'd hoped for.

'The really good chefs don't want to compete,' he sighs. 'After all, they have a lot to lose and what do they have to gain?' The winner of the British round will get an all-expenses-paid trip to Tokyo for the final, where the overall winner gets a training session in Tokyo and a nice knife. Perhaps if they had made a little more of that million-pound budget available for prize money …

Nevertheless, competing today here in London are chefs from prominent restaurants albeit of a kind I would probably never consider dining at (the oligarch canteens, essentially) – Gordon Ramsay's Maze Grill Park Walk, for instance, Saka No Hana and Sushi Samba – although there are also some I am not so familiar with, such as Sam Butler from Shrewsbury's House of the Rising Sun. Sam does not fare very well in the first round. Lined up, his higgledy-piggledy maki look like the Shrewsbury skyline. He has my sympathy: that's exactly how it looks when I make maki.

We move on to the second, 'creative' round. Though the tension remains high, this goes better. Competing chefs must be working at restaurants in the UK, but they don't have to be British. There is a wide range of nationalities competing, including Polish, Brazilian, and one man of Chinese background who was born in Rome. There is even someone from Norwich.

Diana de Carvalho's (a chef from Maze Grill Park Walk) sushi is delicate and attractive, but she uses both Philadelphia cream cheese and mango chilli sauce in her maki, which marks her down in my book. Wojciech Popow from London restaurant Yashin Sushi, meanwhile, has brought along another intriguing range of ingredients including chocolate, smoked salmon and Hibiki whisky jelly, all of which, he tells me, he is planning to incorporate into his single taster for the judges. I gulp nervously and offer an encouraging smile. Tai-Po Wong, from London's Sushi Samba, is also pulling out all the stops. He has a smoker, foie gras, caviar and some freeze-dried crumbs. His final plate, while entertaining with its Jackson

Pollock splashes of sauces, is a little too 'busy' for the Japanese judges.

There are further calamities: contestants are supposed to make two plates of twenty pieces each but with ten minutes to go I notice that the guy from Saka No Hana has finished one, admittedly beautiful, plate but is packing up. I sidle up to him: 'You do know you are supposed to make two plates, right?' I whisper. His face drops, and he springs into action, hastily unpacking his equipment.

Unlike the ten-minute Edo-mae challenge, during the 'creative' round we judges are encouraged to talk to the contestants as they work, this interaction with diners, which usually takes place over the traditional counter of a sushi restaurant, being an important aspect of a sushi chef's work. As one Japanese sushi chef later puts it to me, 'French chefs stay in the kitchen, but a sushi chef must communicate with customers, they have to be monitoring them all the time.'

Sam tells me that he started a ramen restaurant in Shrewsbury, and now makes sushi, too – a career change which would be unthinkable in Japan where ramen chefs and sushi chefs almost never 'cross the floor'. Sam's special ingredient is beetroot. Though by now very hungry, I find myself hoping this is not his sample piece.

While the chefs work, I sit down with Ogawa to find out a little more about his career and the WSSI. Having worked in restaurants in Australia, he opened his own place back in Tokyo in 2003, in Chiba, on the eastern side of Tokyo Bay, but, unfortunately, aftershocks from the March 2011 tsunami destabilised the ground beneath the building and it had to be vacated. He could not face the idea of starting all over again, so instead took a job at the WSSI in 2012. His favourite sushi restaurant in all the world is Sakae Zushi in Chiba, he says, but many of the cheap, conveyor-belt places that I sheepishly confess to frequenting when I am in Tokyo are actually quite good 'because they are chains so they can buy good quality fish in bulk'. We talk about the contestants: 'I can tell that numbers eight and seven were trained by Japanese chefs,' he says approvingly.

Finally, it is time to eat some sushi: the contestants present us each with a piece of sushi to showcase their creativity. Up until now, there has been a judging schism, the Japanese judges preferring a classic style, Møller and I tending to favour something a little more Western, but we all agree that the piece made by Wojciech is the best. The home-smoked salmon, chocolate and Hibiki whisky jelly combine unexpectedly well. But Popow the Pole is not going to the final in Tokyo. It is close, but a shell-shocked Xia Jia Tian from Rome, latterly of restaurant Kouzu close to Victoria Station, is the winner. As his name is called, he remains with the group of contestants literally unable to believe he has won until, eventually, we coax him forward to accept the trophy.

'French food is about having a concept, about creativity, but the work of the sushi chef is more about skill. A French chef will always ask "Why?", but in Japan there is no "Why?"'

It is now some months after the London round of the Global Sushi Challenge. I am in Tokyo for the final, where I will also be a judge. Ogawa-san had intrigued me, and I learned so much from him just in those few hours in Nobu, so I have arranged to meet him at his favourite sushi restaurant, the one he had mentioned in London, Sakae Zushi. We are talking about perceptions of sushi in the West, perceptions which Ogawa has dedicated his life to overturning.

'Thanks to the documentary about Jiro [*Jiro Dreams of Sushi*, about Jiro Ono and his restaurant, Sukiyabashi Jiro, directed by David Gelb], I think people in the West are beginning to realise that the simplicity of sushi hides the fact that it is very, very difficult to achieve at the highest level,' he continues as we sit at the restaurant's counter. 'The sushi chef needs to know about a hundred different types of fish, each one prepared a different way according to the four seasons.'

Sakae Zushi is far out in the suburbs of Chiba, east of Tokyo on a busy residential street. From the outside it hadn't looked especially legendary, although legendary sushi restaurants rarely do. Still, few have picture menus outside like this one.

Ogawa is already seated at the counter when I arrive and introduces me to the elderly bespectacled gentleman standing behind the granite counter. He is wearing a white, short-sleeved chef's coat, a rolled cloth tied around his forehead. The chef is, it turns out, the real reason we are here.

This is Masayoshi Kazato, sixty-six, the chairman and founder of the World Sushi Skills Institute and its parent organisation, the All Japan Sushi Association. Ogawa tells me that Kazato is one of the most respected sushi chefs in all Japan. Though we are far from the high-rolling glitz of Ginza where many of the famous Michelin-starred sushi restaurants like Jiro Sushi are to be found, Sakae Zushi is a regular haunt of Japanese celebrities and politicians, including Prime Minister Abe, Ogawa whispers. The restaurant will be forty years old next year, but its master, Kazato-san, has been working as a sushi chef since he was seventeen.

'It takes ten years to make a good sushi chef,' says Kazato, as he forms the first of our dozen or so glistening dishes: a pretty landscape of precision-placed sashimi. 'The essence of Japanese cuisine is this: the more simple, the more difficult it is to make.'

I taste my first piece of nigiri. It is a slight anticlimax. To my uneducated, Western palate the rice seems very lightly seasoned with only the faintest trace of vinegar and salt.

'In Japanese sushi we foreground the flavour of the fish,' says Ogawa, perhaps sensing that I am a little underwhelmed. 'In the West you try to add extra flavours.' It is clear this is a bad thing, and that low-seasoned rice is a more mature choice. At home, when I make the seasoning for my sushi rice I use around 80ml of rice vinegar for 500g of rice (uncooked weight). Ogawa scoffs at this. 'No, no, no, you should be using no more than thirty millilitres for that much rice!'

Kazato founded the WSSI in 2010 but has been travelling the world expounding on good sushi-making practice – the washing of hands in vinegared water, among other things – since 1995. When Ogawa joined, the WSSI was still in its infancy and, initially, the two men paid their travel expenses out of their own pockets. 'I used over a hundred thousand dollars of my own money, I have three children!' says Ogawa. Now, the organisation enjoys government support and is expanding its certification. Around 500 certificates have been issued to chefs in the US, Australia and the UK – the pass rate is only 50 per cent apparently. Ogawa tells me they are currently developing a coloured belt system akin to that of karate or judo, with five colours to distinguish training levels of foreign chefs. A black belt in sushi might one day be a possibility.

The work of the World Sushi Skills Institute is not without controversy: in Japan there is anxiety about disseminating the secrets of great sushi to the outside world (although *Jiro Dreams of Sushi* did rather let that particular cat out of the bag). 'Some chefs have complained: "Why do you go overseas and tell our secrets? That's wrong! This knowledge must only be in Japan, they must come to Japan to learn,"' says Ogawa. Meanwhile, outside Japan there is resentment at what can sometimes be seen as a superior attitude from Japanese chefs and instructors and a rather limited definition of what sushi is. '[Foreign chefs] are proud of their own skills, yes, but I'm not there to just critique them. When they see my skill, they realise that they can learn.'

A glistening hamaguri clam nigiri arrives, briefly distracting us with its angular, alien form (it looks like it was designed by Frank Gehry). I ask Ogawa to talk me through his apprenticeship as a sushi chef. He began by studying at the Tsuji Cooking School in Osaka,* after that working at a sushiya in Tsukiji fish market. He talks me through the apprenticeship in more detail, it does not sound an especially joyous experience.

'For the first two years they didn't even let me touch a knife. I only did washing-up and ran errands. But you do this to study the

---

* This was the school founded by Shizuo Tsuji, author of the book *Japanese Cooking: A Simple Art*, which had inspired me to go to Japan in the first place a decade ago.

tableware, which is very important in Japanese food. I did the cleaning which is also a learning experience: when you vacuum a room you understand the space. Towards the end of that I began to sharpen knives. During the third year I did basic things like skinning squid, and waiting on tables to understand the communication with the customers. Then I came here to Sakae Zushi for two and a half years where I learned making *maki* in the first year, and then the rest was spent on nigiri and finally the cutting of sashimi.' Ogawa met his wife around that time but they did not live together at first. As with trainee sumo wrestlers, tradition dictated that he must live with the boss of the restaurant during his apprenticeship.

Kazato-san was listening to our conversation. 'Once, when I was in Australia, I heard someone say that you can train to be a sushi chef in a single day!' he adds, incredulous, briefly wafting some slices of mackerel over the grill. A sushi chef's job is to bring forth the essential flavours of the fish, a deceptively complex skill which takes years to learn. 'In Europe, they add taste by adding sauce but we extract the flavour from the fish itself. We don't add anything.'

Eventually, Ogawa left Kazato's tutelage to work in the ANA hotel in Sydney, where he stayed for five years as head chef before returning to Tokyo to open his own restaurant. 'I tried to keep it very traditional in Sydney. There were so many fusion sushi places,' he recalls with not a little disdain. 'Some people think fusion sushi is more difficult but I want traditional sushi chefs to get the respect they deserve. I want more people to know about traditional techniques and styles. The fusion chefs were good, but I think you need to learn the basics of Edo-mae sushi first. Not many of them had, though.'

What is so special about Edo-mae sushi? Only members of the WSSI were permitted to judge it at the Global Sushi Challenge, for instance.

'Technically speaking, Edo-mae sushi is sushi made only with fish caught in Tokyo Bay,' said Ogawa.

'Isn't the water there awfully polluted?' I ask.

'Ha! Yes,' replies Ogawa, blithely. 'You see TVs floating in it, everything!'

I wonder how the sponsorship by Norwegian Salmon squared with this tradition. Competitors in London and in the final in Tokyo had to include salmon in their sushi, but salmon are not found in Tokyo Bay.

'The younger generation demand salmon,' interjects Kazuto. 'Salmon is the number one most popular neta [nigiri topping], you know.'

I also find this rather hard to believe but let it go. I ask instead about tuna. Outside of Japan there is broad awareness that bluefin tuna is endangered and many believe it should no longer be served in restaurants, but within Japan one rarely gets a sense that this impending extinction is high on anyone's agenda and I have never eaten in a sushi restaurant in Japan where tuna was *not* on the menu. I wonder if Ogawa is concerned about the dramatic decline in stocks.

'Yes, very worried,' he says. 'Maybe in the future there won't be much left. Bluefin is very popular in China. They like oily fish. Japanese prefer umami flavour.' I am not sure the Chinese deserve to take the blame for bluefin's decline. 'The best wild bluefin comes from Oma in Aomori Prefecture [this is the north-eastern tip of the main island, Honshu, close to Hokkaido]. They feed on the squid in the sea there, where the cold water meets the warm coming up from the Philippines. The best time is from October to January.' Our meal is at an end. I thank these two tough sushi taskmasters, and head back into the city.

Ogawa, Kazuto and I next meet a few days later in the vast function room of a posh hotel in Tokyo, the location of the final of the Global Sushi Challenge. I will be judging alongside Yoshihiro Narisawa, the multi-award-winning chef of the eponymous Tokyo restaurant, whom I know a little. Another judge will be chef Ryu Hwan Tan of Ryunique, in Gangnam, Seoul, who is new to me but apparently has a growing international reputation, and then there are the WSSI chefs who will also be judging alongside us. Fourteen finalists from around the world have won the right to compete here in Tokyo; all are male. The winner will get a posh knife and a three-day training session in Tokyo; if the Japanese contestant wins, he gets a trip to Norway.

This time, I have had breakfast.

The procedure is the same as in London but everything is on a much larger scale. There are TV crews from Japan, Turkey, Korea, France and elsewhere and, before we get underway, we must endure several extremely dull speeches from important people in the Tokyo sushi scene, and the Norwegian sponsors.

'People think they can come to Japan for three or four months and learn how to make sushi,' Tadashi Yamagata (head of another sushi organisation) tells the assembled crowd of competitors, supporters, sponsors and media – the now familiar refrain. 'But they can't. It takes years. So what happens is that the reputation of sushi abroad is damaged. Now we want to disseminate the correct way around the world.'

Someone gestures to me. Apparently, I also have to say something to inspire our competitors so I take the microphone and mumble a few encouraging words, which I think we can gloss over here, don't you?

Now feeling even more out of my depth than in London, as the competition begins I shadow Narisawa and Ryu, both of whom are in their chefs' whites. Many of the chefs have chosen to use ingredients from their native countries in their sushi: the competitor from Spain substitutes Iberico ham for nori seaweed in his maki, for instance, and the Swedish chef uses dill, which is virtually unheard of in Japanese cuisine, let alone sushi. I'm quite pleased about this as the Japanese are, as we've heard, hyper-chauvinistic when it comes to sushi, but one of the competitors' creations, a salmon nigiri topped with parmesan and pine nuts, will haunt me to the end of my days.

After many hours of deliberation, back in the judges' room we are in agreement: the American and Norwegian contestants were excellent, and I can see the UK's Xia Jia Tian has been practising hard, but Dae-Won Han from Korea just pips the Japanese chef. His sushi is precise, original and has a wonderfully balanced range of flavours. The scoresheets tell a different story, though. Apparently, unseen by Narisawa or I, Han cut his finger at one point, incurring a penalty which, in this close-fought competition, drops him to seventh. Narisawa politely protests but it is explained that for a sushi chef to cut his finger in front of diners is unthinkable. The decision rests.

The award ceremony features a stirring performance from Japanese drummers, and many more speeches. Finally, Ogawa-san takes the microphone as the exhausted contestants in their chefs' whites line up behind him. He thanks the sponsors and the various attendees and then, in front of a crowd of a few hundred, including members of parliament from Japan and Norway, this tireless task-master breaks down and begins to cry. Months of tension are released as he thanks the contestants and praises their efforts, tears streaming down his face.

At the end of it all, the winner is, perhaps inevitably, Japanese: forty-five-year-old Jun Jibiki of Komazushi in Tokyo. 'I felt so much pressure, being the Japanese entrant,' Jibiki tells me afterwards, as he clutches his glass trophy. 'I've been a chef since I was eighteen, so it's maybe not surprising that I had kind of reached a standstill in terms of my development, but this competition, particularly the creative part, has pushed me forward. I really understand for the first time the creative possibilities with sushi.'

'I know how the chefs feel, because I am a chef,' Ogawa tells me, tears still streaming down his face some time later. 'I think the Japanese contestant won because he knew how to cut, because of technique; Japanese chefs have more than ten years of training, every day cutting.'

Two days after the final of the Global Sushi Challenge I lunch at Jiro Sushi, the most famous sushi restaurant in the world. The 2011 documentary about Jiro-san and his working life revealed the extra-ordinary dedication of the now ninety-year-old chef and his team, and the relentless, meticulous hard work that goes into making sushi at the very highest level, day in, day out. It also made getting a reservation more difficult than ever: this time it required a friend of a friend, who happened to be a CEO of Sony Japan, to vouch for me and I am, needless to say, almost hysterical with excitement at the prospect of experiencing this pinnacle of Japanese cuisine for myself.

So how was it?

I realise this is irritating given how difficult and costly it is to get a reservation at what is a surprisingly humble-looking subterranean restaurant incongruously located amid the network of passages and tunnels that comprise Ginza Metro station, but Jiro-san's is the best sushi I have ever eaten.

He had just turned ninety when I dined there but still stands behind his eight-seater counter for lunch and dinner weekdays, and lunch on Saturdays. He moulds the nigiri perhaps a little more slowly these days but still with a steady precision born of decades of honing. He looks like a majestic Galápagos tortoise. He serves his rice still warm, roughly body temperature, which gives a wonderful contrast with the chilled fish, introducing the grains of rice very gently to each other so that they hold together just long enough to transfer the pieces from the counter to their mouth (by hand, chopsticks are not advised). In contrast to Kazato's delicate flavours, and more to my preference, Jiro's rice is bracingly vinegared but balances perfectly with the umami-rich, aged, raw fish and fresh shellfish. The whole experience, though brief and awfully expensive (the meal, without drinks, costs £165), is for me as enjoyable and moving as any piece of theatre or musical performance.

After twenty-one pieces of sushi with the famous, cake-like omelette and slice of absurdly ripe and juicy Hokkaido melon to finish, all eaten in silence but for a few groans of pleasure, my friend and I get up to pay. I am surprised to see Jiro leave his counter to say goodbye. The stern, frowning sushi machine we had watched at work for the last half-hour – who had actually scolded the two Chinese diners sitting alongside us for some unseen breach of sushi etiquette – suddenly transforms into a smiling, chatty old codger.

I ask him how he manages to stay on his feet all day: 'When I was at school, the teacher was always sending me to stand outside the classroom, so I got used to it,' he laughs. How did he celebrate his milestone birthday the other day? He came to work as usual, he shrugs, as if to say, this is what I do, this is my life. 'The life of the shokunin is like a sportsman,' nods his son, Yoshikazu, who one day will take over the restaurant.

As I re-emerge into the Ginza afternoon sunshine, it almost seems wrong that shoppers are bustling by, oblivious to the culinary magic which has just unfolded beneath the streets.

I can't help but wonder how many more Jiros Japan has left in its future. Given the country's seemingly irreversible demographic decline and the economic challenges Japan faces, how many more young men, or women, will be prepared to commit their lives to standing behind a sushi counter, learning how to wash, cook and season rice, fillet, age and slice fish, how to master the grill and the simmering pot?

Chapter 25

Curry Rice

Clutching the handrail, trying not to look down, I finally reach the top of the destroyer's gangplank. It is a warm, clear, blue-sky day. I take a deep breath. The sea air carries the contrasting aromas of fresh paint and curry. They blend surprisingly well.

Awaiting my arrival on deck is a line of five officers in uniform. They are wearing peaked white caps and offer me a sharp salute. Nothing thus far in my life has prepared me for this eventuality. What am I supposed to do? My first instinct, informed by all those battleship movies, is to return their salute, but that would be absurd, wouldn't it? I am not actually *in* the Japanese navy or, as it is properly known, the Defence Force. My right hand twitches at my side like Dr Strangelove's, but I manage to control the urge. Should I shake hands? No, that wouldn't work either, you fool; then they'd have to stop saluting. Instead, I elect to offer several half-nods as I walk unsteadily along the row of officers.

A little over seventy years ago, the Japanese military tried to kill my father. Today, they have invited me for lunch aboard their destroyer, JS *Kirishima*, motto: 'Right, Brave & Power'. Strange, the places food takes you.

I have travelled by train to the port at Yokosuka fifty miles west of Tokyo to try to get to the bottom of a wildly popular, perhaps *the* most popular, Japanese dish. It is foreign in origin but thoroughly indigenous in execution. (I know you already know what the dish it as it is the title of the chapter, but just go along with this, OK?) It is, to me, one of the least lovely of all Japan's popular dishes yet to the Japanese it is the ultimate comfort food, evocative of childhood and schooldays, the simplest of home-cooked meals, one that anyone can make and which everyone does. But first, let's rewind a few days to an audience with the self-proclaimed monarch of this particular dish.

Wearing a gold jumpsuit, an oversized red and gold foam crown and Elvis sunglasses, with an electric guitar slung over his shoulders, the Curry King and I meet outside the entrance to Shimo-Kitazawa Station on the final day of the annual Curry Festival. He is here to welcome new arrivals to this rather lovely district of western Tokyo, known for its independent theatres and hipster hangouts, and to hand passers-by maps of the 145 participating restaurants and cafés.

The festival seems like a good place to start if I want to get to the bottom of this country's fascination for a dish which, to me, is not only perplexing in its ubiquity but also deeply unappealing.

These days several types of 'Japanese' food are broadly recognisable to us in the West: sushi, of course, tempura, miso soup, ramen and perhaps yakitori. Also maybe soba, tofu and gyoza. However, raisu kare – or 'curry rice' – though rarely associated with Japan by outsiders, invariably appears near, or, in the case of Japanese kids, at the very top, of any list of their absolute most favourite foods.

The first time I tried curry rice was in a restaurant specialising in the dish in Roppongi. It had all the spicy zing of workhouse gruel and the texture of baby food. I recoiled at its cloying sweetness, its one-note flavour, the white pepper afterburn and its gloopy, starch-thickened mouth-feel. I remember, too, that they offered me *grated cheese* as a topping. How could they even call this curry, I had thought to myself as I pushed the sickly sweet matter around my plate.

Typically, curry rice is served on a plate featuring clearly deline-ated portions of, on one side, a suspiciously glossy, faecal brown sauce with lumps of unidentifiable meat in it, and pristine, bleached-white rice on the other. That first ever bowl of Japanese curry rice. Sometimes, I later learned, you might get a piece of tonkatsu (breaded pork cutlet) on top, or perhaps instead of the rice there might be some udon noodles, which is a definite improvement, but all too often there were also cooked carrots!

And no one, but no one, likes cooked carrots.

One thing was for sure: this was not curry as I knew it. Where was the symphony of spices, the chilli kick, the nose-twitching aroma? Where was the subtle complexity of a bhuna gosht or rogan josh? Like many English people, I had been weaned on kormas, biryanis and chicken tikka masala as a child, before progressing to madras, vindaloo and then branching off into the endless variety of subcontinental cuisine. I do realise that the 'curries' we eat in British Indian restaurants are often a bastardised version of dishes eaten in the Punjab or Bangladesh, and that even the term 'curry' is a false construct, but having travelled in India I knew that there was at least some relation between what I knew as curry in Britain and what was eaten in the place where it originated. But in Japan, where supermarkets can have entire aisles dedicated to ready-made curry sauce powders or boil-in-the-bag varieties, it almost seemed an affront – 'cultural appropriation', as people call it these days – to Indian culture; they really ought to have come up with another name for their own version. At least the Québécois had the good grace to name their version of chips and gravy 'poutine'.

I wanted to know who was responsible for this outrage. How could a people who had created a dazzling cuisine which I otherwise considered the very apogee of culinary sophistication, the world's most refined and discerning eaters, how could they eat this … this … *abomination*?

To tell you the truth, in the years since I first tried it, I had kind of been in denial of curry rice. I had ignored it; ignored the fact that millions of Japanese people ate this shit every day, that there were thousands of restaurants specialising in it. But the Japanese love curry rice, there was no use pretending otherwise. It was time to confront the skeleton in their culinary closet.

'I think the reason you don't like curry rice is because it's sticky,' the Curry King told me, mildly, when I confessed my antipathy for his beloved dish. 'You see, we mix flour into it so that we can eat it more easily with chopsticks, and they don't do that in India.'

A man walked past in a yellow t-shirt bearing the words, 'Shall We Curry?'

'No,' I thought. 'We shall not.'

I suspected it was more than a little flour thickener that was putting me off curry rice, but I persevered. Why did *he* love it so? 'Compared to other dishes, I get more surprises with curry rice, and I love the power the spice gives you. I realise that Japanese curry is not really curry, it's another food. Really, it exists only for Japanese rice.'

The Curry King told me he ate curry rice at least four times a week and kindly suggested a few restaurants that my friend and I might try. I was intrigued by a place which was serving uni (sea urchin) curry, as uni is one of my very favourite things, less so by another offering 'minced horse tendon keema curry', and totally not by the British restaurant Good Heavens! (the exclamation mark is theirs), which had put 'Fish & Chips with Curry Sauce' on their menu, but the King suggested an Indonesian-style place, Magic Spice, instead.

The smell of curry powder hung heavy in the air on the streets of Shimo-Kitazawa that day. Seemingly every restaurant my friend Yukiko (who had kindly offered to help me navigate a part of the city she knew well) and I passed was serving curry rice.

Usually, a queue is an encouraging sign at any restaurant in Japan but I reserved judgement as we arrived at Magic Spice, which was done up in a generic India-backpacker style. We joined the waiting crowd in the entrance hall beneath a large gold statue of Ganesh beside an array of Magic Spice products: their own brand packets of curry roux, t-shirts, baseball caps. It is rare that I actively dread lunch but the menu offered little by way of comfort (it is reproduced here; the typographical errors are their own):

'Dear the first guest
The curry of the totally new type that the curry of MAGICSPA makes a clear distinction from so-called general curry such as Indian curry and Western-style curry ... It is 'soup curry'.

The magical mystery world represented in this place is an
original of MAGICSPA. ... A form, a flavour, wave motion ...
All is an MAGICSPA original thing, and it is finished space.
And it is becoming the new food culture of the departure from
Sapporo.
I'm hoping you'll throw away old measure (such as a fixed
idea, an established concept) and then have a holy trip into
The unknown world of the spice.'

The flip side of the menu invited us to choose the meat and
toppings we wanted, and the spice level, at least that's what I think
they meant:

More good stimulation! 'Spirit and energy before the public
performance!' 'I want to do a space trip!' ... For such guests,
we have the special hot version, too. (Awakening Aum air)

Other levels of spiceness offered included 'Consciousness flying
in the sky' and 'The entrance to the mysterious world'. Toppings
included camembert, sausage, natto, raw egg, mochi, tofu and something called 'MAGIC no MUSHROOM'. There were also Maitake
mushrooms which the menu claimed had the power to cure both
AIDS *and* cancer. I chose beef and camembert, and the spiciest
version which promised 'The gateway to the world of mystic
hotness of MAGICSPICE'.

The food arrived, the rice in one bowl, the curry soup – dark and
malevolent with pools of oil shimmering on its surface and topped
with crisp rice noodles – in the other. This was far from the classic
Japanese curry rice I was used to, so in that sense a good thing.

It was indeed spicy. Rivulets of sweat began trickling down my
forehead with my first mouthful but the heat was tolerable, madras
level. 'Is it OK? Are you all right?' asked the waiter, concerned. I
nodded. 'Some take a mouthful of the soup, then some rice and
mix it in their mouths, some mix it in the bowl,' he added
helpfully.

So, my first curry rice in years was not at all repulsive, enjoyable even, as was my second – Yukiko and I found that uni curry rice place and, as with anything remotely involving sea urchin, it was gorgeous – but I had to concede these were not really representative of the true, authentic horror of everyday Japanese curry rice. For that, I would have to visit some proper old-school restaurants.

My first was the venerable Grill Swiss in the unlikely setting of a Ginza backstreet – unlikely because Ginza is home to some of the most expensive and refined restaurants in the world, not to mention the flagship stores for brands like Hermès, Chanel and Louis Vuitton out of which I am gently shepherded every time I attempt to browse.

The Grill Swiss is in a narrow street parallel to the main drag and is identifiable by its red-and-white striped awning. Inside, little appears to have changed since 1947, the year it was founded, rare in this fast, churning part of the city. I like the old-fashioned niceties: the complimentary coffee cup of some kind of unidentifiable soup with which to start, the gingham tablecloths, and so on. It is the kind of place where, once you are ensconced in a booth, you feel nothing can go wrong, that you are shielded from the horrors of the modern world. (Although, looking back, it does seem odd to have 'Grill' in your name if you don't actually grill anything – presumably they don't grill the curry.)

Their curry is really not too bad at all, particularly considering it costs just a few hundred yen. First impressions are of a crude but satisfying meaty-marmity flavour before the white pepper burn takes over, eventually to be defeated by a lingering sugary aftertaste. They serve the chocolate-brown sauce separately from the plate of pristine white rice, perhaps a tradition here. There are nice shreds of beef and a funny little silver foil cup of bright red pickled something or other but, oh dear, there are lumps of carrot. Verdict: edible. A good yardstick by which to measure other curry rice.

For my next curry rice I am aiming a little higher. Though Hinoya is a chain, it regularly tops polls and wins awards as being among the best in Tokyo. Perhaps because of this, at the first branch I visit the chef tells me that they have 'run out of roux', though it isn't yet eight o'clock. There happens to be an award-winning tsukemen ramen place next door so I am able to stave off my hunger in preparation for the twenty minutes it takes me to walk to the nearest other branch of Hinoya, in Kanda.

I can smell their curry roux from a hundred metres away as I arrive, and I take a seat at the counter with high expectations for my ¥730 plate. Hinoya's presentation style is striking: overcooked rice pressed into a thick disc, smothered in sauce, with a raw egg yolk planted plumb centre. It stares back at me like some hideous cyclops. I stick my spoon in its 'eye' and taste. It is ridiculously sugary, almost to dessert levels, with the now familiar white pepper burn, but is at least blessedly free of carrots, with tiny, machine-cut cubes of beef and a sauce like an over-reduced *boeuf bourguignon*. I am still no closer to solving the mysterious appeal of curry rice.

It is time to call in the armed forces.

Fast-forward a few days, and I have arrived in Yokosuka, one of Japan's largest naval bases, fifty miles west of Tokyo. Since the late 1990s, Yokosuka has successfully branded itself as Curry Town, attracting thousands to its annual curry festival during which the warships docked here open up to the public to share their unique interpretations of this massively popular dish.

As I wait for my contact to pick me up outside Yokosuka Station's convenience store, I notice that the shelves are full of packets of 'Yokosuka Curry Rice' mix. Outside is a statue of a cartoon duck in a seaman's uniform. The duck, called Sucurry, is Yokosuka's mascot. He is bearing a plate of curry rice with a silver spoon.

As I inspect the duck, a naval officer in full uniform approaches, hand outstretched. This is Lieutenant Commander Watanabe, tall, stiff-backed, mustachioed: the full Top Gun.

'Call me Tadpole,' he smiles. Really? 'It's my nickname.' There it is on his name badge alongside an impressive escutcheon of medals.

After a quick taxi ride during which there is just time to ascertain Tadpole's opinion of his commander-in-chief, Prime Minister Abe ('Very happy with Abe. He's good for the military. I like him'), I am boarding the escort ship *Kirishima* and inspecting that row of saluting sailors just as a submarine glides into port with its crew lined up on deck.

After a surprisingly thrilling tour of its weaponry – 127mm rapid-firing guns, multi-purpose ground-to-air missile system, anti-aircraft guns, anti-submarine missiles: basically I feel nine years old again – we visit the bridge where I am invited to sit in the captain's chair, mounted like a barber's chair with a fetching red fitted cover. The captain himself is otherwise engaged with a five-a-side football tournament.

The *Kirishima* has a crew of 255. Officers eat in the war room, but we join the men in the canteen to sample the *Kirishima*'s special curry rice.

'We eat it every Friday. It helps the men to get a sense of what day of the week it is when we are at sea,' explains another officer called Sawada. It is also a long-standing Japanese naval tradition that curry rice is served on the last day before shore leave which means that the dish has extra special associations for all Japanese sailors.

'Even when the men have retired, that smell of curry rice still means it's Friday, and many still even eat curry rice on Friday long after they have left the ships,' adds Tadpole. As well as this Pavlovian aspect, curry rice is also an eminently practical dish: the galley can feed 250 men in two and a half hours, including washing-up time, all for ¥440 (£3) a head.

Each naval port has its own universal curry roux, the basic flavoured thickener with which to make the curry sauce. It is delivered to ships in one-kilo bags, and each ship then has its own recipe for curry rice involving various secret ingredients and tricks. The *Kirishima*'s recipe has been handed down from chef to chef over twenty years but it is tweaked daily according to who is in charge of the kitchen that week, their preferences, their skill and what supplies they have to hand.

The man in charge today is Petty Officer Komagome, who looks like a Japanese Leonid Brezhnev. He has an entire arsenal of 'secret ingredients', he says, none of which, it turns out, are all that secret:

ketchup, jam, honey, chicken fat, oyster sauce and processed, pre-grated cheese, sometimes deployed all at once he tells me (were I his commanding officer I think I would be a little concerned at Komagome's ability to withstand torture should he ever be captured by the North Koreans). I grimace at the mention of the cheese, but the sailors assure me it is a very common addition to curry rice and has been ever since the British invented it.

Wait, what? The British invented Japanese curry rice?

'Yes, the curry of the Japanese Imperial Navy originally came from the British Royal Navy during the Meiji era,' says Komagome.

I look into this later, and it turns out to be true. Following the British navy's example, curry rice was indeed introduced to the Japanese navy in the 1880s primarily as a cure for beriberi, a disease of the nervous system caused by a vitamin B deficiency. This was on the recommendation of the surgeon general at the time, Kanehiro Takagi. Beriberi was the most significant cause of death in the Japanese military, a symptom of the malnutrition which has often plagued Japan, partly because of their insistence on polishing away the husk of their rice – wherein the vitamin B lies – to make it white. The theory was that the flour in the curry roux would ensure that the food took longer to travel through a sailor's digestive system allowing for more nutrients to be digested, and it worked: curry rice did indeed eradicate beriberi in the Japanese navy within just a few years. Because it arrived via Britain, curry rice was considered a 'yoshoku' or 'Western-style' dish, and it duly appeared on the menu of the early yoshoku restaurants in Yokohama and Tokyo in the late 1800s.

It wasn't only the recipe for curry rice which came from the British. For many decades the curry powder used by the Japanese to make it was made in Britain by Crosse & Blackwell. Those imports came to a shuddering halt, however, with the great curry powder scandal of 1931 in which 'fake' powder was found to be in circulation – according to the *Japan Times*, there were numerous arrests and a diplomatic incident ensued. After that, domestic production began in earnest, with instant curry sauce mix being introduced in the

1950s. Today, most convenience stores sell boil-in-the-bag curry, and entire aisles of Japanese supermarkets are dedicated to the dozens of variations of 'curry roux' made by the likes of S&B, Vermont Curry and the biggest brand, House Foods.

Naval curry rice as a cultural phenomenon is a more recent development, with its origins in a community outreach project initiated by the defence force here in Yokosuka in 2001. That was followed by the first Yokosuka Curry Festival in 2014, which drew 30,000 people and was such a hit that other naval ports, like Kure and Sasebo, followed suit. So successful has the whole naval curry promotion been that the Ministry of Defence in Tokyo is currently engaged in a project to create a definitive joint forces curry involving the combined efforts of the army, navy and air force. 'But don't worry, it won't be a threat to naval curry,' Komagome assures me.

It is time to eat. Taking a compartmentalised pressed tin tray I join the queue, ignoring the hot dogs and strange, rubbery pucks of omelette, to reach the vat of steaming brown slop that is today's Kirishima Curry Rice. I fill the largest indentation half and half, lumpy curry and a hefty chunk of rice, with a couple of pieces of lettuce for appearance's sake, and return to the table.

The bad news first: there are cooked carrots in the sauce. Did I mention nobody likes cooked carrots? There are also potatoes, which are more acceptable, and the beef is sliced rather than cubed – apparently that's just how it arrived (from Australia) that week. It has a deep, beefy flavour, isn't too sweet, but there is that by now customary white pepper assault.

As I eat to the sound of several dozen clattering spoons on trays, a thought suddenly strikes me: in 1942 the Japanese had invaded Singapore, capturing hundreds of British servicemen, many of whom later perished in internment camps. Among those who escaped was a twenty-two-year-old sergeant major in the Royal Air Force, Stanley Victor Booth, my father. He told me that, on hearing the Japanese were about to enter Singapore, he and his comrades literally dropped everything they had with them on the quayside and boarded a mango boat for Sumatra, escaping from the enemy with hours, if not minutes, to spare.

My father held no particular grudge against the Japanese for their conduct towards him during World War II, so I am sure he would have been delighted by a turn of events which has seen me hosted for lunch on a Japanese destroyer. I weigh up whether to share all of this with my lunch companions. Is it unfair, or even inappropriate, to burden them with my sentimental backstory?

I begin to tell them the story but halfway through I can feel myself becoming a little emotional. My father died more than a dozen years ago, before I even began visiting Japan. Yes, I think to myself. He would have loved this. He would have loved to hear about this day.

I take a deep gulp of tea, compose myself, and make it to the end of my story. I don't know what I was expecting by way of a response, but my new friends seem sympathetic, and smile back.

'So, how does this compare to British Royal Navy Curry Rice?' Komagome asks as I finish my lunch. 'Which was best?'

'Oh yours, definitely yours,' I say, and raise my cup of tea as a toast.

Chapter 26

Yakitori

I've been to Torishiki several times, but it never seems to be in the same place twice.

Everywhere is difficult to find in Tokyo: you can take it for given that for virtually all of the places we visit in this book my family and I will have spent at least half an hour lost, trying to find it. Picture me sweaty and tight-lipped, clutching a crumpled scrap of paper which I will occasionally brandish at innocent passers-by while my family pretend not to know me. Well-meaning strangers draw a blank, and I let out a deep, almost existential sigh, before finally turning on 'data roaming' in a desperate, prohibitively expensive attempt to find out where on earth we are.

It doesn't even matter if I have visited a place before. Every time I come to Torishiki, for instance, I spend a good deal of time in a frantic, spiralling orbit of Meguro Station with random digressions down dark alleyways and, each time, this chic little yakitori joint suddenly appears at the end of the same alleyway that I have checked three times already. It is the Brigadoon of restaurants. It doesn't help that its entrance is the epitome of discretion: an unmarked pale wooden door, draped with a white noren curtain, set in a windowless charcoal-coloured wall. It looks more like an exclusive kaiseki restaurant than a yakitori joint.

That is not entirely inappropriate as this is arguably the best yakitori restaurant in Tokyo; in fact, it might well represent the future of yakitori globally, as its ambitious chef, Yoshiteru Ikegawa, explains when I finally settle behind his horseshoe-shaped counter for a chat.

'I want yakitori to be thought of in the same way as sushi. I want yakitori restaurants to have that same image, the same prestige around the world,' he tells me.

'Yakitori' literally means 'grilled chicken', although various vegetables, pork, cheese, even nuts, can be involved. Usually yakitori places are smoke-filled, low on comfort, with tatty beer ads pinned to the wall, a model of a waving cat on the counter, and a prominently placed air-conditioning unit caked in dusty fat – a 'quick and dirty' kind of vibe.

Torishiki, on the other hand, has a Michelin star, and Ikegawa is one of only a few yakitori chefs to work on the 'omakase' principle, as practised by the better sushi places, where the chef selects the courses you eat without a menu. But one star and acclaim from the *New York Times* and others are not enough. As Ikegawa explains, he wants nothing less than to be the Jiro Ono of yakitori.

'There are a lot of similarities with sushi, you know. They both look like simple ways of cooking from the outside. There's just the meat, the salt and the tare, or the fish and the rice, and you serve the customer directly, but yakitori is very complicated if you do it well. I want Japanese chefs to start spreading the story about high-quality yakitori like they have with sushi. I think it can get much better quality and much more refined. There is still so much potential.'

It is late afternoon and, as we chat, Ikegawa prepares for the evening service, gliding with smooth purpose about his small, open kitchen, occasionally removing a large fan from the belt behind his back to give his fire a quick waft, or hammering down the charcoal into an even spread in the oblong grill behind the cedar-wood counter.

Ikegawa, forty-three, grew up in the eastern Tokyo district of Koiwa. The way he describes it, his childhood was permanently wreathed in yakitori smoke from the restaurants clustered in the alleyways close by Koiwa Station.

'I spent all my pocket money on yakitori,' he grins. 'Back then, yakitori was definitely a low-class kind of food. All yakitori restaurants were very casual, very smoky usually. But by the time I was twenty, I had made up my mind that I wanted to be a yakitori chef and started to plan how to make that happen. My father [a printer] was against it. He didn't think I would be good enough to make a living.'

At this stage, others might have approached an established yakitori restaurant for a trainee position, but Ikegawa instead spent most of his twenties just eating as much grilled food as possible. 'I was working in an office by day but in the evening and during my time off I was eating yakitori, seeing it from the customer's point of view. Finally, I found the restaurant I wanted to train in: Toriyoshi.'

Toriyoshi's owner was Yoshito Inomata, a venerated yakitori master. He had been the first to offer wine as an accompaniment to yakitori and, as a result, had already begun to attract the attention of French culinary tourists. But Inomata, more used to teenage apprentices, was extremely reluctant to take on a trainee of such comparatively advanced years.

'He made it clear that he expected me to work twice as hard,' recalls Ikegawa. 'I really had to prove myself. They gave me all the rubbish jobs. For the first year, I was not even allowed to touch any of the chicken meat. Many other trainees quit in that first year. The boss was watching who would survive. He never directly taught us techniques, but that's normal in Japanese kitchens: you just have to learn by watching. But I never thought of giving up. Quitting was not an option.'

Ikegawa spent years two, three and four of his apprenticeship learning how to prepare the meat for the grill, taking care of the customers, and in particular observing the way Inomata timed the meal.

'He used to say, "To make good yakitori, the most important thing is to brush up on your personality skills, then you can understand your customers better." Timing is so important. I am like a conductor, and the diners' breaths are like musical notes.' He turns away to tend to a simmering pot, then back again. 'When you exhale you can't eat, so I try to sense my customers' breathing. I have to be alert all the time to my customers, to serve the women first or, if there is a group, then the oldest guest, but I need to check on all the relationships. I have to figure out who is hungry, who eats fast, who is more interested in talking to their companion. I have to feel the atmosphere, watch the body language to time the meal to maximise their satisfaction.'

Looking back, when I've eaten here before, the pacing of the meal has been perfect. Ikegawa-san usually starts quite quickly, placing a few skewers in rapid succession upon the hefty ceramic plates on the counter before you, then slowing the pace to let you digest and catch up with your companions. Sometimes he can almost seem to be teasing you (or, at least, someone like me who eats far too quickly), making you wait longer than you might want, whipping your appetite up into a frenzy of anticipation with the wafting smoke and sizzling chicken juices. You watch, rapt, as he tends his grill like a brilliant xylophonist, turning skewers a specific number of times (it varies depending on the cut of meat: some he turns up to ten times), removing others to dip in tare (again, several times), judging the cooking time of each to within seconds. Now I think about it, this also explains the slightly stilted way he moves about this open kitchen, purposefully pausing to face different customers as he attends (or appears to attend) to some or other task.

Ikegawa claims that he can remember every single skewer he has ever served and to whom he served it. I wonder about all the conversations he must have overheard and memory-banked. He mimes tucking a secret away in his breast pocket: 'I am all ears but I put confidential information in my pocket.'

Though he often had sharp words for his young yakitori padawan, Inomata was a relatively kindly teacher who taught by example. 'Often in traditional Japanese restaurants the boss can be very tough, emotional, angry, but he was very logical, and he worked the hardest of us all so everyone followed.' But it was four years – *four years* – of 'oimawashi' work, being the 'dogsbody', before Ikegawa was allowed to actually place a skewer of meat over hot coals. During those years, he would work in the restaurant from nine in the morning to around midnight, then go home and practise making yakitori himself until the early hours. He studied the history of yakitori which, he says, evolved in Turkey where, of course, they still cook on metal skewers, before moving to Asia where they substituted bamboo for the metal, arriving in Japan during the Muromachi period (1336–1573). The modern-style yakitori joint was established in the post-war era when chicken was the only available meat, and yakitori places were usually yatai, or street carts. 'It was food for workers, up in Ueno, or Tsukiji. But most of the yatai were cleared away for the 1964 Olympics,' he tells me.

A good yakitori chef can break a chicken down into over thirty different parts – some of which I never even considered edible, like the trachea or kneecap. Ikegawa is a little more selective and serves around twenty different types of chicken skewer, along with some seasonal vegetables (his Brussels sprouts are unprecedentedly good), tofu and quails eggs, finishing the meal with a rice bowl and minced chicken (there are no desserts). It is a symphony of textures, not all of them immediately appealing to a Western palate: I have still not really reconciled myself to the crunchy-chew of nankotsu – cartilage – for instance. The cuts range from almost raw tenderloin with a dab of fresh-grated wasabi to deeply flavourful thigh meat, as well as innards like liver (the trickiest part to cook), heart, rubbery skin concertined on the stick, and, my favourite, the chouchin. Otherwise known as the 'lantern', this is the chicken's uterus and fallopian tube, removed with the soft, orange ovum still attached before either egg white or shell have formed; there can be as many as twenty of them per chicken. It looks like a little knapsack on a stick, and the 'eggs' pop satisfyingly in your mouth.

Of course, good yakitori costs: you can pay as little as a couple of hundred yen per skewer at a hole-in-the-wall yakitori joint. Torishiki is about ¥6,500 yen (£35) for a full meal, but that's still nothing like the cost of a meal at a top sushiya, which can easily run to four times that.

Ikegawa uses one-hundred-day-old chickens raised close to Koriyama in Fukushima. The breed is called date-dori, a cross between a Japanese chicken and the fabled poulet de Bresse from eastern France. 'They are really healthy, free-range, they eat when they want, they are really strong. In the winter they taste better because they eat more, so they exercise more, the liver is more rich.' The liver is the litmus of yakitori: if the liver is sweet with no trace of bitterness then the chicken is likely to have lived a good life. The liver at Torishiki is pillowy soft and tastes like chicken candy.

Ikegawa has recently experimented with other birds like duck, quail and even swallow, and has also given great thought to the type of charcoal he uses (hard-wood *binchotan*, from Wakayama – which smokes less and burns more slowly); to how the juices which drip from the skewers create smoke when they hit the embers and in-directly flavour the meat; to the salt; and, of course, to the tare, the mahogany-brown sauce into which he dips certain skewers during grilling (others get just salt). Based on my experiences trying to extract recipes for tare from other yakitori chefs, I assumed his was a big secret.

'No, no secret, it's just soy sauce, mirin and zarame sugar,* but when I opened the restaurant in 2007 my master gave me some of his tare from his restaurant. It must already have been twenty years old and, over the years, I suppose because I dip so many skewers in it, the meat must give it a special, umami flavour.'

Ikegawa suddenly stops. Sweat glistens on his shaved head and drips down into the rolled hachimaki cloth tied around his brow. He looks me in the eye. 'Why don't you come over here and give it a go?'

And with that invitation I circumvent four years' yakitori appren-ticeship and find myself squeezing sideways through the tiny back kitchen, its walls covered with stacks of plates and glasses, to find myself behind the counter of Torishiki.

---

* A large-grain, amber-coloured sugar, common in Japanese kitchens and with a lighter flavour than Western refined sugar. I think Japanese sugar is a really import-ant but often overlooked ingredient when it comes to recreating Japanese flavours outside Japan.

The view is very different here, in the centre of the horseshoe-shaped counter which, in a short while, will be ringed babbling customers. I can see Ikegawa's grill in all its meat- and ash-encrusted glory, thick with the smoky, black, sedimentary build-up of a million cooked chicken skewers. It looks like some ancient sarcophagus retrieved from the Valley of the Kings. Beside it is a large, red ceramic pot, vessel of the fabled tare. The dense, dark-brown liquid cascades slowly down its sides like primordial umami-ooze. Ikegawa hands me an apron, a fan and a skewer of thigh meat and gestures, go ahead. I place it on the grill, noting how the smoke is drawn efficiently away under the counter by his super-quiet induction system. Ikegawa gestures to my fan; I waft the embers which glow a diabolical red; smoke rises, hissing as the juices from the meat drip onto them. He gestures again for me to turn the skewer and, moments later, to dip it into the tare and return it to the heat, and so on until it is cooked and I am invited to taste my work: the succulence is astounding, the meat releases a powerful wave of flavour which carries on and on until well after I have gnawed the skewer clean. (As sushi chefs prefer you to eat their nigiri with your hands rather than using chopsticks, Ikegawa advises that you always eat straight from the skewer rather than removing the morsels of meat onto a plate with chopsticks.)

Ikegawa's evening guests are due. It is time to leave but I have just a couple more questions. I am always curious how the shokunin copes with the monotony of working in one relatively limited field for years on end. After all, most of us seek some variety in our work. I ask if he can ever imagine getting bored cooking chicken over coals. 'No, not at all. I want to be a specialist for all my life,' he says. 'Young people have so many choices these days that they quit too easily. The most important thing is to have a passion right from the start.'

Torishiki has one Michelin star. Is he aiming for more? 'I don't know if that's possible, I'm just doing what I do, as best as I can. For sure, more of that kind of recognition would help to promote yakitori outside of Japan, make people realise it can be as high an art as sushi.'

The next afternoon, Lissen, Asger, Emil and I take the commuter train out to Koiwa where Ikegawa grew up amid a cloud of chicken fat-laden charcoal smoke.

My family is not impressed, and wonder aloud why on earth I have brought them here. It's true, this is not the most salubrious part of Tokyo: the warren of alleys by the station boast as many Thai massage parlours as restaurants and Ikegawa had himself warned me that most of the decent yakitori places had long gone, but there was one place he still recommended: Toriki. We are guided to its first-floor entrance by a kindly, aproned waitress from another izakaya a little way down Koiwa's pedestrianised high street. It is early evening and Toriki, a ramshackle room with various simmered vegetable dishes lined up along the bar, tapas-style, the requisite beer posters on the walls and boxes of unopened condiments in the corner, is empty; the chef, an older gentleman in white t-shirt with a lit cigarette dangling permanently from his lower lip, is preparing his *mise en place* for the evening. It doesn't look all that promising, but our 'yakitori sets' are delicious: five sticks – gizzard, thigh, wing, liver and skin, along with mustard, a slice of lemon, and no chopsticks – for a few hundred yen. It is a long way from this to Torishiki, and the quality was obviously a few steps down, but, then again, in some ways it was not so different. Deliciousness has many forms and, in Japan, is found in many places.

Chapter 27

Yanagihara

I have worked in Michelin-starred kitchens in Paris, I have cooked for large numbers of people in small, unfamiliar kitchens and I have made dinner for famous and revered chefs (not to mention my mother-in-law), but I have never been this out of my depth while wearing an apron.

I am attempting to filet an eel but the skin of this long, slithery thing is as tough as plastic hessian and I am making an awful hash of it. The poor creature now looks as if someone has taken a blunt hacksaw to it. My teacher pauses behind me, reaches around my waist and takes my hands in his, like a golf pro showing a newbie a grip. It is an alarmingly intimate action for one man to perform upon another in public – particularly as we have only just met, and he hasn't even bought me dinner – but I acquiesce and soon there are two, skin-free eel fillets on my chopping board.

My visit to the Yanagihara School of Traditional Japanese Cuisine had begun to go awry before I had even entered its front gate. The school is located in one of the poshest parts of Tokyo, close to the American Embassy in Akasaka. When I arrive, I find myself unable to open the gate to enter the small, meticulously kept front garden in front of this elegant four-storey building, its exterior clad with expensive dark slate tiles. I push and pull, but the damn thing seems to be locked. Eventually I buzz the intercom and ask for help. A moment later, a handsome clean-cut man of a kind one could imagine reading the news on Japanese TV, comes to my rescue.

'It's not locked,' the man smiles sympathetically. 'See?' And he *slides* the gate open to the right.

The man is Naoyuki Yanagihara, the thirty-seven-year-old scion of this three-generations-old cooking school. He guides me into the entrance hall where a dozen women aged from their mid-thirties to early eighties are waiting for his cooking class to start. I put on the standard Japanese indoor plastic slippers and a flowery apron I've borrowed from a friend, and follow the group upstairs to the demonstration kitchen.

The air is rich with the aroma of fresh dashi. Three elderly women (the eldest of whom, I later learn, is eighty), each in their own floral pinny, buzz around the kitchen preparing the ingredients for the cooking demonstration which is about to take place. It is a similar set-up to my alma mater, Le Cordon Bleu in Paris, with a large central island with hob and sink, overhead TV screens to show the close-up work and a blackboard behind.

Naoyuki introduces me to his mother, Noriko, who, together with his father, Kazunari, is still very much involved in the day-to-day running of the school – she as executive director in charge of etiquette and table manners, he as president. As we talk, the elder Mr Yanagihara, now seventy-four, dressed in a pale blue lab coat with elasticated cuffs, joins us. He mentions that NHK had recently phoned him to check some food facts for their anime series of my book, and we chat a little about the programme.

I have come to the Yanagihara School for several reasons. I had heard its name mentioned reverentially by various people in the Japanese food world among whom the Yanagihara family is legendary. This is particularly with regard to its dedication to keeping alive the traditions of Kinsa-ryu, the style of cooking which evolved alongside the tea ceremony from the early seventeenth century onwards, first in Kyoto, then in Edo (or Tokyo as it is now known). Yanagihara students are an unusually loyal and dedicated bunch; the oldest (not here today, alas) is ninety-six, another has been attending the school for fifty years. It also has a reputation for being exclusive, costly and popular with ladies of leisure: the equivalent, perhaps, of Leith's in London, or a traditional Swiss finishing school.

Mrs Yanagihara, a formidable-looking woman in her late sixties with a daunting glossy hairdo and a faultless carapace of make-up, presents me with her business card.

'I've read your book,' she offers, brusquely.

Now, 'I've read your book' is a fine thing to say to an author so long as you follow it up with something along the lines of 'And it was amazing, the single greatest book I have ever read.' Something like that. But it is the very *worst* thing you can say to an author if you then just leave the silence hanging, as Mrs Yanagihara does.

I try to compose myself. Conscious that teaching etiquette is Mrs Yanagihara's forte, I fumble to offer my business card but can only find a horribly mangled one in my coat pocket. I dust off the lint, and hand it to her. She does not look impressed, instructs me to hang up my coat, turns, and leaves me with the two dozen women who are milling about chatting, tying aprons and readying their notebooks for the day's class. I notice to one side a single, rather lonely looking white man in his early thirties with lanky hair. I sit at the front. There are some awkward moments during which many of the women giggle shyly and whisper behind their hands, and try to find seats away from me. Late arrivals are forced to sit beside me.

(Re Mrs Yanagihara. It now occurs to me that virtually all of the people I have met in Japan who have been self-proclaimed etiquette experts have also been among the rudest people I have met. For instance, at a book event in Kyoto once, a woman approached me as I was signing copies, handed me a card which described her as a 'Mannerist' – I don't think it was a reference to the late Renaissance art movement – and asked if I was related to the late author Alan Booth, who had also written about Japan. 'Oh, that's disappointing,' she said when I told her that I wasn't. She then looked at me as if I had perpetrated some kind of fraud and stalked off. Meanwhile, on another occasion at a dinner in Japan I sat next to a woman who had gatecrashed the gathering and then spent the entire evening explaining to me how I had no understanding of Japanese manners whatsoever, while chewing her food with her mouth open like a cat throughout.)

Mrs Yanagihara coughs and rustles some papers, indicating that she requires silence. She begins the class by showing the latest magazine articles her son has been featured in, or written, and then introduces me, but I am busy taking notes at the time and not really paying attention.

'Stand up!' Mrs Yanagihara barks. I realise she is looking in my direction. I pause. Really? OK. I do what I am told, and take an awkward bow.

Her son, Naoyuki, enters, now wearing a knee-length white lab coat. He is going to show what gradually dawns on me is the *advanced* class on how to make traditional dishes from the Okayama Matsuri ('matsuri' means festival; Okayama is a city on the coast of the Inland Sea, west of Kobe). Maintaining a pout of concentration throughout, he proceeds to give a fascinating and brilliant cooking demonstration of such controlled skill and artistry that, at times, I quite forget that I am supposed to be taking notes, a lapse which I will later come to regret.

One of the dishes is the eel which he fillets in a matter of seconds, brushes with a tare and then grills, swamping the room with a mouth-watering aroma. Another features yam, which he grinds to a thin paste in a suribachi and surikogi (a Japanese-style ridged mortar and wooden pestle) but which he then somehow, miraculously, is still able to divide into pieces, lift from the bowl, wrap in nori and deep-fry, all using just his chopsticks, an astonishing display of technique. Meanwhile, he fillets a kohada (gizzard shad), blanches an octopus arm and prepares some sushi rice, pouring the seasoning vinegar over it via the broad back of a spoon, a nice trick to better distribute it more evenly. He prepares lily bulbs for simmering; transforms a turnip into a hexagonal, edible bowl, now beautifully translucent; and finely chops some brown ribbons which looked like wet tights (these, I later discover, are dried gourd ribbons, or 'kampyo', often used as an edible string in traditional Japanese cuisine, here chopped and added to the rice). Live shrimp are despatched into boiling water, then an ice bath, and then into soy sauce. And so on.

It is a virtuoso performance by a chef in his prime. He is so smooth, in such total control and command. Watching him make a Japanese-style omelette in a thin rectangular pan, wafting the base of the pan only vaguely in the vicinity of the gas flame to delicately set the eggs' proteins, then flipping it using his chopsticks with a sublime economy of motion, is like some kind of Noh theatre. All of this he does in silence, the only noise that of the extractor fans, the scratching of students' pens on paper and the odd fluttery-eyed sigh. The demonstration ends in silence, too; no applause.

Naoyuki approaches me as the rest of the students move over to their workstations in the other part of the L-shaped room where they will begin to make the dishes they have just seen demonstrated.

'So, Michael, are you ready?'

'Hmm?' Ready for what, I wonder. Our interview?

'To join your group. Let me introduce you.'

It seems that I, too, am now expected to cook all of the dishes together with a group of five students, all of whom have been attending his classes for years, in some cases decades.

I catch the eye of the lone Western male student. His name is Ryan and he is from Texas. I thought this was a home-cooking class, I hiss to him desperately.

'Yes, using "home cooking" to describe this can sound almost insulting,' he sympathises. 'This is kaiseki level cooking, make no mistake.'

Ryan has lived in Japan for seventeen years and, as a supplement to his language studies, he had wanted to learn how to cook authentic Japanese cuisine. 'I asked around to find which cooking school to come to, and this one was generally considered the most serious for non-professional cooks,' he says.

Naoyuki interrupts to introduce me to my 'team' – Noriko, Junko, Nitani (this was her second name, I didn't get her first), Setsuko and Michiko. Michiko is rather stern, with glasses hanging on a chain around her neck like a librarian; Nitani-san is super-smiley and tiny, barely reaching up to my hip; Setsuko tells me she travels all the way from Himeji for the class – three hours by Shinkansen; Noriko, the youngest, speaks the best English and it is she who patiently guides me through the four hours of cooking, concealing well her irritation at being lumbered with the hopeless *gaijin* (foreigner).

They set me to work making the omelette. This may not seem a big deal but is nevertheless a gross misjudgement of my abilities. Though I can make French-style omelettes in my sleep, Japanese omelettes are a much more demanding art requiring a special rectangular pan and an experienced eye for temperature control. I have never made one before but, miraculously, the first I turn out is pretty much perfect. The next, though, is a mess of overcooked eggy ribbons. I also ruin the shrimp by peeling them before I cook them which renders them horrid, grey, chewy curlicues. And then comes the eel, which I at least manage to skewer through its eye in order to fix it to the chopping board, but mess up royally thereafter.

Naoyuki rescues me with his golf-swing assistance, and, slowly, my team of capable cooks and I work towards the end of our multicourse, Okayama festival dishes. When we are done, some time after everyone else is finished (entirely my fault, although no one openly blames me), we eat together at our workstation.

Afterwards, I finally get some time to talk with Naoyuki. I am keen to hear his view on the current state of Japanese cuisine.

'Two things have happened in the last few years,' he says as we sit in the upstairs TV studio (the school has its own TV studio). 'There was the earthquake in 2011, and the UNESCO World Heritage status awarded to Japanese food in 2013. The first, I think, made people realise how little they knew about cooking. For two weeks, some people in Fukushima could not buy food, they didn't have electricity or gas. Lots of Japanese cannot even cook rice, you know, but our students, they can cook rice over a wood fire, so we teach useful skills which are disappearing. A lot of new students came to us after that.'

He admits the impact of UNESCO's award was probably greater domestically than internationally. 'Japanese people realised Japanese cooking was very cool for people outside of the country, that we have some real treasures, and that foreigners were coming here for the food, to see Tsukiji and things like that.'

The Yanagihara school does not claim to be a cooking school for professional chefs, like Le Cordon Bleu; it is a place to train the next generation of home cooks in the ways of past home cooks. It's great that people go to nice restaurants, but they don't realise that Japanese food culture begins with the family, in the home. They need to learn about techniques, ingredients, the seasons. That's why we only teach Japanese cooking, not how to make pasta or pizza.

'My grandfather was taught by his mother, he was the first male to learn to cook in his family. He started the school in the 1950s because he was already worried that the traditional style of Japanese cooking he had learned was breaking up. The Japanese were eating a lot of bread, using oils for frying, which is not the Japanese way. Japanese cuisine is a cuisine of water, not oil. He realised that Japanese food culture is made by the housewives, not the restaurant chefs. The wives and mothers create the palate of their children when they feed their babies. That was why my grandfather felt we should teach the housewives.'

Wasn't this approach perhaps a little outdated? Didn't men have an equal responsibility in the kitchen?

Naoyuki hesitates. 'Yes, but men are more busy. It is a Japanese problem. They work late, and a lot. Sometimes when they retire they come here to study. I know that women can't make food every day, but they can on Saturdays and Sundays. These should be the days when they spend time with their families, not go out to restaurants. They should be at home, making Japanese food, but even the grandmothers these days don't know how to cook. A lot of Japanese cooking teachers don't even know traditional Japanese food.' He shakes his head in despair.

Naoyuki's grandfather, Toshio, died when Naoyuki was twelve years old, after which his culinary training was left to his father, but his grandfather was able to pass on a special symbolic gift before he died.

'In Japan, it is a custom that on the sixth of June in the year you turn six, that is the day when, if you start something, you can become an expert,' recalls Naoyuki. 'That was when my grandfather gave me my chefs' knives.'

Naoyuki has recently been named a Japanese Cultural Envoy, an honour usually reserved for practitioners of traditional arts – dancers or musicians – but following the UNESCO announcement the Ministry of Cultural Affairs felt they ought to have a representative from the culinary world. In a pattern that seems familiar from my dealings with the Japanese – who love formal gestures but don't always think them through in terms of content – everyone involved felt it was a great honour, but no one seemed to be clear about what it entailed. Another well-meaning but vague hope involves the 2020 Tokyo Olympics. It will be a major opportunity to show Japanese food to the world, Naoyuki feels, but he is not quite sure how Japan will make the most of it yet.

'I don't know what we can do, but we have some study groups looking at it. I heard there were lots of cultural things with the London Olympics. I think the most important thing is to show the world what real Japanese cooking is. There are a lot of fake Japanese restaurants around the world, but if chefs know what is the true Japanese style, that might change and authentic Japanese restaurants will increase.'

Towards the end of our conversation, as I am getting up to leave, Naoyuki's wife enters the studio, carrying their seven-month-old son, Shutaro. We coo over the baby for a while. He is adorable. It is eleven at night now and Naoyuki has been up since six to go to Tsukiji to buy fish. He and I are both flagging, but the next generation of the Yanagihara cooking dynasty, in whose hands the destiny of traditional Japanese home cooking may well lie, is wide awake and bright as a button.

Chapter 28

Cake

I am becoming obsessed by obsession, by the single-minded dedication and discipline of shokunin like Jiro-san, the Arita potters, and soba and mochi masters Hibiya and Horiguchi. I have got it into my head that I want somehow to pass on to my sons some sense of their unwavering focus on the *process*, rather than on the transient *results* of their endeavours; if they can understand what is becoming for me some kind of a self-evident 'life truth', I think it will serve them well in the coming years.

Since my first visit to Japan I have been fascinated by the meticulous perfection of Japanese patisserie. Having lived in Paris for three years I know my way around a fancy cake shop, but I had never seen cakes as delicate and precise as those in Tokyo. I have spent literally hours trawling the depachika – the department store basement food halls – marvelling at glass cabinets filled with immaculate Mont Blancs, mille-feuilles, operas and macarons.

Japanese patisserie is, I think, one of the few areas where cuisine approaches art, at least in the purely decorative sense. I was going to qualify that by stating it would be ridiculous to say that I find *meaning* in an eclair but, actually, I probably do – a 'religieuse' experience, you could say (*Cough* One for the cake nerds, there), after all, Proust found meaning enough in a madeleine. Put it another way, can you think of any other handmade product which exhibits this level of technical accomplishment, is this pretty to look at, this satisfying sensually, not to mention in terms of one's appetite (well, if you eat enough of them …), for sale anywhere in the world for the same price as a crappy cup of Starbucks' brown water? Original paintings, sculptures or ceramics made by masters of their art are way out of most people's reach; the same goes for 1960s Ferraris, Charles Eames chairs or Fabergé eggs. Even in the dining world, a meal at a Michelin-starred restaurant will often run to three figures, as will a decent bottle of Bordeaux, yet in the glass display cabinets of the Tokyo patisseries every day you will find original examples of the apogee of their form, made fresh by the greatest practitioners of their art *in the world*, craftsmen and women who have spent years perfecting their technique, and on sourcing and understanding how to work with the very best ingredients, all on sale for just a couple of quid a pop.

I've always wanted to meet one of the people behind these incredible pieces of patisserie. What drives them to work with such fanatical precision and dedication within such a tiny framework, and for so little financial reward? I also have a nerdy curiosity about the technical challenges of creating those helium-light mousses or keeping biscuit bases crunchy beneath a moist fruit topping. Within that 'little bit (two inches wide) of ivory', as Jane Austen described her canvas, there can be as many as seven or eight components – sponge, mousse, ganache, fruit, jam, sugarwork, biscuit, ice cream, sorbet, glaze, crème pâtissière, Chantilly – using maybe twenty basic ingredients, all assembled into often perilously fragile, transient, gravity-defying constructions.

Hidemi Sugino is Tokyo's most revered patissier. He is the first Asian to win the Coupe du Monde de la Pâtisserie (in 1991), the cake world's Bocuse d'Or, and was named the best pastry chef in Asia in 2015. Sugino is a master of his craft at the very top of his game. Famed for making the most beautiful 'entremets' – Russian dolls of the cake world with different layers of perfectly matched flavours and textures – Sugino's creations boast the most delicate mousses made with the bare minimum of gelatine and sugar, and the most airy sponge bases. Initially, his cakes appear to be nothing particularly extraordinary or innovative, the flavour pairings are the familiar coffee and caramel, raspberry and pistachio, mint and chocolate, and so on; they exhibit none of the shock avant-gardism you sometimes find in Europe where you see everything from olive oil

to coffee grounds or cereal milk (actually, even *mother's* milk) used
in desserts. He just uses chocolate, nuts and the standard palette of
patissier's fruits – raspberries, blueberries, peaches, strawberries –
seasonal, of course, so summer might bring coconut and passion
fruit, chestnuts dominate in autumn, citrus in winter and so on.
This is classical French patisserie yet it is executed at a level rarely
seen even in Paris.

Having initially worked as a young man in the kitchens of Tokyo's
legendary Hotel Okura, Sugino continued his professional journey in
Paris, learning his craft at Patisserie Peltier, now sadly defunct. He had
moved to Paris in 1989 to do a *stage*, or internship, at another restaurant,
but one day on a trip to buy a birthday cake for his niece at a different
patisserie, Sugino disembarked at the Duroc Metro station by mistake
and found himself looking in the window of Peltier. He was dazzled.
He bought a cake, tasted it, and his life was changed for ever.

'It was so fabulous, a *tartelette orange*,' he tells me one day when
I meet him at his Tokyo store in an otherwise featureless backstreet
in Kyobashi. For a moment, he is transported back to that Damascene
moment over two decades ago. 'I particularly remember the pastry
– it was so perfectly cooked.'

Sugino-san plucked up the courage to return to Peltier and ask
if there were any opportunities to work, unpaid, and inveigled his
way into what was at the time one of the great dessert kitchens in
Paris. He ended up working there for three years, mastering pastry
and macarons, mousses and *pâté à choux*, and all the other miraculous
substances which make up the patisser's armoury. Clearly, something
extraordinary was awoken within this man during his time at Peltier
as, within two years, he was lifting that first prize in the Coupe du
Monde de la Pâtisserie on behalf of Japan. It was and is the international peak of competitive cake-making and his victory came as
a great surprise to all, not least Sugino himself.

'Back then, the Japanese were known for their decoration, but
they were not so good at flavours,' he recalls. He had trained for
the competition for six months, unheard of preparation in those
days. 'When the final announcement was being made, I remember

they said the third place first. It was Canada. The French team was so confident they would win, but then they announced the second place was France. I just thought Belgium would win. It was so dramatic when they said, "First place: Japan".'

Sugino maintains the Coupe du Monde changed neither his life nor the course of patisserie in Japan. The latter had been well under way since his former boss André Lecomte had arrived to take charge of desserts at the Hotel Okura in 1963.

Now forgotten by most, Lecomte's arrival was a seismic moment in the history of European cuisine in Japan. Lecomte stayed in Japan until his death in 1999, training an entire generation of patissiers and almost single-handedly introducing proper bread-making and Viennoiserie to Japan via his shop in Roppongi, which was the first of its kind in Japan. According to his obituary in French catering trade bible *L'Hôtellerie Restauration*, by the time Lecomte passed away this plump, pink little man, who back in France had been orphaned at the age of thirteen, had built up an extraordinary empire of five shops, a restaurant (Le Toucan), a brewery, four tea rooms, a factory and a catering company employing 200 people.

Lecomte began his career with an eight-year apprenticeship at the George V Hotel in Paris, but was working for the Shah of Iran when he was encouraged by a French tour operator to move to Tokyo ahead of the 1964 Olympics. That first Tokyo Olympics was another of the major food moments in Japanese history. It was the first time that French chefs were introduced to the beauty, simplicity and seasonality of Japanese cuisine. From that awakening, nouvelle cuisine was born, which rejected the heavy sauces, the fat and dairy of Auguste Escoffier and the nineteenth century in favour of simplicity, seasonality and more considered plating.

Back in the early sixties, the Hotel Okura was pretty much the only top-quality Western-style hotel in all Japan; when Lecomte began working there he was its only foreign member of staff out of 1,500 people, but soon word spread of his extraordinary desserts which were so very different from the adzuki- and mochi-based wagashi to which the Japanese were accustomed.

Lecomte married a Japanese woman, Yasuko, who ran her own tea room, and he soon began supplying food to the city's foreign diplomats and, eventually, to the Emperor himself. In 1968 he transformed his wife's tea room into a French bakery, and went on to cook for visiting dignitaries including the Pope and various royals, as well as a long list of visiting French presidents: Pompidou, Giscard d'Estaing, Mitterrand and Chirac. There are still branches of A. Lecomte in Ginza and in department stores in Tokyo. He paved the way for the likes of Robuchon, Bocuse and other French chefs to conquer Japan with their own restaurants and branded products, a trend which continues today.

It seems as if Lecomte was struck, too, by the Japanese sense of duty and dedication. Perhaps this was why he stayed so long in Japan. *L'Hôtellerie Restauration* quotes him as saying, 'In Japan, we never relax. The Japanese work a lot. I like them. Daily discipline is the key to all success.'

On the other hand, there are all sorts of horror stories from foreigners who have worked in the kitchens of Paris, from Orwell to Gordon Ramsay, and the Japanese do seem to suffer the most. The great Japanese kaiseki master, Yoshihiro Murata, shuddered when he recalled his time in French kitchens when I first interviewed him some years ago. I wondered how Sugino had been treated by the French?

'I counted myself lucky to have been allowed in, but the treatment was very bad. For example, we were not allowed to use the same showers as the French chefs, we had to shower along with the workers from Mauritius or the washing-up staff from Africa. Sometimes the French chefs asked me, "Why are you so yellow?" and I would tell them it was because I ate too much sweetcorn. I'd ask them, 'Why are you so white? Because you eat too much wheat?"'

Sugino eventually returned to his home city of Kobe, where he opened his own patisserie. It is telling that Sugino is a Kobe boy. In Japan, Kobe is synonymous with Western-style patisserie; it is Cake City: the central shopping district is full of amazing patisseries. Dozens of them. Ever since it had been one of the first Japanese ports to open up to the outside world in the late nineteenth century, Kobe has been considered the capital of cosmopolitan sophistication and fashion, and cake remains one of the most obvious manifestations of this. Sugino opened his first shop in 1992 in the Kitano district, traditionally home to the city's large expat population (I urge you to visit Kitano if you can, by the way: it has some of the strangest and most charming museums in the world, housed in the old colonial mansions of consuls and traders from Spain, Britain, France, Holland and Germany). In 2001, he moved to Tokyo and opened this store in the Kyobashi district of central Tokyo.

The store opens at 11 a.m., by which time there is usually a queue of a dozen or so fans. The most popular creations sell out within an hour. You have to be quick to grab one of the ten examples of the Ambroisi he makes a day – this is an ethereally light chocolate mousse cake with a raspberry jam, pistachio mousse and pistachio 'joconde' (a biscuity sponge) at its core, all covered in a chocolate glaze with a gloss like the paint on a brand new Lexus. This is the piece which won him the Coupe du Monde in 1991. The recipe, which I found translated online, is extraordinarily complex and precise, calling for thirty-eight different quantities of ingredients, including 38g of pistachio paste (not 37g, or 39g). He only uses 4g of gelatine to set 550g of cream/milk/eggs, an unusually low ratio. Another of Sugino's hallmarks is that he minimises the sweetness of his cakes. There is no sugary throat burn with his desserts.

By the time I arrive for my meeting with Sugino in the early afternoon, all of the Ambroisis have been sold and the cabinet in the front of the shop is already looking sparse. In front of me is a customer trying to make up her mind. As I inwardly urge her to get on with it so that I can try some cake for myself, Sugino appears from a door to the rear of the seated area where daintily dressed Japanese women are already tentatively nibbling at their prized patisserie. He sees me, the only foreigner in the store, scowls to himself – I was early – turns to mumble some instructions to a server, then retreats once more into a side door.

A couple of minutes later, at the exact time of our appointment, Sugino returns, now smiling, and invites me to join him at one of the tables where we talk for a while. As we do, a plate with three of his pieces arrives, much to my relief.

'You want to try them first?' Sugino asks, correctly interpreting my distracted manner. I tuck in first to a raspberry and pistachio mousse which defies the laws of physics with its lightness, and then a nine-layer apple cream piece, made with butter from Hokkaido ('more mild-tasting than other butters'). They both look fairly conventional but the balance of flavours is exceptional, the moderate sweetness allowing the raspberry flavour to shine through, and the textures are ethereal. Then comes a chestnut and chocolate mousse; I may at this point have disgraced myself with some inadvertent groans of pleasure. When I finally lift my head from the plate, I see Sugino is watching me intently. I tell him how wonderful his cakes are, and his face – chubby cheeks, close-cropped hair, neatly trimmed goatee – relaxes into a smile.

Famously – in pastry circles, at least – some of Sugino's patisserie are so fragile that he forbids customers from taking them away from the shop; they can only be consumed in situ. It seems he cannot bear the thought of his desserts being eaten in a less than perfect state. Others, like the Ambroisis, are made in very limited numbers. Why, I wondered, did he not make more, so he could sell more and make more money? Why didn't he have other outlets, or stalls in depachika like many other famous patissiers did, both French and Japanese?

'Because I make them all myself. Do you think Pierre Hermé works in all his shops? For me, quality is everything. I have no need for money. Number one: I love to work. But it was only after I turned sixty [up until this point I had assumed he was in his early fifties but he is sixty-two] that I started to enjoy working.'

Even at Christmas time, his busiest season, Sugino does most of the work himself, with help from just a few assistants, working fifteen-hour days to create around 800 Christmas cakes. A recent

Japanese TV documentary revealed the physical toll this takes on him. The cameras followed him on a visit to his chiropractor, shuffling zombie-like, clearly in agony from standing for hours every day. The documentary made him famous in Japan for his almost masochistic dedication, showing him repeatedly submerging his hands in a bowl of iced water to keep them cool while working with heat-sensitive ingredients. 'The mousses can be so delicate that they melt,' he tells me. 'So the moulds and my gloves are also cooled before I start, especially in summer.'

So, if not money, what was the motivation for this kind of extreme work ethic? 'The source of my motivation is the smile of my guests. With the Christmas cake, I have been making that for twenty-five years, and the reaction from guests is amazing, so I always want to meet their expectations.' It was essentially the same answer I had received from all the master craftsmen I had met in Japan – they do it for their customers. Their expectations give them the energy to keep going, to improve. Their pleasure is reward enough.

Up in his stainless steel-lined atelier next to the store Sugino shows me this year's Christmas cake, a pear and fig concoction, not yet finished. He had been struggling with a fig mousse component because, apparently, figs have an enzyme which melts gelatine. The solution, he eventually discovered, was not just to use fig purée, but pieces of whole fig, too. How long had he been trying to solve this?

'Fifteen years.'

Despite the fairly conclusive evidence to the contrary, Sugino claims to have no particular technical ability. He is 'all thumbs' he says, 'not so good at delicate work, but my skills are getting better. The answers always come through working every day.'

He uses Valhrona chocolate, none of your bean-to-bar nonsense for him. That seems sensible: whatever we might want to believe, making chocolate is, really, an industrial process not to be undertaken lightly by bearded men in braces and leather aprons in hipster ghettos. But why, I wonder, did none of his current range use traditional

Japanese ingredients, like matcha powder, yuzu or adzuki – all of which have been embraced by the Parisian super-patissiers?

'I've never used yuzu or matcha because everyone else is using them,' he tells me. 'I don't like to copy others. I only once made a cake based on another chef's recipe but my staff said it was not my style. I don't think of my works as being Japanese or French. They have the spirit of France, yes, but it is a bit like the Buddha: he was born in India, but Buddhism exists in Japan and Thailand with a different form. The spirit of Buddha is still alive here.

'I don't think that patissiers in Japan are highly skilled. According to my standards, the level is not so high. I think many Japanese patissiers rank as upper-middle. There are no particularly excellent patissiers in Japan. That's the difference between Japan and Paris.'

As well as the latest special Christmas cake (for which orders usually begin in early November), Sugino was also working on a new book which he considered to be his legacy. I assumed it would detail the complexity of his professional output, but no. 'It will be for home cooking, ordinary ingredients, so that people will be able to make them in their kitchens.'

As I am leaving, I still don't feel I have even scratched the surface of what makes a man like Sugino tick. Where does he find his determination, how does he sustain his discipline? He stops wiping down a work surface, and smiles.

'What drives me?' he says, slowly shaking his head as if he doesn't really understand it himself, or perhaps hasn't even given it much thought. 'Some power, some spirit.'

CHUBU/TOHOKU

Chapter 29

Mochi

The two men raise their heavy wooden mallets in the chill Ibaraki air. Charcoal smoke briefly envelops them, obscuring their vision and rendering their task even more perilous. The first man pauses, mallet held shakily aloft, as the second brings his weapon crashing down onto the mound of steamed rice, before wrestling it free from the sticky white mess. He stands clear and now the first man does likewise, smashing his mallet-head into the rice with a resounding 'thwump'.

By now I am already familiar with the traditional methods for making mochi thanks to my time with Horiguchi-san in Minowa, so who are these two men risking shattered craniums to beat the hell out of a couple of kilos of rice in a hollowed-out tree trunk? And why is a young woman crouching beside them recording the dull thwacking of their hammers on her tape recorder?

One of the men is Rarecho, the talented forty-four-year-old anime artist who has been responsible for turning me and my family into what must go down as the least likely animated characters since SpongeBob SquarePants. Rarecho is wearing his trademark beanie hat and black-framed glasses. The other is a local man, Takabumi Suzuki, eighty, dressed in an orange baseball hat, plaid shirt and grey slacks, his face creased with smile lines. Suzuki-san has agreed to show me, Rarecho, the sound technician, and a small army of animators and producers who have assembled this afternoon at a former high school, now a culture and crafts retreat, how to make mochi the traditional way.

We are here to research a new, extra episode of the cartoon series, an extended New Year's special on the theme of 'osechi ryori', the dishes eaten on 'O-Shogatsu', or New Year's Day – probably the most important holiday in the Japanese calendar.

There are many osechi ryori dishes which are unique to this time of year, but for most Japanese New Year is synonymous with mochi. This is why, up in the hills of Ibaraki, Rarecho and Suzuki-san are engaged in the 'mochi-suki', the perilous practice of pounding rice with oak mallets, called 'keyaki', in the 'usu', a chunk of hollowed-out tree trunk (in this case a 130-year-old cedar) which, before the advent of machines, was the only way to make mochi (there is one other way: each year at Yokohama's Hakkeijima Sea Paradise, they entrust the mochi-pounding to walruses).

Making mochi this way is still an evocative experience for many Japanese. It seems an almost spiritual ritual with the power to bring a people, who can seem to have become rather isolated by the relentless progress of twenty-first century technology, back in touch with their agricultural past. The smell of the charcoal and the cooked rice has awoken something in the group here: nostrils twitch, smiles spread, a giddy mood is blossoming.

Suzuki-san stands aside and invites me to take over in concert with Rarecho, each of us taking turns to bring our mallet crashing down onto the large ball of rice like members of a chain gang breaking up a large rock. Now, Rarecho is a wonderful artist, but I am literally trusting him with my life as, one slightly mistimed strike, and his mallet could come crashing down on my cranium, and likewise mine upon his. But we take it slowly, making sure the other's head is clear of the hammer zone.

Every once in a while Suzuki-san stops us, dabs some more water on the rice to stop our hammers sticking and gives it a quick knead, slapping it back down into the tree hollow like a super-dense bread dough. I am grateful for the pause. It is hard work pounding mochi. Rice farmers used to consider this a 'day off', their New Year's holiday, Suzuki tells us. Apparently, an awful lot of sake would have been consumed during the mochi-making which is a frightening thought. Rubbing my sore biceps, I joke that they should make it an official sport for the 2020 Tokyo Olympics. Someone else says it helps if they imagine the rice is the face of their boss.

After a good half-hour of pounding, there comes a brief, even more dangerous phase of mochi-making in which one man massages the dough by hand in between repeated hammer-pounding by the other (it is at this stage that you would add sugar if you were making sweet mochi), then, finally, Suzuki-san lifts up the finished mound of mochi – enough of it to fill both arms – and we follow him inside. Here, he shows us how to pinch a piece of the dough between our thumbs and forefingers, and then twist it off into a bite-sized morsel. We then roll the pieces either in adzuki bean paste or kinako – toasted, ground soy bean powder, one of my absolute favourite Japanese ingredients.

The third option is to add the mochi clumps to a light vegetable broth, 'zoni'. There are many regional differences with this New Year's soup: in Kanto, eastern Japan where we are now, they typically use chicken and soy, while in Kyoto the New Year's zoni is made with white miso; in Kyushu it's a fish broth with grilled shrimp; on Shikoku they use sweet mochi, and so on.

It is this zoni mochi which nearly kills me.

Every 1 January, several elderly Japanese choke to death on mochi. I had never really understood how this was possible, having eaten tons of mochi in the past with no difficulty. It is ironic, then, that the first mochi I make myself very nearly does for me, too.

We have literally just been talking about the annual deaths caused by mochi and I had expressed my usual bemusement: 'I just don't understand how anyone could be stupid enough to choke to death on a piece of mochi!' I say, shaking my head.

I take a bowl of the broth, slurp a little and pluck out a pristine blob of mochi with my chopsticks. This is the first time I have eaten mochi in a savoury soup and so I am completely unprepared for the challenge of dealing with a super-slippery, squash-ball-sized piece of pounded rice. It slides down my throat before my tongue and teeth are able to coordinate to render it more digestible, lodging

there like Augustus Gloop in the chocolate tube. I struggle for a
few seconds as the terrible realisation dawns that I can't actually
breathe. Sheer Englishness prevents me from drawing anyone's
attention to this, so instead I launch into an involuntary gagging-
bucking-rocking, like a cat with a recalcitrant furball, eyes bulging,
face reddening, panic rising. Finally, I manage to swallow the damn
thing whole like a python downing a goat (I am sure it creates a
visible bulge in my throat as it goes down). I feel it slowly descend
to my abdominal area like a gold brick falling through quicksand,
where I suspect it resides to this day, like some monstrous
interior goitre.

I breathe a sigh of relief that I have managed to deal with the
mochi myself and haven't had to seek humiliating assistance, and
pluck another one from the soup. It is delicious.

Afterwards, I chat a little with Suzuki-san. 'In the old times they
said mochi gave you more energy. Farmers would take ten pieces
with them when they worked in the fields, with a lot of sake of
course,' he says. He recalls a time when communities would gather
at New Year to make mochi together, and at other times to help
each other with harvests, or even funerals. 'Now they just employ
a company to do it,' he sighs. He also remembers when people
would visit shrines regularly, and the womenfolk would gather at
the crescent moon. 'There were always festivals, all the time, to
please the kami.' These are the gods which are said to inhabit natural
and even manmade things: trees, rivers, rocks, washing machines
and so on, thousands of gods, all to be appeased, cajoled and
persuaded according to the animistic principles of Shintoism.

Days later, I see there is still a small piece of mochi encrusted in
my phone case as, once again, I take a deep sigh and turn on data
roaming. I am lost somewhere in central Tokyo, in search of Rarecho
and the team. We are due to meet for the second element of our
research for the new programme – an osechi ryori lunch featuring
traditional New Year's Day dishes, prepared for us by octogenarian
Hisae Ooka.

Finally having found them, we walk together to the quiet, upmarket residential district where Ooka-san lives. Her home for the past forty years is an apartment unusual for the Japanese capital in both its large size and extensive carpeting, with that familiar memento-cluttered, hermetically sealed atmosphere of grand-mothers' homes everywhere.

Ooka-san has taught cooking for most of her adult life. She first learned at the Yanagihara cooking school with the grandfather Toshio Yanagihara himself, attending classes every fortnight for over ten years. She also found time to become a high-jump champion and athletics trainer, something she continues to do even at this advanced age.

Straight-backed, with her hair stiffly coiffed, Ooka-san is an imposing figure of a woman. She is dressed in a polka-dot blouse with a black skirt, with black pearls and a gold bracelet. After the usual introductions in her living room, she shows us through to the dining room.

Traditionally, it is forbidden to actually cook anything on New Year's Day, Ooka-san explains; everything must be pre-prepared, which of course has an impact on the types of dishes served. She has spent more than a day and a half preparing our meal, with help from two assistants, one of whom is her grandson, Koyata. It is a kaleidoscopic spread, featuring twenty-five different dishes made with over fifty ingredients. There are carrots pared into flowers; tiny mountain potatoes; even tinier silver fish; strips of squid; glossy edamame beans; one dish is flecked with gold leaf; there is yellow omelette; and pink and white strips of kamoboko (minced, steamed fish), somehow contrived into knots. Several other of the dishes are unrecognisable to me, and all are served in elegant gold and black lacquer boxes with red interiors, along with red and blue Arita bowls. For each guest, there is a fan-shaped, gold lacquered plate and a choice of crystal sake cups offered from a tray.

We begin with a sip of rather bitter herbal sake, traditionally served only at New Year. 'I believe happiness is in the circle of people, and food is the best way to gather that circle,' pronounces

Ooka-san, indicating with a formal nod that we may commence eating.

As with other forms of traditional Japanese cooking, symbolism and meaning abound within Osechi dishes. Take the herring roe which Ooka-san served for us. The 'kazunoko', as it is known, was poached in dashi and had an eyebrow-raising crunch-pop texture (it is almost a treat to find one of the eggs in your teeth hours later) but the eggs also symbolise fertility and have particular significance for people wishing for children (or grand-children) in the coming year. The name itself has the kind of double or even triple meaning – Japanese people relish that kind of thing: 'kazu' means number and 'ko' means child, but in the language of the indigenous Ainu people of northern Japan 'kado' means herring.

Among the many other dishes on the table are kuromame – black soy beans – 'mame' meaning both 'bean' and 'health'. Not all of the meanings revolve around wordplay, some are visual puns: the pink and white of the kamobuko knots (fish paste steamed into a rubbery textured product) symbolises the rising sun, symbol of Japan itself, of course, while the bent-backed pose of the cooked shrimp is supposed to evoke the elderly. There is usually some gold or yellow included in an osechi ryori spread – both are celebratory colours – in this case they are represented in a sweet potato mash with chunks of whole chestnut and gold leaf.

'The chestnuts must be whole. You cannot cut them into smaller pieces,' warns Ooka-san. 'They symbolise nuggets of gold, and we want whole gold!' Some of the Osechi taxonomy loses a little in translation, however: I can't quite grasp how one can 'see the future through the holes in the sliced lotus root', for instance.

As we begin to eat, it strikes me that many of the osechi ryori dishes, like the potato-chestnuts, are unusually sweet: lots of other ingredients have been simmered or steeped in mirin, sugar, vinegar or soy.

'Yes, sugar and vinegar were traditionally used to preserve New Year's food for three days, so the women didn't have to work,' says

Ooka-san. It still seems like a huge amount of work for the woman of the house to provide herself with a day or two off.

'It is important to pass down our ethnic character. These traditions and festivals all have a special meaning, and New Year's is the biggest,' she continues. 'We have passed down these dishes in my family from generation to generation; my aunt was a cooking teacher who worked until she was ninety-six – she has just turned one hundred. The first thing to teach the young is educating their palate, teaching them what good produce tastes like.

'These have been our life force, they've helped us survive all kinds of difficulties. For me, these kinds of things are the basis of belonging to my family and I am happy that all my grandchildren are learning them. These celebrations are profoundly meaningful for every family and if they stop, their meaning is lost. They have already been lost for many people in Japan. These days many just buy pre-made osechi ryori. I understand that women are working full time so they want a holiday at New Year like everyone else, so they order from the Internet. I did that once when my husband passed away but no one liked it in my family, and I will never do it again.'

Now Ooka-san has a question for me. She had once had an exchange student from England to stay. Why was the girl so fat? she wonders. I am afraid we are all getting a little larger in the West, I reply.

To change the subject, I wonder whether men might bear some of the responsibility for preserving Japan's traditional foods. 'Maybe we are at a turning point now,' Ooka-san says. 'Women will work more and I hope more men will go into the kitchen. That would be a good way to keep these traditions alive. Men are more focused and determined, so there is great potential there.'

The food looks like a jewellery display which I think is why I am a little taken aback that it also tastes so wonderful: the umami power of the sea bream cured in konbu is quite extraordinary, for instance. The fish is sandwiched between konbu for a couple of hours which firms up its flesh and intensifies its flavour. It is one of those dishes you yearn for long after it's eaten.

As well as eating, the New Year is also a time for reflection and, as the meal comes to an end, Ooka-san begins to reminisce about her childhood during the war.

'I can remember being evacuated from Tokyo, seeing the dead, I can remember the terror,' she says. The table falls silent. 'I remember bombing, and running with a blanket over my head to the temple, having to divide an orange between four people, or a single fish for a whole family.'

We gather ourselves to leave, bellies now groaning from the abundance that modern-day Japan has given us. I ask Ooka-san if she finds life in modern Tokyo too frenzied and fast, compared to her childhood.

'No,' she shakes her head vigorously. 'I am a track and field star, so I've always been fast in everything, and, not only that, I am accelerating because time is running out!'

Chapter 30

Koji

Soy sauce and sake have been exported from Japan to Europe for 400 years; I always find it strange to think that soy sauce was served at Versailles during the reign of Louis XV in the mid-1700s, but it's true. Of course, back then the exports from Japan to Europe were on a minuscule scale. For most of the next four centuries, the culinary influence was probably stronger in the other direction, from the West to Japan. Initially, as we have heard, this happened via the gates of Dejima, and the influence accelerated dramatically after World War II, since when the Japanese have wholeheartedly embraced the Western wheat and meat diet, but it wasn't until after the Tokyo Olympics of 1964 that the influence really began to flow in the opposite direction.

That was the year that one of France's pioneering TV chefs, Raymond Oliver – who since 1948 had owned and run one of the greatest restaurants in Paris, Le Grand Véfour – accompanied his country's Olympic team to the Japanese capital. Oliver was exposed to Japanese food and in particular the kaiseki meal which had a direct influence on the emergence of nouvelle cuisine in 1968, eventually mutating into the often overblown multi-course menus now so popular at ambitious restaurants around the world.

Paul Bocuse, another of the nouvelle pioneers, made his own pilgrimage to Japan in 1972 followed by other titans of *les grandes tables*, Michel Guérard, the Troisgros brothers, Roger Vergé and Fernand Point, all of whom played their part in the simplification and a lightening of classical French cooking. That first wave of Japanese influence on French cuisine focused more on techniques, presentation and the structure of the meal than introducing Japanese ingredients to the French. Nouvelle cuisine was still mostly founded upon French ingredients (although I do remember reading of that other great moderniser of the Parisian dining scene, Alain Senderens, 'mounting' soy sauce with butter later on in the 1980s). The first major wave of Japanese ingredients to arrive in France probably started with Joël Robuchon in the mid-1980s. A fervent Japanophile, Robuchon was one of the first, if not *the* first, to incorporate yuzu into his dishes; in the same decade wasabi mayonnaise would momentarily become all the rage, too (albeit not made with fresh wasabi root; we are still talking about the stuff in tubes). Then, in the 1990s, the molecular crowd also found their way to Japan, led by Ferran Adrià, head chef and co-owner of the most influential restaurant in the world at the time, El Bulli, on Spain's Costa Brava. Among other Japanese secrets he 'discovered' agar-agar, a setting agent made from powdered algae, also known in Japan as 'kanten' (although, technically, the two are made from slightly different types of algae). Adrià realised that agar-agar did not melt when it was heated, which meant that he could serve hot gels, plus, of course, vegans can eat it. Then there was kuzu, a flavourless starch, better at thickening sauces than traditional flour; and the technique for coagulating soy milk to make tofu, which was adapted for the modernists' celebrated and much-imitated 'spherification'.

Since then, many other chefs have picked up on a yet wider range of Japanese food products, from the smoky-meatiness of katsuobushi (dried bonito fillets) and the umami power of konbu, to the Szechuan pepper-style tongue-tingling effects of sansho pepper or the aromatic zing of shiso leaves. The French pastry crowd fell in love with matcha and yuzu, of course; panko breadcrumbs and nori are now sold in my local supermarket; and, I may be wrong, but though they had been eaten in parts of the Mediterranean for millennia, I suspect the world only really fell in love with sea urchin because of the Japanese.

So what's next? Is there anything left in the ransacked Japanese pantry? Are there any ingredients or produce yet to be 'discovered'?

We've already met umi budo, the Okinawan sea caviar, and awamori, as well as Kyushu's sweet and juicy Kurobata pork, and shochu, of course. Then there are the many varieties of Japanese teas which are only just now finding a wider market in the world. In terms of raw produce, I love myoga, the softer, sweeter Japanese ginger, though I still don't see it that much outside Japan, and the same goes for the various sansai – spring mountain vegetables, like butter-burr, fiddlehead ferns and the like. Yuzu is already moving into the mainstream but yuzusco (tabasco) and yuzu kosho – salted yuzu pith with chilli – have huge potential and, I'll say it again, yuba – soy milk skin – is a miracle, whether fresh or dried.

And then there is koji, the mysterious mould which has been used in the production of soy sauce, shochu, mirin, miso and sake, among other things, for hundreds if not thousands of years in Japan and elsewhere in Asia, and which is also beginning to arouse the interest of the more adventurous, experimental chefs in Europe and America.

I have heard about this strange substance, koji, initially at sake makers I visited in Kyoto ten years ago, but many times since at miso and soy companies. Koji is a kind of fungus – Japan's official national mould, no less – which is added to steamed rice or grains to begin the fermentation process. The mould releases enzymes called proteases and amylases which develop or 'break down' the proteins and starch in the rice (in the case of sake) turning them into sugars on which the mould feeds. Koji's Latin name, as we have seen, is *Aspergillus oryzae*, which to me always sounds like a cross between a mental illness and a type of pasta (Asperger's orzo?). But what actually *was* koji, what did it look like, how did it taste and where did it come from? I had always envisaged koji arriving at the brewing room in some kind of nuclear waste container borne by a man wearing a biohazard suit. Perhaps there was some steam escaping from the container, and everyone stood back when it was opened ... but, in truth, I didn't really know.

To find some answers, I took the Shinkansen from Tokyo to Niigata with Asger and Emil, leaving Lissen alone for some R&R in the big city.

Niigata is one of the great centres for sake production. Japan's two longest rivers reach the coast here bringing with them not just pure, soft water, but fertile soil from the mountains which is deposited on the marshlands, reclaimed since the sixth century for fertile rice paddies. During the course of a year this part of the Sea of Japan coast experiences comparatively extreme contrasts in heat and cold – again, good for the fermentation process required for sake. Niigata has always been among Japan's most prosperous cities. When the Victorian writer and explorer Lady Isabella Bird, who generally tended more towards obnoxious condescension when describing Japan, travelled from Tokyo to Hokkaido in 1878, she described Niigata as 'A handsome, prosperous city of 50,000 inhabitants … so beautifully clean that I should feel reluctant to walk upon its well-swept streets in muddy boots.'

There are still ninety sake breweries located in what, these days, is a still very clean (hardly unusual in Japan) but oddly empty city. My sons and I arrive one bright, sunny spring day, check into our hotel and take a walk around, visiting first the city's history museum and then the Toki Messe congress centre, incongruously huge for such a somnolent city with its skyscraper office tower overlooking the ferry port where boats leave for Sado Island, Korea and Russia.

The next morning, at the Imayotsukasa Sake Brewery Co. Ltd, we are welcomed by CEO Masayuki Habuki and his American employee, Jarom Reid. Founded in 1767, Imayotsukasa is one of the most famous sake breweries in Niigata, in part because it sticks bloody-mindedly to the traditional way of doing things: washing the rice by hand, storing at least some of its sake production in cedar barrels rather than metal tanks, and never adding alcohol, as many other breweries do.

Jarom, a friendly, handsome fellow, used to work for Delta Airlines. He fell in love with sake while compiling its in-flight drinks menu, and moved to Japan over a decade ago to learn more about the country's national drink. He asks us to put on some little plastic slippers. 'There are lots of live cultures in here, and we don't want outdoor shoes contaminating it,' he says. 'We are not even allowed to eat natto when we work here because natto bacteria are too aggressive, they kill our sake koji.'

We follow Jarom and Habuki-san through the brewery's atmospheric old wooden buildings as they explain the process by which sake is made. Most of it I am familiar with thanks to other brewery visits over the years but they keep referring both to 'koji', and something called 'koji kin'. The first time Habuki-san does this, I nod, as if I understand, assuming I must have misheard. By the second or third time, it is too late to ask for clarification. That would be embarrassing but, as the tour progresses, it becomes clear that I have missed something very important amid all this talk of 'inoculated rice' and 'koji rooms'.

I stop them: 'Sorry, but what *is* koji kin? Is that just another name for koji?'

Jarom looks at me with some sympathy. 'Let me start again,' he says.

Koji kin is different from koji, he explains. Koji kin is the actual fungus in its pure form, the domesticated spores of the aforementioned *Aspergillus oryzae*. To start the fermentation of an initial, small batch of partially steamed rice the sake brewer will sprinkle the koji kin – thousands of live spores – from a container covered with a fine wire mesh over the rice. At Imayotsukasa they usually make this starter rice in batches of 300kg. The brewer then leaves the rice, swaddled with blankets to keep it at about 30°C, for three days. This takes place in a wood-panelled koji room – the muro – which looks and functions rather like a sauna, keeping the rice and its mould nice and toasty. This process turns the rice which has been inoculated with koji kin into koji – or, in English, 'malted rice'. If you add a little yeast to this koji, then transfer it all to a large tank with water and a larger quantity of polished rice (the more polished the rice, the higher the grade of sake you end up with, though this does not necessarily guarantee the best flavour – another, long story), after fermenting and pressing and it will eventually become sake.

'So, where do you make the actual koji kin?' I ask, trying to mask my frustration.

'Oh, no, we don't make it,' says Jarom. 'We buy that from another company, in Akita. I don't think any sake brewers make their own koji kin. There are only a handful of companies who make koji kin in Japan. It is a very long and involved process which needs lots of care and attention, but it is *so* important.'

At this moment I feel like some traveller from Greek mythology who, having solved all the riddles and surmounted the challenges set before him, believes the treasure is finally within his grasp, only to find yet another wizened gatekeeper with a riddle to solve. But Jarom promises to put me in touch with Imayotsukasa's koji kin supplier, and I decide there and then that I must go there to honour my koji kin quest.

Meanwhile, we cross the busy road outside the brewery to visit two sister companies to Imayotsukasa, the first a magnificent traditional miso factory, the other a unique food retailer.

As we walk Jarom explains that this part of Niigata, an area called Nuttari, was once the very epicentre of Japan's fermentation industry. Back in the days when rice was Japan's most valuable currency, Niigata, as the most prominent rice-growing area, was not only the most populous and wealthiest city in Japan, but in *all Asia*. In those days, the road through Nuttari was lined with companies making sake, soy and miso and selling it to Japan via this highway, which stretches all the way to Tokyo, as well as via Niigata's large port to overseas markets.

The shop we were visiting was Furumachi Kouji, a light and modern space decorated in a contemporary Japanese Zen style, with a grey stone floor and pale woods. This is Japan's only shop dedicated to koji products: there were different types of koji marinades for tenderising and flavouring meats; koji curry sauce (the koji thickens the sauce without flour, and sweetens it without sugar, making it suitable for coeliacs and diabetics); amazake – best described as sweet, thick sake but with either no alcohol, or low alcohol levels;

and even chemical-free koji beauty products (soaps, face creams, sunscreen). At the counter they served yeasty-sweet koji ice cream.

Koji contains numerous vitamins (especially vitamin B) and minerals, is high in calcium, with a wide range of amino acids and, because it grows naturally sweeter at round 55°C, there is no need for added sugar. It also renders food more easily digestible; as with all fermented or 'rotten' foods, in a sense it pre-digests it for you and contains many of those micro-bacteria which we are constantly being told are beneficial for our physical and even mental wellbeing. It is also said to reduce blood glucose, making koji products an obvious area for research in terms of dietary products for diabetics. If it weren't so expensive koji could in theory be used to make a sugar substitute.

The amazake is particularly intriguing and, again, I think it has huge potential internationally. Though it seems to be growing in popularity in Japan, in part because of its perceived health benefits, I somehow hadn't really paid it much attention before (perhaps because it doesn't have much alcohol). The first we try, a standard amazake, has a sweet, toasted flavour reminiscent of cereal milk. The other, a recent innovation, has added fermented lactic acid harvested from sake lees (the leftover rice after sake has been made) lending it a wonderfully complex, refreshing sourness.

Jarom has been patient, kind and informative, but I think he senses my disappointment at not actually coming face to face with the fabled fungus itself, *Aspergillus oryzae*.

'Just a minute,' he says, disappearing up some stairs at the back of the shop. He returns carrying two dishes. 'This is koji. Malted rice,' he says, offering me a bowl of what looks like half-cooked, then dried, ivory-coloured rice. I ask if it is safe to taste. Yes, of course, he says. The koji rice is malty tasting and sweet with a mineral aftertaste. Then, with a flourish, Jarom produces another saucer, this time bearing a small mound of what looks like unusually dark green matcha powder.

'This is koji kin,' says Jarom triumphantly. 'Is it safe to taste?' I ask again, looking at the dish of fungal spores. 'Go ahead,' he says.

I dab a finger in the powder and put it on my tongue, expecting the heavens to open and celestial light to beam down upon us, but I have to report that koji kin, this miraculous source of all that is good in Japanese cuisine, is both odourless and flavourless.

That evening, searching online for more information about koji and koji kin, I find a fascinating TED talk by 'culinary innovator' Jeremy Umansky, who works with Cleveland chef Jonathon Sawyer's Italian restaurant Trentina. Umansky explains how he has used koji as a cure on a range of produce including scallops and beef. With scallops it makes them more intensely flavoured and densely textured, like chicken apparently. With beef, koji speeds up the ageing process, supposedly reducing that of dry-ageing beef from thirty days to three. In slides, he shows how the scallops and beef grow a furry white coating as the koji releases enzymes which break down proteins. I actually found my mouth watering as I watched this, which is odd. Could you imagine using mould in your home cooking? Many believe it is on the way. Even more fascinating, in a typically 'blue sky' bit of TEDism, Umansky speculates that further research might reveal that koji has unforeseen medical properties; that it could be used by farmers to break down stubble in a field and act as a fertiliser; and even that it could be used to create biodegradable packaging or construction materials.

'It is true, some fungus can be very strong, they can kill insects and other unwanted micro-bacteria and fungis, but unlike chemical pesticides and insecticides, they don't kill the good bacteria and they die in water so they don't linger in the soil and food chain.'

It is some days later. I have travelled, alone this time, towards the eastern tip of Honshu. Dr Hiroshi Konno of the Akita Konno Shouten 'Applied Fungal Technology' company is telling me all about the fascinating possibilities of *Aspergillus oryzae*. You could say he is a *fungi* to hang out with (or, please yourself).

Having spent the night in the city of Akita, I had taken a local train to the small town of Kariwano. Though covered in snow for much of the winter, Akita Prefecture in spring is the greenest place

I have ever seen. Its lush valleys and forested mountains seem to teeter on the brink of being subsumed by verdant undergrowth.

Kariwano station is little more than two platforms and an overpass, but a team of local ladies in pinnies and white gloves – most likely volunteers working for free – are busy cleaning every inch of it. There is a single, rusty taxi outside but Akita Konno is just a short way down the high street, so I walk.

Dr Konno, in his late fifties with a fantastic thick, bushy, Tom Selleck moustache, welcomes me a few minutes later at the company's reception whose walls are decorated with striking electron-microscope blow-ups of different fungi which look just like coral. Beneath the photos is a display cabinet with odd, conical glass containers, each with a different type of *Aspergillus*, ranging in colour from ivory to brown to olive-greens.

As is often the case when I interview people who work in scientific or highly technical jobs, much of what Konno-san tells me flies straight over my head and it is a struggle to keep him to layman's territory, but this is what I learn about koji kin (and Konno-san has read the following – not the bit about Tom Selleck – so we should be on safe ground):

Koji kin, also known as 'moyashi', or 'seed koji', is a pure, domesticated version of the ambient fungi (fungi found just hanging about the place) used for hundreds of years in Japan to make their various fermented foods and drink. It is just one of thousands of different types of fungi, enzyme and micro-bacteria Akita Konno sells for the making of miso, soy, sake, shochu, awamori, mirin, katsuobushi, vinegars, pickles and natto, among other products. Each of them needs a specific type of fungus – sake requires a koji which turns the starch in rice into sugar and alcohol, for instance, while miso and soy sauce need a koji that can decompose proteins to create deliciously umami-rich amino acids and peptides. Some koji increase in temperature quickly, some slowly. Black koji (*Aspergillus luchuensis*), used for awamori, produces a lot of citric acid which is good for fending off other unwanted fungi in the warm climate of Okinawa where it is made, but is bad for sake (although, interestingly, one company in Niigata has recently started using it to make sake: bet that's funky). The *Aspergillus* usually used for shochu is also quite high in citric acid to cope with Kyushu's similarly warm climate, while *Aspergillus glaucus*, the type used for katsuobushi, is unusual in being what Konno-san termed a 'perfect fungi', which means it contains both male and female fungi. The fact that fungi had different genders was news to me, but apparently miso, soy and sake use 'imperfect' fungi.

What would happen if you used, say, a miso koji for making sake? 'You could make a sake with it but most excellent sakes have a simple taste, so you don't want too many amino acids, not too much umami,' says Konno-san. 'A hundred years ago, sake makers would have started the fermentation naturally because they simply weren't aware of the different types of fungi, so you may well have had people making sake with the "wrong" one.'

Konno's great-grandfather, the founder of the company, was Seiji Konno, born in 1882, and the scion of a centuries old sake and soy maker. By all accounts a man of meticulous habits (as a hobby he would make charts to record the accuracy of his watches), Seiji studied the microbiology of brewing at Osaka Higher Technical College and was the first man to isolate and propagate the types of *Aspergillus oryzae* suitable for making soy sauce and sake. This was the first so-called 'domesticated fungus', and the *Aspergillus oryzae* that the company sells today can be traced back over a hundred years to the one isolated in Seiji Konno's laboratory.

'We never isolate *Aspergillus oryzae* from nature, we always use this domesticated fungus,' Konno-san tells me. 'The difference between the two is like that of a wild pig and a farmed pig. Ours is a pure culture. Before, they used some old rice from the last batch of sake in the same way you make bread with a sourdough starter, but that would be a mixed culture, you could never be sure how the end product would taste.' (Later, via email, Konno-san expanded on his pig simile: the domestic pig was bred from wild boars and just as the boars' tusks degenerated because they weren't used, so have the toxins in *Aspergillus oryzae*. Prior to his great-grandfather's research, one can only imagine the number of Japanese people who died trying to figure out why one particular batch of rotten rice created delicious sake and the other, which looked and smelled exactly the same, but made Uncle Hiroko go green and die.)

As well as selling koji kin to food producers the length of Japan, the Akita Konno company also exports to Europe, the USA and Indonesia where a type of koji is used to ferment beans for tempeh, a tofu-like product made from soy beans. But the various koji kin were only one of its product areas. Konno produces more than 10,000 different cultures in all, including brewer's yeasts, enzymes and bacteria for the food industry. There is one which is more troublesome than the rest. The type of fungus – actually a bacillus – used to make natto, the frankly disgusting, odiferous fermented soy bean gloop loved by many Japanese as a healthy breakfast treat, is particularly virulent. It grows very quickly – taking just twenty minutes to begin its cell division. The awful whiff of natto should give one warning of its potency but, just in case, the thirty staff at Akita Konno are forbidden from going from the natto bacillus production facility to any of the others on the same day.

Dr Konno, in a pink polo shirt and blue slacks, takes me on a tour of the factory, first to a lab filled with laser scanning micro-scopes and electron microscopes – big, clunky, grey machinery with massive computer screens of a sort last seen in 1980s sci-fi movies. Shelves are lined with test tubes containing all manner of moulds and fungi. We surprise some technicians who are in the midst of a sake tasting.

'Sake brewers send us samples for analysis and we advise them on blending,' explains Konno. 'And we also make sake ourselves to test our own koji.' He shows me their special freezers which store their 'seed bank' of fungi at $-80°C$. Then we put on some fetching white wellies to see koji kin being made, entering a special part of the factory through an alarming air-lock system which surprise-blasts me with a shock of air with the force of a hundred hair dryers. 'Sorry about that,' laughs Konno-san. 'Koji is a living thing, it can mutate easily and frequently. It's like breeding a dog: we have to

keep it pure. That's why sake brewers are afraid to make koji themselves in case it mutates. Keeping a pure environment is very
important.'

In the air-locked room, rice is soaked then steamed, cooled and
inoculated with the seed culture. It germinates here for a day in a
huge perforated steel drum where it is cooled, before being transferred to wooden trays, covered with muslin, to incubate further
for five to six days. The wood allows the transfer of air, says Konno.
A worker clad head to foot in white hat, overalls and boots brings
us some he made earlier: a seed tray, a bit like a cat litter, filled
with rice which has now turned a uniform, and rather fetching,
dark green.

The room is uncomfortably warm and smells, frankly, of old
socks, but eventually it will produce some lovely fungus spores which
will then be mechanically sieved from their host rice. Just 70g of
these spores will be enough to ferment 200kg of rice to make sake.

'This kind of solid fermentation is really a Japanese specialty,'
Konno explains proudly. 'In Europe and America you brew beer, for
instance, which is not solid, kernel fermentation, it is liquid fermentation only, which is very primitive. But this kind of fermentation
we do in Japan produces many more enzymes which I think will
have many more applications in medicine in the future.'

Several chefs in the West have been experimenting with koji. As
well as Umansky, in New York David Chang has fermented pork
fillets to make a version of katsuobushi he called 'porkbushi', as
well as pistachio- and chickpea misos; in Copenhagen, the Nordic
Food Lab have made pea miso, or 'peaso', and a garum made from
fermented crickets. Konno has heard about their experiments but
they were nothing new as far as the Japanese were concerned. Shio
koji (malted rice in a brine) and amazake are commonly used in
domestic kitchens for marinades, pickling and other purposes.

'The first use of koji was probably four thousand years ago in
Japan; definitely it has been used for a thousand years in Japanese
food culture, to make miso and so on. Koji has always been used
in Japanese home cooking, in dried form on rice, in pickles. Sake

lees with koji and salt makes a wonderful marinade for chicken legs.' There had been a lot of interest recently in making koji ice cream and amazake from a producer in the Czech Republic, he adds, but Konno-san has greater ambitions than just selling koji to chefs.

'My dream is to create a koji that can ferment like yeast,' he says excitedly. 'Imagine if you didn't need to use yeast to make sake! How great that would taste. And then imagine if you could create a koji which fermented fructose. Sake yeast ferments glucose – the starch in the rice becomes glucose – but if you could ferment starch to create fructose then you could make wine from rice!' My mind was now on full boggle. How on earth could you do that? 'It would require a little genetic manipulation and, at the moment, that is not allowed with microorganisms in food production because of the fear that someone might create some killer fungus,' says Konno sadly.

Naturally occurring fungi can, of course, also be deadly. *Aspergillus flavus*, for instance, which grows on the soil in warmer countries, closely resembles *Aspergillus oryzae* but is poisonous. In 1960 an outbreak eventually traced to Brazilian-grown peanuts used in poultry feed caused the death of 100,000 turkeys in the UK. That incident caused a big stir in Japan precisely because of the close resemblance of *flavus* to *oryzae*. Meanwhile, *Aspergillus fumigatus*, which is airborne, is deadly for people whose immune systems are vulnerable and is thus especially unwelcome in hospitals. Hence, these days the production of *Aspergillus* is very closely regulated by the Japanese government.

I left Konno's industrious hive of mould production a little wiser about the miraculous properties of *Aspergillus oryzae* and its potential but I always struggle with the abstract nature of the sciences – or, basically, stuff about stuff you can't see.

It was time to get back to basics, to return to the world of the tangible, to feel the soil between my fingers,* to delve deep into the roots, the very *soul* itself of Japanese food.

* Minus any *Aspergillus flavus*, obviously.

Chapter 31

Rice

I am standing up to my knees in mud. My bare arms are burning in the sun but I can feel the pleasant chill of the wet, grey mud through my rubber boots. Frogs are chirruping and from the corner of my eye I see something slither away into the grass.

'This paddy is deep and soft so the rice will be really tasty,' the Greatest Rice Farmer in the World (TGRFITW) tells me. 'Each field has its own character but this one is tougher to work which is why we use this.'

TGRFITW – known to his friends as Katsuyuki Furukawa – gestures to the machine in front of me. I try to turn but my feet remain stuck stubbornly facing his direction. I am literally a stick-in-the-mud. One at a time I wriggle my feet free using both hands to pull the tops of my rubber boots up and turn around accompanied by lurid squelch-sucking noises. The rice planting contraption sits menacingly in the field looking like a cross between a skidoo and a sewing machine. I don't understand how Furukawa-san is comfortable about letting me loose on one of his precious paddies with something the size of an American supermarket trolley which is also motorised.

The machine has two handlebars: you click the right-hand lever to release the brake, do the same with the left-hand one and you set the monster in motion, he explains. Both functions can operate without you holding the handles which, it will soon become apparent, is a major design flaw when the machine is being operated by a novice.

Suspended immediately in front of the handles is what looks like the paper feeder tray on a photocopier. This 'hopper' (I suppose you'd call it) is filled with oblongs of overgrown turf which are, in fact, patches of young koshihikari rice plants from Furukawa's greenhouses. These gorgeous green sprouts – a beautiful, soothing verdancy – are the reason we are here. We have two fields to fill with these young shoots today, and another two tomorrow. It's time to get planting.

Ahead of the hopper trays is a small petrol engine driving the whole shebang, and beneath that is some clever sewing gubbins which automatically plucks two clumps of shoots and then divots them into the waterlogged mud. Each clump contains roughly three rice plants which, one day six or so months hence, will be enough to provide enough cooked rice to fill two bowls – an ancient measurement known as a 'go' in Japanese. The machine plants the rice in two neat rows about forty centimetres apart at roughly twenty-centimetre intervals, two times per second. The idea is that the person in control of the machine follows behind, tiptoeing along a narrow path between the two straight rows of newly planted seedlings, lifting off the planting lever at the end of the field and executing a neat, 360° turn, before re-engaging the left-hand lever for the return leg.

I take a deep breath, whisper the instructions to myself out loud and release the left handle, but then panic slightly at the sudden, high-pitched infernal racket this initiates as the planter begins to deposit green shoots into the mud. I promptly forget all of Furukawa's instructions. It is like my first driving lesson all over again. In the few seconds delay, I have already planted a dense clump of rice shoots all in one place, like a bad hair transplant. Furukawa patiently suggests that I also release the brake. The scenery lurches as the machine suddenly pulls me forward. Unfortunately, my wellies remain firmly embedded in the mud. In a split second I have to make a decision: either carry on in my socks and leave my boots behind, or let go of the machine. I choose the latter and watch the rice-planting skidoo chug onwards at an unfortunate tangent away from the previous – perfectly straight – row of new plants. Furukawa-san springs after the machine, moving at surprising speed as if on points, like a ballet dancer. Asger and Emil hop into the paddy to help me, also moving at an impressive rate. And thus my humiliation is complete.

This is not how I had foreseen our trip to the rice paddies of Fukushima. I had such lofty ambitions for our rice-planting experience. I wanted Asger and Emil to meet Furukawa-san and to learn about his extraordinary dedication to growing The Best Rice in the World (I'll get to his credentials in a moment), and to get a sense for the work involved in farming in general.

In 2011 the tsunami and ensuing nuclear disaster devastated the coastal part of this prefecture, killing thousands and destroying buildings and infrastructure. Though Furukawa's farm, here in Koriyama in the central zone of Fukushima Prefecture, is far from the epicentre and separated from it by a mountain range, the disaster threatened to destroy the market for his rice, and with it his livelihood. But Furukawa kept going, exhibiting a very Japanese type of noble stoicism. I wanted my sons to hear about this and also just to experience the sheer physical hard work of a rice farmer, the endless slog in unpleasant conditions that ultimately results in those ridiculously cheap bags of little white grains which we take for granted on our supermarket shelves back home. I wanted them, also, to meet, simply, a very nice man who conducts himself with unassuming dignity and is key to his community and, in a sense, his country.

I was on a more personal mission, too. I hoped finally to understand the meaning of rice to the Japanese. For many years, in fact since I first travelled to Japan, there has been an elephant in the room in terms of my understanding of Japanese food, and that elephant is rice. I knew how important rice is to the Japanese; it is perhaps the single most significant ingredient, not just in Japanese cuisine, but also as an elemental part of Japanese culture. After all, 'gohan', the word for cooked rice, also means 'meal'. I knew that every proper Japanese meal should finish with a bowl of steamed white rice. I knew that one shouldn't leave one's chopsticks sticking out of a bowl of rice because this is a symbol of death, and that it is frowned upon to leave any rice in the bowl at the end of the meal. Having asked innumerable Japanese what their favourite meal is, or what they would choose as their last meal, I also knew that 'just a bowl of rice' was the most common answer to both questions. But I also knew that, personally, I found plain steamed white rice deeply uninteresting. I usually left my bowl at the end of meals in Japan, enduring the slightly pained expressions of my fellow diners as I did so.

Earlier, while interviewing the Osakan Michelin-starred chef Fujiwara, he had referenced legendary Kyoto restaurant Sojiki Nakahigashi, one of the most difficult places in the city at which to make a reservation, and where the lunch menu can sometimes be entirely focused on rice. The chef, Hisao Nakahigashi, one of Fujiwara's mentors, is an influential figure in Japanese cuisine, but unknown beyond Japan. When I had met him, Nakahigashi, a handsome man in his mid-sixties, was affable enough yet I sensed within him an iron core. He has owned his restaurant, close to the Ginkaku-ji temple, for twenty years and every day he forages in the mountains surrounding Kyoto for many of the plants and vegetables he uses. He served me his four-course rice menu for lunch one time when I visited with a Japanese TV crew for a documentary. The meal started with 'niebana', deliberately undercooked rice served straight from the donabe, the traditional earthenware pot in which it was cooked in front of us, using water from a well in the restaurant's backyard. This rice, organic and sun-dried from Yamagata Prefecture, north of Niigata, reappeared in the second course alongside some himono, salted, sun-dried, then grilled fish. In the third course, 'okoge', the rice was deliberately browned, making it nice and crusty (it is a universal truth that everyone, no matter their race, creed or colour, likes the browned, crusty rice in the bottom of the pan best of all), before taking a final bow floating in a bowl of hot water with ume and perilla. It was an ascetic, thought-provoking experience, and unquestionably the best rice I had eaten up until that point, but it was still, you know, *just rice*. While expressing my – sincere – enjoyment about the lunch for the cameras, there remained the nagging sense that I had missed something.

White rice contains little of nutritional value; all the vitamins and minerals are in the husk, which is removed to make it look white, so why eat it, other than to fill a hole which I would much rather fill with dessert? For the last three decades in the West we have been told that brown rice is the thing to eat if we want the healthy rice option, and I have done, even though it tastes like the bits our pet rabbit leaves behind at the bottom of his bowl. A diet based on the consumption of white rice was, let's not forget, the reason the Japanese sailors suffered from beriberi back in the nineteenth century. To my taste buds it didn't have much by way of flavour, either. And I also knew that more and more Japanese were coming to a similar conclusion; consumption in Japan has halved since the early sixties. This is normal: a decline in rice consumption invariably coincides with an increase in a country's GDP: the richer people get, the less rice they eat. Today, the Japanese currently rank a lowly fiftieth globally in terms of per capita rice consumption. Rice was, then, yet another of those traditional food products which younger Japanese people appeared to be rejecting, along with tofu and tsukudani, funa zushi, homemade dashi and sake.

This is why there was no rice-themed chapter in my first Japan book all those years ago. I knew at the time I should investigate it but the subject neither interested me, nor could I find a way into it, a story to tell about rice. Until, that is, I met Furukawa-san for the first time, which had happened seven months earlier, prior to me and my sons turning up in his fields to help with the planting.

I wasn't sure what to expect of my first trip to Fukushima Prefecture. Of course, I had seen the footage of the devastation wreaked by the tsunami in 2011 but Furukawa's farm was about fifty miles away from the coast, so presumably it had been protected from the flooding. Of course, I did ponder the consequences of any air-, water-, or land-borne nuclear contamination. After the tsunami, I know some expats in Tokyo had reacted by leaving the city for ever. One prominent Japanese food figure of my acquaintance had bought two different types of Geiger counter for use in his home in Tokyo; other Japanese people I asked admitted they had immediately stopped buying anything grown in Fukushima. Despite the assurances from the Japanese government that all produce was being screened for radioactive contamination, many had switched to sourcing their food from the western part of Japan, or overseas. (Oddly, whenever I asked these people about eating fish caught in Japanese waters, they expressed no reservations. 'It's OK, they are not fishing off the coast of Fukushima,' I was assured. 'But fish swim, right?' I would think to myself. The bonito, or katsuo, for instance, migrates hundreds of miles up and down the Japanese coast each year. What was to stop contaminated fish from making their way down the coast to be caught off Shizuoka, for instance? But the conversation would usually mysteriously change at this point, and we would all tuck into our sashimi.)

Arriving back in November 2015 to spend a couple of days filming in Furukawa's fields for the intro to that NHK New Year's special episode, the city of Koriyama appeared unaffected by the 2011 disaster, at least physically. Small and low-rise by the standards of most Japanese cities, it had a slight *Back to the Future* feel, as if all development had halted around about 1988.

My first meeting with Furukawa-san, dressed in his regulation outfit of blue overalls and a John Deere cap, was staged and repeated a couple of times for the cameras: I disembarked from a taxi and strode over to meet him as he cut some rice stalks with a small scythe (we were visiting towards the end of the harvest time). Despite the artifice of the situation, I was immediately taken by his unaffected welcome to me and the crew. Furukawa's broad, suntanned face fell naturally to a relaxed smile. He was fifty-eight years old and had been a farmer for forty of them, but looked ten years younger. Though he was busy finishing the harvest, he was patient as we repeated our conversations, again for the cameras, and I 'helped' with various tasks in the fields. Over the course of the day I was filmed cutting the rice stalks with a scythe, and stacking them in bundles up against thick, tall wooden poles to dry in the sun, in a traditional manner these days rarely seen in the Japanese countryside.

We broke for lunch. It was finally time for me to taste Furukawa's rice. His daughter-in-law had prepared some onigiri – fist-sized clumps of rice pressed together in a triangular shape, and wrapped with a sheet of nori, usually with a small piece of something savoury in the middle of the onigiri – tinned salmon, konbu tsukudani, ume, or pickled Japanese plums. The onigiri rice grains glinted in the sun. They seemed to radiate their own light source. I took a self-conscious bite, watched by a dozen people and two cameras. The rice had a lovely, lingering sweet mineral flavour but I was failing abjectly to summon some kind of transcendent revelation, some 'aha' moment in which I suddenly understood why steamed white rice resonated so powerfully within the Japanese soul. It was just very, very nice rice. Excellent rice. The best rice I had ever eaten, for sure, but still rice. The homemade pickled ume I was also offered, on the other hand, were much more interesting. Rather embarrassingly, my reaction was far more demonstrative when I ate the plums than when I ate Furukawa's rice. Oh dear.

We returned to the harvesting and conversation. I noticed his fields were full of insects – spiders, crickets, weird alien flying things – as well as frogs and lizards. He explained that most of his paddies were fully biodynamic. 'There is no point in fighting nature, so I just leave it to the power of the soil,' he said.

Furukawa started out as a flower farmer but had suffered from constant allergic reactions to the large amounts of pesticides they used, so had changed to farming rice. Over the years, he researched various kinds of organic farming until, in 2002, he attended a seminar about farming with Chinese herbal medicine, exactly the same type of bitter powders that are prescribed for humans.

'I tried a tomato that had been grown with this method and, to be honest, it was nothing extraordinary,' he said, offering me a taste of the herbal powder from a five-kilo bag (it was extremely bitter). 'But I gave it to a one year old baby who hated tomatoes and usually threw them up, and the baby loved it.'

He started slowly to convert his fields to this new system, despite many strange glances and snarky comments from his neighbouring rice farmers. He scattered the powder – ground oyster shells is a key ingredient – on his fields as fertiliser. It wasn't cheap at ¥100,000 (£700) per hectare and his yield was half that of his neighbouring farmers who used both pesticides and chemical fertilisers, but today Furukawa's rice sells for ¥1,600 (£12) compared to low-cost rice which can be as little as ¥650 (£4). (For some fields he also uses a rather fraught and even more expensive process, which I witnessed when I visited the second time with my sons, involving a much larger, ride-on machine which simultaneously lays down rolls of black carbon paper and plants rice through the paper, and which, when it went wrong, which it often did when the paper got damp and torn, reminded me of my own efforts to put up wallpaper.)

Crucially, within two years of starting with the Chinese powders, Furukawa won the largest, most prestigious, and most rigorous rice competition in Japan, beating two thousand other entrants. As with Japan's No. 1 restaurant that we had visited, Yanagiya, my thinking here is that any rice that is deemed the best in Japan has got to be up there among the best rice in the world, hence TGRFITW. Not only that, but Furukawa went on to win the competition for the next *five years* in a row – 2004, '05, '06, '07, '08 – eventually beating 4,000 competitors in the final year. Finally, the Osaka-based rice growers' union in charge of the competition begged him not to enter again, giving him a special diamond award in '09 instead. It was a relief, actually, he chuckled. 'Every autumn as the competition approached, I would get this unapproachable aura of pressure and stress around me. It got really crazy, I would get so irritable, it was better not to be nominated.'

His neighbours still think he is crazy, apparently, but among the rice growers of Japan as a whole he is a hero, a guru attracting young, idealistic farmers from across the country who visit to learn his methods, and is invited to give speeches up and down the land.

Did he enjoy rice farming, I wondered as the camera crew packed up at the end of our day's filming. As with a lot of the shokunin I had met, I don't think Furukawa had ever been asked this before, or perhaps even considered it. He paused and then said, 'I do what I like. But doing everything by myself, in the fields and at home, is so tough.' He used to be married, he said, and has a son and a daughter, but is now divorced. Later on, over a dinner at his house, he admitted to me that he only actually learned to cook his own rice after his wife left. 'I would like to marry a strong woman, I would prefer to be number two in this house!'

Furukawa had invited us all to dinner after filming – more osechi ryori/New Year's dishes in keeping with the programme's theme. He lived in a traditional single-storey wooden building with an enclosed deck, or *engawa*, out front, and two open-plan tatami living rooms at its heart. Here, pride of place went to not one but two small shrines: one Buddhist the other Shinto.

'I pray to Shinto gods once a day to say thanks for my health and peace in the family, nothing to do with the farm or money,' he said as he showed me around. 'I just want my family to be well.'

Fast-forward seven months to the following June, 2016, and Asger, Emil and I have come to Koriyama to help Furukawa plant rice. Eventually I do get the hang of his planting machine, although Asger and Emil master it far more quickly than I and are soon marching up and down the paddies in perfectly straight lines. With their help, we finish the two paddies before the light fades.

That night, over another dinner, this time of temaki – featuring, of course, his wonderful rice – back at Furukawa's farmhouse conversation turns to the 2011 disaster.

'I was at home with my grandson in the garden,' he recalls. 'I was watching my house shaking badly, the roof was breaking.'

Out of fear of contamination, people stopped buying his rice literally overnight, even in local shops. The 'Grown in Fukushima' label, once the mark of some of the best produce in Japan, suddenly became a curse. 'It looked for a while as if I would have to stop farming altogether.'

The Fukushima authorities did what they could to alleviate the public's fears, posting the results of all radioactivity produce checks online, but Furukawa went a step further, undertaking his own independent tests of his rice and posting the – completely safe – results on his homepage.

Still, sales ground to a halt. Farmers on the coast received subsidies from the government but not here in the centre of the prefecture. 'The government tries everything to pay less,' he says. 'I don't trust them. Nobody does.'

Furukawa was invited by supporters and well-wishers to move his farm to another part of Japan but he couldn't abandon his home town, the place where he grew up. In the end, his business was saved by the Takashimaya department store chain. Its flagship branch in Nihonbashi, Tokyo, began promoting Furukawa's rice and supported him financially. But still it took him two years and a lot of debt to return to any kind of economic stability. Many of his neighbouring farmers gave up; several committed suicide. Furukawa now has to sell his own rice directly as there is no longer a profit for a distributor. Happily, he told me that the phone had started ringing right after NHK's New Year's Day transmission of the programme we had made about him – a welcome boost for orders.

Beyond the impact of the 2011 disaster, I asked him why, if rice was so central to the Japanese psyche, consumption in general was in such a decline.

Most farmers these days are only interested in volume and efficiency, not quality. And the government is the same. A while ago, they reduced the number of different quality categories for rice from five to three, so the first category now includes what used to be second-grade rice. If you eat rice grown with chemical fertiliser, it doesn't taste so good. People have forgotten the taste of good rice. They have begun to think rice has no flavour.

'Actually, my main aim is safety, not flavour. If it is safe the consumer will buy it, but the good taste is a by-product of that.' I had asked him something similar – what was the secret of his great rice – when we had been making the documentary the previous year. 'The most important thing is gratitude,' he had said back then. 'There are gods that dwell in the rice, in the soil and in our tools.

If you keep a feeling of gratitude for all these things, and use them with love, I think you will make something good.'

In my grand vision, my second visit to Furukawa's farm was supposed to provide Asger and Emil with some important real-life lessons about dedication, diligence, discipline, all those 'D' words, which for me are tied in with the key Japanese principles of selflessness, community and hard work. But in the end, the lessons end up being largely for my benefit.

I had been anxious about whether Asger and Emil would be able to keep helping all day, whether they could handle, or be bothered with, the hard work, but though Asger would later admit the days with Furukawa-san had been the hardest work of his life ('and, don't forget,' he added, 'I used to have a paper round'), the reality was that my sons came to my assistance more than once. It was *they* who were anxious about *me*, they who were looking out for me. It was they who saved my skin. It turned out that they were better at just about every aspect of rice farming than I was, and they worked hard all day, not just doing the fun stuff with the machines, but raking dead straw from the fields and helping to lift great clumps of clay from the paddies: man's work. By the end of the second day, as we surveyed four (almost) perfectly sown rice paddies, I think we all felt a slight proprietorial feeling towards them.

At one point, early in the first day, I had started to explain to Emil how to plant the rice by hand, something Furukawa had asked us to do in the corners of the fields where the machines had been unable to reach.

'But he didn't do it like that, he did it this way,' Emil had protested, showing me. And he was right; it was I who had misunderstood. This kind of thing had happened before back home many times, of course, particularly with various technological challenges such as connecting the computer to the TV, or having it explained to me that my phone had a torch function so I didn't need to take photos with flash just to find a keyhole in the dark. But I think that, somehow because this was old-fashioned physical labour out in field, the kind of thing I ought to have had an upper hand with, it was much more of a watershed; it was the moment when I realised for the first time that my sons no longer really needed my guiding hand; it was the moment, without being too soppy about it, that I went from Daddy to Dad.

As I stood there up to my knees in wet mud watching over my youngest son's shoulder while he focused on planted rice by hand, that line from the Cecil Day-Lewis poem 'Walking Away' came to mind. Across a school playing field Day-Lewis describes watching his young son depart from him, essentially into manhood, and ' ... like a satellite wrenched from its orbit, go drifting away'.

Perhaps this, then, was *my* meaning of rice, this was what our days spent planting in Furukawa's glistening green fields were supposed to teach me: stop worrying, they are up to it, let them go, off into the world. The world will be lucky to have them, as you have been.

HOKKAIDO

Chapter 32

Uni

We have one final trip to make, to Hokkaido, where our first journey in Japan had begun all those years ago. It is now summer, a couple of months since our rice-planting escapades. I arrive a couple of days before the rest of my family which gives me time to visit what I have been led to believe is the ultimate food destination in Japan: the port town of Hakodate.

Over the past few years I have read so much about this city, supposedly the greatest place for seafood dining in all Japan (which, given that Japan is the pre-eminent seafood nation, once again probably means in the entire world), thanks to its history as an important fishing port for some of the richest fishing grounds in Japan. Hakodate had the best sushi in Japan, according to one writer, while others had written breathlessly about the restaurants by the harbour in and around the Morning Market which were said to serve the most amazing donburi, a bowl of steamed rice topped with cured salmon roe, or uni, or crab or other seafoods, all for ridiculously low prices. I couldn't wait. I was rather glad, actually, that my family would not be witness to what I knew full well would be a grotesque, unedifying overindulgence on the part of their paterfamilias, particularly as this was the height of Hokkaido's uni season.

More than anything, I came to Hakodate with the goal of gorging myself on these golden orange tongues of delight: uni, my absolute favourite thing to eat in the world.

I arrive in the evening to find the Morning Market closed (the clue is in the name, I suppose). I wander by the old brick warehouses along the harbourfront, growing more and more dejected at the coachloads of Chinese tourists disembarking at the average looking conveyor-belt sushi restaurants and chintzy tourist boutiques selling glass dolls, music boxes and fancy chopsticks. There are large 'Tax Free' signs everywhere, which is rarely a sign of quality or authenticity. Is this what all the fuss was about? At the end of the promenade I come to a sign indicating the direction of 'Japan's oldest concrete telegraph pole' nearby. Right now, it seems the more interesting alternative.

I check into my hotel a tram ride away on the other side of the narrow peninsula on which Hakodate squats, and ask for a recommendation for a sushi place. There is one nearby, the receptionist tells me, producing a map. By now almost dizzy with hunger, I find the restaurant, Sushi Kura, a tiny place with its chef working behind a half-filled counter. He takes one look at me as I stand in his doorway, my right index finger raised beseechingly to indicate I need just one seat, and shakes his head. He has no room. It is way past eight o'clock. The Japanese tend to eat out early, particularly outside of the big cities, so it seems unlikely that the empty seats will fill up from now on. 'Omakase?' I venture, meaning that he can serve me what he wants, and also hopefully reassuring him that I am not a total newbie when it comes to sushi, that I won't cause any trouble. But no. The chef is adamant.

As I stomp back to my hotel, I hatch a plan. I shall ask the receptionist to ring the restaurant to check if it really is true that they are fully booked. The receptionist duly rings the restaurant. I can tell from the tone of the conversation that there are indeed spaces available but then the receptionist says the dreaded word, 'gaijin' – 'foreigner', but not in a good way.

'Nooo,' I hiss, waving my arms around. 'Don't tell them that!'

The receptionist puts his hand over the receiver. 'You speak Japanese?'

'Erm, yes,' I lie.

On my triumphant return to his restaurant a few minutes later, the chef tries his best to hide his irritation and duly serves me twenty or so pieces of sushi in complete silence. It is good sushi, but far from great. Mid-ranking by Tokyo standards. This is an objective critique, you understand, nothing to do with the fact that I ate the entire meal quietly seething with vindicated rage.

Being turned away from a restaurant or bar on account of not being Japanese has happened to me before in Japan. Indeed, just two days later, in Sapporo, a waiter won't even bother to claim his izakaya is full, he will simply say: 'Japanese only', and close the door in my face. I find it impossible to imagine a restaurant in London turning a potential diner away because they aren't English, even if they don't speak English. After all, restaurants are part of the *hospitality* industry. Is it unreasonable to expect them to be hospitable, even towards foreigners, particularly in a country which so prides itself on its tradition of 'omotenashi', the highly refined Japanese notion of excellent service?

After my sushi meal, I have paid and am about to leave. I look across at the chef. Making sure I have his attention, I lift one hand up, palm down, and waggle it left and right in the universal 'Meh' gesture, indicating this was what I thought of his sushi. He looks at me, holding his long, thin sashimi knife in one hand, and for a moment I think he might attempt to fling it in my direction. Clouds of confusion scud across his face but he returns to his chopping board.

I should have taken a tip from a friend of mine. Though Japanese herself, she experienced similar treatment in a wine bar in notoriously snobby Kyoto a while back. The hostess initially denied her entrance but my friend insisted and took her place at the bar. As she sipped her grudgingly served wine, my friend then had to endure the hostess talking loudly for the entire time about how irritating she found non-regulars. Too mature an individual to engage in the kind of childishness to which I had resorted, my friend instead exacted her revenge as she left with clinical intent by taking one of the bar's business cards and placing it in her purse next to some yen notes. When my friend had first told me this story, I had waited for the punchline, but that was it. Placing someone's 'meishi' next to money is akin to spitting on it, or grinding it under your heel. It is a gesture of deep disrespect as money is considered unclean.

So, Hakodate and I do not get off to a great start. The next day, hoping to rebuild our relationship, I make straight for the Morning Market using one of the city's charming old trams. It turns out I have chanced upon a *really* old tram, over a hundred years old. The driver and conductor are wearing period costume, which is rather lovely. My mood is once again optimistic. It is time, now surely, to sample the world's greatest seafood.

At the Morning Market I scout out the dozens of stalls and restaurants there selling fresh-grilled scallops, massive scarlet crabs, their legs trussed up with rubber bands like bunched fists, and the famed donburi. I plumped for a uni donburi at Uni Murakami, the market's most famous uni shop. And it is great, it is fine, but I can't help feel the rest of the market is not quite what I had hoped for. The prices are Tokyo-high: ¥2,000–4,000, (£15–30), for a donburi – the most expensive being the uni. There are no bargains here and the bowls are considerably smaller than those shown in the picture menus. Worse, the quality of produce just isn't what I had been led to expect. Mass tourism – in this case, of Chinese people – had done what mass tourism does everywhere in the world: it had changed the essential character of the place to one focused almost entirely on parting one-time visitors from their money. I have never before in Japan been harangued by traders trying to get my attention, for instance, but this happens to me in Hakodate, and it makes my nose wrinkle a little. After my uni donburi I sit down in a crab restaurant and immediately the waitress takes great pains to make sure I realise there is a cover charge and 8 per cent tax. Both are quite normal in Japan but clearly she has experienced problems with this. After forty minutes my food has yet to appear and I leave.

I need more uni-therapy. At the heart of the Morning Market is an indoor food hall, the Market Square, selling local produce – himono (sun-dried fish), smoked salmon, konbu, fancy Hokkaido melons, and more live seafood. I stop by a stall with a few uni and pay a thousand yen for a single sea urchin. The stallholder opens one up for me to eat as if it were a hard-boiled egg and I scoop out thick pale yellow tongues, the size of my thumb. They taste almost floral, sweet but mildly briny too with a creamy, fatty texture and a lingering, haunting flavour. Fantastic. I'm feeling a bit better once more.

The centrepiece of the food hall is a large tank of live squid around which snakes a line of Chinese tourists, including many children, all waiting for the chance to catch their own lunch with little fishing rods. With not much else on their dance cards, the squid are easily hooked – through their bodies, eyes, wherever – and lifted from the tank to be prepared immediately and served up on paper plates, still very much alive.

Live squid sashimi is another Hakodate speciality. I order some at a nearby place. The plate arrives bearing a squid so recently dismembered that it doesn't seem yet to have realised. The unfortunate cephalopod continues not only to twitch its various detached body parts, but to pulsate its camouflage. A bit late for that, I think to myself, as I tentatively pluck at a slice of its body, only to find a nearby tentacle grabbing hold of it. I'm rarely squeamish about food, but I do feel a little sympathetic towards my lunch.

A couple of days later I find myself at Sapporo's Nijo Market, where the story is the same: a once fantastic seafood market feels like just another stop on a coach tour with high prices and substandard food and service. Growing increasingly desperate, I head on to Otaru, another coastal Hokkaido town, an hour by train from Sapporo, famed in particular for its sushi. But what modest appeal Otaru once boasted as a wealthy trading and herring harbour has also long been lost to the relentless kettling of tourists from the station to the kitschy drag of souvenir shops on Sakaimachidori, and then on to the early-twentieth-century warehouses beside the canal close to the harbour. These warehouses feature in every single photograph of the town and are apparently famous from many TV dramas, but to me they resemble the less salubrious parts of Birmingham. The sushi is far from bad, but given the much vaunted context, still far from excellent.

It is all very disheartening. I feel cheated, somehow; as if something halcyon has been lost: Hokkaido's seafood heart seems to me no longer to be pumping. Where am I going to gorge on my dream uni? There is only one answer: I am going to have to go to the source.

This is how stupid I am. I have booked one of the most expensive hotels, if not *the* most expensive, on Hokkaido, boasting one of the greatest views of any hotel in the world, for one night only, but I both arrive and leave after dark. I dine in the top-floor restaurant which has by all accounts the most staggering panoramic view over a gigantic lake-filled volcanic caldera but, as it is night time, I gaze out instead at my own face reflected back from the pitch-dark windows. But never mind: I didn't come here for the view. I came for the *Gargouillou*.

This is French chef Michel Bras' restaurant at the Hotel Windsor in Toya, awarded three stars in the 2014 Hokkaido Michelin guide; alma mater of some of the greatest chefs in the world at the moment (Shinobu Namae, of L'Effervescence in Tokyo and Alexandre Bourdas from SaQuaNa in Honfleur, Normandy, to name two); and a place I have been dreaming of visiting ever since I was lucky enough to meet Bras and cook with him one afternoon in Copenhagen five years ago (he showed me how to avoid cutting off the tops of my fingers when slicing fennel bulbs on a mandolin, for which I am eternally grateful).

I have a principle (much mocked by Japanese friends) of only ever eating Japanese cuisine when in Japan (at least, I avoid restaurants which are straightforwardly French, Spanish, Italian, Mexican, and so on), but I had decided to break my self-imposed embargo in order to try Bras' iconic *Gargouillou*.

Often erroneously described as the greatest vegetarian dish ever (it usually features some air-dried ham), it is true that the *Gargouillou* is one of the most influential dishes of modern times, replicated in top restaurants around the world, from New York to London, Paris and Copenhagen. In essence just a plate of seasonal vegetables, flowers and plants, the *Gargouillou* is deceptively complex, with each of its sixty or so components cooked a specific way for a specific time, or indeed left raw, and all of them meticulously plated amid various colourful sauces to resemble as much a piece of abstract art as dinner. It is easily the highlight of my meal, the rest of which is a fairly typical, Michelin-approved, stream of neurotic, tweezered dishes; even Bras' equally famous innovation, the molten chocolate dessert, was a little underwhelming, its theatricality dulled by over-exposure from the freezer department of every supermarket in the world.

After the meal, I sleep fitfully, partly because I am annoyed with myself that I have blown such a huge amount of money on what was actually a rather soulless, chintzy hotel with a view I was completely unable to enjoy, but also because I have set the alarm for 4 a.m. and rising at that time will be a new and frightening experience for me. And, sure enough, getting up so early and making my way in the dark to a small harbour at Usu, on the Uchiura Bay coast in south-western Hokkaido, is easily among the top twenty most harrowing experiences of my life. But, boy, is it worth it in the end.

Usu is home to thirteen uni fishermen; Ashihara-san, once one of them, now retired, has been kind enough to offer to take me out in his *isobune*, the special, narrow, fibreglass boat, about four or five metres long, white on the outside, pale blue inside, used for fishing for uni and abalone.

'When I was a child, the seabed was covered in uni, completely black with them,' Ashihara shouts above the noise of the outboard motor. 'But that has all changed. These days, we have to buy fifty thousand young uni every year from Okushiri [an island on the other side of the Oshima peninsula] and leave them here to grow.'

They leave the babies for four years before harvesting – a process called 'seeding' – feeding them with dried, ground starfish in the meantime. There used to be twice as many uni fishermen here back in his childhood, he adds, but over the years their numbers have been depleted due to old age, retirement and death. (Later, I check and the decline was actually far greater; fifty years ago, 130 fishermen had uni permits in this harbour alone.)

We sail out between the rocky, wooded islets which guard the entrance to Usu harbour, and continue a few hundred yards further out to sea. Soon, several similar boats come into view clustered around some black rocks. Each of the boats is curiously tilted to one side. As we draw closer, through the gauzy early morning light I can see the reason why: the fishermen are leaning over the sides of the boats using large black masks, like glass-bottomed buckets, strapped to their heads, to search beneath the surface of the sea. Every once in a while, one of the men will rise back into the boat, lifting up a pole almost as long as the boat itself. The poles have three short metal prongs on the end, into which are wedged dark, round, fuzzy shadows: sea urchins.

Following a massive collapse in uni stocks in the waters around Japan in the early 1980s, the uni harvesting season is now closely regulated. It varies around the coast of Hokkaido, but here in this part of Uchiura Bay it runs from mid-June to mid-August. The reason for our early start today is that the fishermen only fish until 7 a.m. after which they must rush to process the haul before the distributors arrive. In the winter, the fishermen go after even more valuable commodities: abalone and sea cucumber.

After half an hour or so, with fog now rolling in, we follow the fishermen back to the quayside and help unload their catch among the mountains of yellow and orange buoys, barnacle-encrusted nets and plastic crates on the quayside.

I am introduced to Masaki Fujino, seventy-three, who fishes here together with his forty-year-old son. During his career, Fujino has fished for everything – grouper, abalone and now, as he has grown older, the slightly less arduous uni. Today has been a good day.

'I've caught too many!' he jokes as they unload the blue plastic crates filled with the precious prickly balls from their boat. Huge, oil-black crows stand like nightclub bouncers on mounds of glossy brown konbu as swooping seagulls compete noisily for scraps. Cats lurk by the scallop tanks. Fujino and his son have harvested around 130kg of uni today; there are about eight urchins per kilo, but after processing they are left with about 15 per cent edible matter.

(Technically, the edible part of the uni are its gonads, although they are often erroneously referred to as 'roe'. Personally I think 'tongues' or 'lobes' are more palatable euphemisms.)

'It's been a good season. Other areas of Hokkaido have been hit by bad storms but the sea is quiet here. The price has doubled,' Fujino tells me. It wasn't so long ago that uni were considered virtually worthless. 'In my father's time, no one cared about uni, it just wasn't profitable,' another fisherman told me on a later visit to a different harbour. 'Only the fishermen ate them, and their families.' Today, demand for uni is increasing globally and domestically but, as Ashihara had said, the main problem with supply in terms of Japan is the decline in the number of uni fishermen. Those who aren't retiring, or dying, are switching to scallop farming or, in particular, fishing for sea cucumbers, which are more profitable. As a result, since the late eighties the domestic supply of uni has fallen by about 60 per cent, and the Japanese are now reliant on the Russians for much of their uni. In Russia, the uni grow to more than twenty centimeters in diameter. 'But they taste terrible,' says one fisherman, disapprovingly.

Edible sea urchins are found just about everywhere in the world. They have been eaten around the Mediterranean at least since Roman times; I've seen them depicted in mosaics in Pompeii, and in the 1980s a major industry grew up off the California coast farming them. I have even dived for uni in the Arctic off the coast of Norway – which was cold. But the Japanese eat most of the world's supply; according to the book *Echinoderm Aquaculture* by Nicholas Brown and Steve Eddy – around 80 per cent of the global catch, 50,000 tons in all per year, worth over £200m.

The uni caught in the waters of Hokkaido are generally considered to be the best in the world. There are two main types of sea urchin caught here: the murasaki, or 'purple' uni, which is a very dark purple, almost black, and has long spines; and the bafun uni, which is dark brown and has shorter spines – its nickname is 'horseshit uni' because it vaguely resembles a lump of horse manure. Fifteen or so years ago the bafun was the far more common of the two, making up around 90 per cent of the catch. These days, Fujino tells me, that proportion has reversed. An almost two degree temperature increase in the sea, coupled with an explosion in the hardier murasaki population – which can basically eat anything, including each other, and rocks – has decimated the fussier, more vulnerable bafun, which tend to eat mostly konbu.

'Bafun are more sensitive to the change in temperature from the sea. Purple sea urchin never die,' says Fujino, bony but straight-backed with skin the colour of teak, and dressed in blue rubber dungarees. (He is also wearing extremely cool 1970s-style steel-framed glasses with pale brown lenses, but not, I suspect, with the intention of appearing cool.) 'Ninety per cent of the bafun population has gone, and that's a shame because we used to have the best bafun here, it was the gold standard at Tsukiji.'

And here's the kicker: guess which type of sea urchin is the most delicious? The bafun. 'It's *so* much better,' one fisherman will tell me the next day, when I make another uni trip to the port of Suttsu, on the other side of the Oshima peninsula. He explains their superior flavour by the bafun's umami-rich, konbu-centric diet. 'The sweetness, it is extremely sweet, so different,' he rhapsodises. Without doubt, among those in the know, among those who have a really bad case of uni addiction, it is the bafun that are the most sought after.

In Uchiura, Fujino says, the bafun population is now effectively zero and the few which survive here are very difficult to find as they tend to hide right at the root of the seaweed. Bafun are still found further north, particularly around the Rebun and Rishiri islands off the northern tip of Hokkaido, but, if its current trajectory continues, the species may eventually become extinct there too.

The largest purple uni grow to about fifteen centimetres, bafuns to ten. They can live ten to fifteen years but taste best at three to five years. The fishermen harvest them from the seabed four to five metres beneath the surface using long poles either with the three-pronged claws I saw them using in Uchiura Bay, or more sophisticated grabbing claws. It is technically possible to farm uni – further east on the south coast at Attsukeshi they are doing this – but very difficult to make a profit as the costs are high and they take so long to mature.

Speaking with the various Hokkaido uni fishermen I met, I would often touch on the perplexing issue of identifying the gender of uni. I never got the same answer twice and it came to be a kind of game for me to hear their different explanations. Some told me uni can be both male and female simultaneously: hermaphrodites. Others said they changed gender during the course of their life, or even during a season. You can tell the sex from the shape of the mouth, one added, but declined to elaborate. Another told me that pale yellow urchin tongues indicated it was male, while the deeper orange was female, which is definitely not true. His friend shook his head and told me that pale tongues were a sign of stress, which might be true, although their feed also has an impact. Basically, bafun tend to have darker orange tongues, an almost rusty, reddish orange, while mura-sakis' are more yellow. Another fisherman said female uni tasted better than males, which I think might be true (the females of every species often do taste better) though his friend disagreed and said there was no difference. My conclusion so far is that sea urchins are born asexual, but at some point they do pick a team and stick to it. The only real way to tell – if you'll forgive the graphic nature of what follows – is to open it up, remove its gonads and see what kind of goo they spontaneously expel: a white discharge is sperm, orange is eggs and thus a female.

As Fujino and I chat by the harbourside the last uni boat struggles in under the power of its elderly, hollow-cheeked fisherman. Its outboard motor has broken down and so he has to punt it in using his uni pole. His equally aged wife in white wellies and rain gear, bent double by arthritis, struggles down the slippery, algae-covered concrete ramp to the water to help him bring the boat in. The two have probably spent their lifetime on these waters, in this harbour, and now those lives are approaching their end amid yet more struggle. As the mist rolls in, it is all a bit Hemingway-esque: the old man and the sea urchin.

The couple take their harvest into the processing hall where the other fishermen plus a crowd of about fifty helpers are now seated hunched on empty soda crates next to open tanks housing live flounder, clams, scallops, octopuses and sea cucumbers, which look like weird, spiky sausages. Though they can survive in their natural habitat for up to two hundred years, uni are sensitive creatures and do not last long out of the sea. Once landed, they must be opened as quickly as possible so that their precious edible innards can be preserved. The helpers are all cheerily scooping out yellow tongues from the spiny shells of the uni using special long, thin spoons, like something a dentist might use to check your molars, and rinsing them with plastic sieves in buckets of chilly sea water.

I sit down alongside Fujino-san who, together with his son, has brought in by far the largest haul today. His group of helpers are gathered in a circle dressed in a colourful array of anoraks and plastic overtrousers; some are wearing white rubber gloves, others have bare hands. They have only an hour or so to 'fillet' several large piles of spiky black balls but they seem relaxed, chatting and laughing.

Fujino scoops out a tongue from a purple uni for me to try. It is sublime. The most delicious thing I think I have ever tasted: simultaneously sweet but rich with umami and a subtle briny after tang and a rich, smooth, creamy texture. I ask if he is going to taste, too?

'I never tire of eating uni, but I don't eat a lot. It's a precious product and, also, they are very high in cholesterol,' he says. But all around, the helpers are, I notice, happily popping the broken pieces from imperfect uni tongues into their mouths. This, it turns out, is their renumeration for their efforts today. Remarkably, they are all working here for no pay, as is always the case. Fujino only ever pays them a small petrol allowance. The helpers, some of whom have been coming here to prepare sea urchin for twenty years and who include his wife, Fujiko, apparently enjoy the camaraderie, as well as the free samples. 'It's very normal in farming and fishing communities here on Hokkaido,' says Fujino. 'We all help each other.' His son is kneeling on the floor on a piece of old polystyrene cracking

the purple uni open using a special, spring-loaded trowel-like implement which splits them neatly in two. The helpers then remove the
tongues with the spoons or tweezers, pecking at them like birds,
and rinse them in the sea water before placing them in small metal
pails. At one point, someone finds a baby uni. It is carefully placed
in a separate bucket to be taken back out to sea by the son. In front
of me is a pile of the discarded shells, their spines are still twitching
(which they will continue to do for a few hours, I am told). The
son turns his attention from opening uni, lifts a rubber-booted foot
and crunches down the empty shells to make room for more.

Would I like to try? Fujino asks, handing me a bucket, a sieve
and a uni spoon. I pick an urchin from the pile of newly opened
shells; its spines tickle my palm as they continue to twitch. It smells
of fresh ocean brine, sea spray, iodine. Inside are the familiar golden-
yellow tongues but these are criss-crossed by brownish tubes which,
I soon realise when I accidentally burst one releasing barely digested
lumps of seaweed, are the creature's intestines.

Suddenly, a miraculous find: one of the other fisherman's helpers
approaches Fujino, shyly offering an uni in his hand. It is different
from the long-spined, purple uni we have been working with. This
one is brown with spines more like the bristles of a nailbrush, just
a centimetre or so in length. It is a rare bafun uni. Would I like to
try it, gestures Fujino? I would. He opens it, and offers me the two
halves from which I scoop a couple of precious tongues, rinse them
in my sea water, and then eat.

In all honesty, I wouldn't say the bafun uni is *better* than the
murasaki uni, but its darker orangey lobes have a subtly different
flavour – sweeter, less iodine, a glorious taste, the kind of taste
that forces you to close your eyes so you can enjoy it in blissful
isolation.

Once you have processed your uni there are various ways to
preserve the tongues. In the days before refrigeration, they would
use the *itauni* method, covering them with salt for eight to twelve
hours so that they expelled their water, then preserving them in
shochu. Refrigeration and quicker transport methods revolutionised

the uni trade forty to fifty years ago, allowing uni tongues to be preserved for up to a week – in effect, this technology created the domestic, now global, market as it exists today. Alum preservation is also widely used, although some say it makes their flavour a little astringent. Alum will be used for the uni we are preparing that day, Fujino tells me, disapprovingly (he hates the taste but concedes it dissipates after about twelve hours). A sterilised sea-water technique has recently been developed to avoid the alum flavour.

Once all the uni have been emptied, we carry the small tin buckets full of golden lobes to another hall on the harbourfront. The elderly couple with the broken outboard motor have worked alone, and though they had only a small catch are the last to finish, bringing their meagre two pails of uni tongues into the bidding hall just in time. Here, their contents are strained into colanders for the wholesalers to inspect. For an uni lover, it is a mesmerising sight: seventy-one buckets full of uni arranged in neat rows. I have never seen so much sea urchin in my life. A handful of younger, slightly better dressed men are inspecting them: these are the wholesalers.

The actual 'auction' had taken place a few moments earlier without me noticing. The wholesalers had bid, not for individual buckets, but for the right to be first to choose, and so now they place their cards with their name on the buckets they fancy. Today, the uni are selling for ¥7,000–9,000 (£48–62) per kilo: there is roughly half a million yen-worth (£3,500) on the floor of this shabby warehouse. It will be worth a million once it gets to Tsukiji where the lobes will be arranged by hand in neat rows on faux-wooden trays, but by the time it is served, typically as a topping for gunkan maki – sushi rice wrapped in lightly toasted nori – on the freshly planed cedar counters of the finest sushi-ya in Ginza? Heaven knows. Many millions.

After the uni are sold, Fujino invites me home for a cup of tea. He lives beside a gorgeous sandy beach and earns extra money renting out his front garden for visitors' parking. Inside, his house is a homely jumble. I take the sofa, he sits on the floor cross-legged with ease, straight-backed like an ancient yogi. As his wife makes me tea, we talk about the future of Hokkaido uni. A black cat with an infected eye, like a pale blue marble bulging from one side of its head (a fish bone injury, apparently), jumps up onto the low table before us.

'Every year, two or three fishermen retire and they are not replaced. There is no one to replace them,' he says as he sips his can of coffee. 'I plan to stop in about three years. Eventually, this whole community will vanish. The shops and schools have already closed. It's such a pity, especially as the price of uni is only going up. Last year, and for a long time, I was getting six thousand yen per kilo, this year it's nine thousand.'

As if warming seas and dying fishermen were not enough to contend with, Fujino and the other uni fishermen I spoke to had also spotted smugglers in these waters. The smugglers weren't usually after uni; rather, they mostly sought abalone but above all sea cucumbers, not so popular in Japan, but highly prized in China.

'Yes, I've seen smugglers, and I called the coastguard,' Sumio Kawaji, the fisherman I met at Suttsu told me later. 'But there are only two coastguards for this whole stretch of coast and, anyway, if the smugglers see them approaching, they just throw their catch in the sea. And even if they get caught, the fines are not so bad. It's a big business. Yakuza.' The smuggling had started around ten years ago. Fujino's son had helped capture eight yakuza sea cucumber smugglers the previous February – he had seen the lights of their boat at night from his house. They had been caught with 100kg of sea cucumber on board. 'I was very angry at them,' the son had told me back at the harbour. 'It is against sustainability.'

Sustainability is not a word you hear much in Japan, so it was heartening that the uni fishermen seemed at last to be concerned about the continuation of the local uni population, and their livelihood. Let's hope they are not too late.

Chapter 33

Whisky

The first thing I hear as I leave Yoichi Station is the sound of bagpipes coming from a small shop across the road. Incongruous in a small Japanese town on the Hokkaido coast you may think, but actually it makes perfect sense. At least one man considered Yoichi to be as close as you could get to Scotland while still in Japan.

The man, Masataka Taketsuru, is a legend in the world of whisky. Born the third son of a sake brewer near Hiroshima, when he was eight legend has it that Masataka fell down the stairs and broke his nose, an accident which is said to have miraculously granted him a superior sense of smell. At Osaka University he studied zymurgy – or fermentation – but became more interested in Western-style distilled spirits than sake. Against his father's wishes, he went to work for Settsu Shuzo, an Osakan spirit manufacturer which at that time was struggling to recreate the newly popular spirits first introduced to the Japanese by Commodore Perry (who brought with him a 110-gallon barrel of whisky when he sailed into Tokyo Bay in 1853, as a gift for the Emperor). In 1918, following a few unfortunate incidents – the result of trying to make liquor using fruit juices and perfume – Settsu Shuzo sent him to Scotland to learn the mystical art of whisky-making (reading between the lines, Masataka's fastidious precocity seemed to get up a few people's noses at the company, and they wanted to get rid of him).

Aged just twenty-four, and with hardly any English, he sailed to Scotland and enrolled at the University of Glasgow as the first Japanese to study the chemistry of distilling. On graduating, this mustachioed, bespectacled Japanese man did the rounds of various distillers to ask for an apprenticeship. The first few turned him down but eventually he was taken on at a couple of places – Hazelburn and Longmorn – to learn the dark arts of whisky-making.

Over two years, Masataka learned about distilling and blending, but that knowledge was not all he took back with him from Scotland. While giving a judo lesson to the brother of a university friend, he met a young Scottish woman, Jessie Roberta 'Rita' Cowan, with whom he fell in love and, much to her parents' disapproval, married at a registry office.

By the time Masataka returned to Japan with his new bride, the original company that had sent him to Scotland was struggling with the economic depression following World War I and no longer had the funds to start up an ambitious whisky programme. Masataka found himself unemployed, and he and the pretty, pale Rita survived for a while on the money she earned teaching the piano and English language classes. Eventually, another company, Kotobukiya (later to become drinks giant Suntory), took him on and in 1923 he helped to start the Yamazaki Distillery, these days a fabled whisky maker whose premises you can still see from the window of the Shinkansen from Kyoto to Osaka at the base of Mount Tennozan, an area famed for the quality of its mountain water.

In 1934, after a dispute with the man who owned Yamazaki, Masataka left to found his own distillery, Nikka, in Yoichi, up here in Hokkaido. Dai Nippon Kaju (the Great Japanese Juice Company), as it was then called, launched its first whisky in 1940, running a sideline in apple juice (which continues to this day) to cover their costs before the first bottles were ready.

I have arranged to meet Yoshikazu Koyano, who works at the distillery, which I arrive at after a short walk from the station. He has kindly offered to show me around. The Nikka complex is made up of a dozen or so grey-stone, red-roofed buildings which do actually look like something you might find in the Highlands.

To make whisky, Koyana explains, barley is first left to sprout, a process which is then arrested by drying. They originally used locally sourced peat for the drying at Yoichi, but now import the barley ready sprouted and dried from Scotland. The malt is then cracked

and mixed with hot water, and yeast is added to commence fermentation. The yeast is Nikka's own.

'That is very important,' says Koyano. 'It gives a very aromatic,
strong flavour.' We are standing inside one of the still houses. The
copper stills look like giant ear trumpets. They are coal-fired, straight,
pot stills, he says: the coal creates a higher temperature which
enhances the toasted, almost burnt notes which characterise Nikka
whisky, and the straight pot captures all the flavours rather than just
the most volatile ones caught by stills with a bulge in the middle.
Together, these factors make Yoichi whisky darker, with a stronger
flavour.

We visit the casks where another little piece of Hokkaido magic
takes place. 'We are close to the sea here, and the ocean breezes
affect the whisky while it ages in the casks. It gives our whisky a
slight ocean flavour,' my guide tells me. They produce 40,000 litres
a day, the most expensive of which is the twenty-one-year-old
Taketsuru, which retails for ¥15,000 (£103) per bottle, but has been
known to fetch five or six times that at auction.

In recent years, Japanese whisky has pretty much conquered the
world. There is little argument that they make as good, if not better,
whisky here than in Scotland, Ireland, America or anywhere. As we
walk through the distillery grounds, I ask Koyano what he thinks
the great secret has been behind the success of Japanese whisky.

'My feeling is – and it's not just Japanese whisky, but many things
– that we Japanese take an idea about how to make something, and
then try many different ways, trial and error, until we come up with
something acceptable. Japanese distillers have been forced to rethink
or learn processes for ourselves. We start with the traditional way
– like using coal to fire the stills – but in other areas we are not
afraid to be innovative with different wood for the casks, different
distillation methods.'

What Koyano is talking about here is 'kaizen', the Japanese notion
of constant, gradual improvement and, he's right, you find it everywhere. Kaizen is the basis of how all those chefs and farmers I have
met on my travels operate, the ones who strive each day to make

the best yakitori, the best ceramic plates, grow the best rice, or mix the best cocktail that they possibly can, identifying weaknesses in their technique or produce, constantly refining the process, honing their skill, questioning every aspect of their work. Kaizen is most famously associated with Toyota's inexorable rise during the 1970s and 1980s which reached its apogee with the launch of luxury Mercedes-basher Lexus, developed following painstaking analysis of European brands, what made them great and how they could be surpassed. One characteristic of kaizen, which is perhaps unusual in what is otherwise often a very strictly hierarchical society, is that it involves everyone in the production chain, from the tea lady to CEO. All are aware of their role in achieving excellence, and in the relentless drive to improve upon it.

It is a philosophy which has certainly rewarded the Japanese whisky industry. In 2001 Nikka's Yoichi Single Cask won *Whisky Magazine*'s Best of the Best award, probably the most seismic moment in contemporary whisky history; it won Distiller of the Year in 2015. The same year, the Yamazaki distillery made headlines around the world when its 2013 Single Malt Sherry Cask was named the best single malt in the world by the *Whisky Bible* (the whisky version of Robert Parker's wine guide), which awarded it 97.5 out of 100 and described it as a work of 'near indescribable genius'. It was the first time a Japanese whisky had topped the *Bible*'s list.

Domestically, too, the whisky market is booming. The first boom was in the golden years of the 1980s when the Japanese economy was rampant, but there has been a second boom more recently when the popularity of the whisky highball exploded, particularly with female drinkers. Since then, Yamazaki and Nikka have left the Scottish whisky industry reeling with their consistently high quality and, at the top end of the market, smaller Japanese distillers have also begun to create their own legends, like Hanyu, which makes the mythical Ichiro Card series of fifty-two different single malt whiskies matured in barrels made from a variety of woods and featuring playing card labels (a complete set sold for close to £319,000 at a Bonham's auction in Hong Kong in 2015). Another small

Japanese distiller, Karuizawa, makes probably the most expensive whisky in the world – £88,000 was paid for a single bottle of its 1960 production. No wonder most of Japan's distillers are expanding as fast as they can, making the country now the world's fourth largest buyer of barley. One recent trend is making whisky from home-grown, Japanese barley. It is still a very limited resource but more and more rice growers are reportedly switching to barley to feed the domestic whisky producers. Another trend is using unusual woods for the casks in which the whisky is aged: Yamazaki uses casks that have been used to make umeboshi – the sickly-sour Japanese plum wine – or ones which are made from the rare mizunara, a Japanese oak.

In terms of the kaizen approach, I once read something interesting about the whisky industry. When the US drinks company Jim Beam merged with Suntory, the American partners were constantly irritated by Suntory's efforts to get them to modernise and innovate. While the Japanese were keen to find improvements, the folks at Jim Beam saw no reason to change a recipe which had worked for decades. There are, of course, plenty of Scottish distillers who maintain a similarly vice-like grip on the past by adhering stubbornly to tradition. Dewar's slogan for its White Label whisky, for instance, is 'It never varies'.

I ask Koyano whether he thinks that kaizen spirit of constant improvement is still alive in Japan. And if so, why, then, is the country's economy declining?

'I don't think it has changed much, no,' he answers after a few moments' reflection. 'But, of course, everyone's economic situation was much worse after the war, so perhaps there was more desire, more drive then, we still had to work for just the basics, just to live. These days everyone more or less has a pretty good life.'

He still feels that there is room for improvement in terms of Japanese whisky. 'I don't think we have at all reached or surpassed the level of Scottish whisky. Scotland is still Japan's sensei.'

Koyano and I are now standing outside a handsome, European-style house, like something you might find in a Dundee suburb.

This was where Rita and Masataka once lived. Across the way is a museum dedicated to them and the history of the distillery they founded. Along with some fantastic 1970s adverts for Nikka featuring Orson Welles and Rod Stewart, there are many personal mementos from the couple, including 'Masataka's favourite table tennis bat', 'Rita's favourite sewing machine', 'Rita's favourite golf club', and dozens of black and white photos of bear hunts, skiing holidays and fishing trips. There is a particularly arresting shot of Masataka riding an ostrich wearing a bowler hat (Masataka, that is).

The museum does its best to play up the extraordinary love story of the Japanese whisky obsessive and his young Scottish bride, a relationship which must have been severely challenged during World War II when Rita was put under constant surveillance as a suspected spy. As one caption puts it:

'She dared to live in the Orient with only Masataka's love to depend on. Rita thrust herself into a different society, defying her anxieties, always believing in Masataka's dream ... The couple now sleep on a hill similar to one in Rita's hometown. The whisky distillery of their dreams can be seen clearly.'

Masataka died in 1979, having outlived Rita by eighteen years (they had no children). Their story has recently been used as the inspiration for a hugely popular, 150-episode morning drama series, *Massan* (Rita's nickname for her husband), by NHK. It had been partly filmed here at Yoichi (really, they made 150 episodes, each fifteen minutes long), after which visitors to the distillery had tripled to 900,000 a year. 'Yoichi people are very proud of the distillery,' Koyano tells me. 'Especially since the TV series which made the town a tourist destination.'

Koyana-san and I part outside the Nikka gift shop and bar where visitors are offered free samples of the company's single malt and blended whisky. It is still morning so perhaps not the best time to be tasting hard liquor, but I take one of each of the drinks on offer and sit down by a window overlooking the distillery grounds. First, the single malt. I approach the tumbler with a little apprehension after Koyano-san's description of it as 'strong and dark' as I tend to prefer lighter, smoother whiskies, but it is really excellent: delicate, sweet and fruity. My second sample, the blended whisky, is, however, as rough as moonshine and horribly bitter, borderline undrinkable, in fact (and an alcoholic beverage needs to be truly execrable before I reject it entirely).

It is not perhaps the highest note on which to end my trip to Nikka but as I totter, slightly tipsy, back to the station, I am glad to have seen the Yoichi Distillery. Its improbable existence and enduring success seems to me yet another example of Japanese bloody-mindedness, and a living tribute to the art of kaizen.

Chapter 34

Melons

I had another reason to be heading for Sapporo with a spring in my step. My family are joining me for this final leg of this journey in our own footsteps. Having travelled by plane, car, train, bicycle, bus, zip wire, various forms of ferry and boat, not to mention a rice planting machine, we had yet one more form of transport lined up to convey us around Japan's northernmost island. I meet them at Sapporo's New Chitose Airport, and we head off together to collect it.

I think I speak for my family when I say that the campervan waiting for us on the forecourt of a rental company just outside Sapporo is not the luxurious Winnebago of our dreams. I had envisaged a magnificent pantechnicon featuring all the technological wizardry Japan could throw at it – something Metallica might use to tour Canada in – but instead here is a gussied up, frankly hideous, Toyota van.

I know what you're thinking: 'Aren't *all* campervans hideous?' But this one comfortably surpasses the usual aesthetic shortcomings of the genre thanks to the orange and red decals besmirching its flanks, which make it look as if passenger and driver have vomited out of their respective windows. Inside, it has also lost the shower and toilet it clearly once boasted: all that is left is a rather smelly cupboard with a now incongruous loo roll still in place on the wall.

As we all squeeze in to take a tour with the rental company man, we discover that the vehicle is the opposite of the TARDIS. Somehow, it is even smaller inside than it appears from the outside.

Where will we sleep, we wonder. The man points to a parcel shelf above the driver, and two more narrow shelves at the back of the van above the rear wheels. There is then a brief blur of activity as he swiftly transforms the dining area into another bed but sadly none of us bear effective witness to this process; the consequence being that, later that night, as we are hoping to retire for the evening, we are unable to accurately replicate what he did. During the rest of our trip, whoever sleeps in that particular berth will slowly sink like a disappointing soufflé to the floor during the course of the night.

But still, we are excited to hit the road. We can go anywhere, camp anywhere, we are free as birds. Except for the thing with the bears, of course.

Looking back, it was a mistake to read up on the bears before we left home. Hokkaido is home to 3,000 brown bears, and these are not koalas. Hokkaido bears are a close relative of the grizzly, weighing up to 380kg. I read that there are around 80–150 bear attacks in Japan each year, and already this year four people have been killed. To distract myself from thinking too much about the bears, I started looking into the other dangerous residents of Hokkaido which, a quick Google reveals, include a very poisonous viper called the mamushi; a hornet the size of a hummingbird; and most chilling of all, a venomous, red-headed centipede, the mukade, which can grow as big as your hand and likes to live in shoes and cupboards. Whatever you do, do not read the comments under articles about mukade online. Or see *The Revenant*.

Like everyone, I enjoyed watching Leonardo DiCaprio have his guts ripped out by a bear in the Oscar-winning movie on the flight to Japan, but, boy, do I regret it at three o'clock that first night camping in the wilds of Hokkaido when, having ignored my insistent bladder for a good half-hour, I finally clamber down from my coffin-like bunk and tiptoe outside to take a hyper-alert wee, my head swivelling this way and that like a demented meerkat at every rustle from the undergrowth. (It turns out that on this occasion the rustling is an especially beautiful fox.)

Our first stop that first morning had been a farming region east of Sapporo, where I had arranged to meet a man who grows the famous and costly Hokkaido melons, known and puzzled over around the world.

Sometimes described as the Kobe beef of fruit, and requiring a similar amount of cosseting to the famous cows, this pure-bred special variety of cantaloupe melon is among the strangest of all Japanese obsessions.

We've all seen the travel shows where the disbelieving host visits a store in Tokyo which sells these pretty green melons for over a hundred dollars a pair, packed in straw in elegant boxes to be offered as gifts. They really do exist. In Tokyo you see them in all the depa-chika, and in dedicated fruit stores which look more like jeweller's than grocer's. I recently read a report about melon thieves stealing an entire harvest from a farmer and, most famously of all, every year, there is an auction in the former Hokkaido coal-mining town Yubari, which grabs headlines around the world because someone invariably pays a ridiculous amount of money for the first melons of the season. This year a pair of these first-of-the-season, or 'hashiri', Hokkaido-grown melons sold for an eye-watering ¥3m (£22,000). That's more than my car cost. A lot more.

I had long been fascinated by the mysterious appeal of these costly green orbs to the Japanese. What was so special about a fairly ordinary looking melon which, back home, was freely available in supermarkets for a couple of quid? Of course, not all Hokkaido melons sell for thousands of pounds, but many do sell for the kind of money I pay for a decent chicken, or bottle of wine. But why melons? Why not peaches, or figs? And why *so* much money?

To find out, we have come to Hobetsu, a little south of Yubari, where we will meet melon farmer Tomomichi Koboyashi. He grows a type of cantaloupe – the IK Melon – originally developed by his grandfather and father in the early 1970s and bred to be even better than those from Yubari. His grandfather had lived in Yubari, but moved further down the hill in search of better soil and climate. What happened next has gone down into Koboyashi family folklore.

'My grandfather moved from Yubari to Hobetsu forty five years ago because there is not so much snow here, and it melts earlier, so we can get to market with our melons earlier,' Koboyashi tells us as we sit on a battered sofa in his cluttered barn. All around us are perfect specimens of his green-skinned, orange-fleshed melons, carefully placed on old Persian rugs. 'He was trying to cross an Earl's Favourite with the Yubari king melon but, one day, one of the horses they used on the farm escaped and trampled over all his seedlings, mashing them all up together. My grandfather tried to salvage what plants he could, and, from those, the IK Melon was born.' It is only after some cajoling that Koboyashi, a quietly spoken man in his mid-forties with a thick shock of bristly dark brown hair, red t-shirt and khakis, brings himself to admit that the IK Melon is 'more excellent' than the Yubari.

Today, he grows about 10,000 a year, selling them to neighbours and passers-by for 'just' ¥1,000 (£7) each, but they fetch many times that in Tokyo. He offers us each a slice, and we slurp happily away on the deep orange flesh. It is very good, at the absolute peak of ripeness, but also extremely sweet, perhaps too sweet for my taste, as in fact all the many other melons we try during our time on Hokkaido will prove to be. Koboyashi measures the sweetness of our melon with a refractometer: it scores a 12.5. At the height of the season, his melons can score as much as 18.

So, why melons? Why has this particular fruit been elevated to such a ridiculous status in Japan?

'Because apples and grapes are autumn fruit,' he says simply. I wait for further elaboration. We all look confused.

'And melons are summer fruit?' offers Asger.

'Yes,' says the farmer. 'So the timing is right for Obon gifts, you see?'

Ah, now I get it. It just happens that the melon season coincides with Japan's biggest gift-giving holiday, Obon, the few days of the year, in late July/early August, when people return to their family homes and tend the graves of deceased relatives. As we would later find out when we visited Yubari itself and see an exhibition about the history of the melon, back in the 1970s a concerted marketing campaign helped persuade the Japanese of the melon's suitability as the perfect Obon gift. Above all, it is the fortuitous timing of its season that has so elevated the melon to the status of Gift No.1.

And the annual record-breaking auction? 'That's just a publicity thing for the grocer who buys them. He gets his company on national TV, it's great exposure.' And the melon harvest thefts? Koboyashi had not experienced this but he had heard of farmers who slept beside their greenhouses to deter thieves who usually struck at night, as did racoons, foxes and – gulp – bears.

Before we leave, Koboyashi-san gives us a quick lesson in how to assess a Hokkaido melon. It is all about appearance, little to do with flavour or aroma, so I should forget my usual supermarket habit of sniffing and pressing the base of the fruit.

Of course, the melon should be perfectly spherical and firm but 'the netting should be elaborate and fine, not too raised'. He invites us to feel the outer surface, or 'reticulation', of two different melons, and it is true; on one the netting is raised and ragged, on the other smooth and fine. Crucially, the melon must still have its perfect 'T'-shaped stalk in place. 'The stalk tells you a lot even if you can't eat it. If it's not there, then the price goes down by fifty per cent. I know it seems crazy, but Japanese buyers have a stereotyped image of how a melon should look, and the stalk must be there.' To that end, Koboyashi always aims to get his melons to market the same day they are harvested.

'I love melons so much, sometimes I talk to them without realising it. I want to grow better and better melons,' Koboyashi tells me as we clamber up into our campervan. 'I want to develop a new type of melon that will give my customers emotion when they try it, I want them to be moved by it, experience real joy.'

As we drive away, I ask Asger and Emil what they think of Japanese melon worship. 'They are absolutely not worth the money,' says Emil. 'Not even close. Mormor's [his Danish grandmother's] rasp-berries taste much better. Never judge a book by its cover, and never judge a melon by its skin.'

'Or its little branch-ey thing at the top,' chimes in Asger.

Chapter 35

Bears

We leave Hobetsu and head east, our mouths agape at the grandeur of Hokkaido's scenery.

The 'mountains tumbled together in most picturesque confusion, densely covered with forest and cleft by magnificent ravines' is how Isabella Bird described the island in 1878, a description which still holds true as far as I can see. Through forested mountains and lush valleys we sweep along immaculate, largely empty highways. It is a staggering, *Lost World*-type landscape with volcanoes steaming silently in the distance. Closer to our first campsite, outside the city of Obihiro on the great Tokachi Plain on the southern coast, the scenery transforms from hyper-Austria to prairie farmland, with cute Midwest-style barns, and bucolic fields of potatoes and corn.

That first overnight – the one with the foxy fox encounter – brings a rude introduction to camping, Japanese-style. Japanese campsites have virtually no facilities, we discover. At this one, there are no showers. Not a single one. The idea, we eventually figure out, is that campers are supposed to traipse to the nearest onsen hotel, about half a mile away, to wash, but the onsen does not open until midday. It is interesting to see the Japanese out in the wild, though, an unusually intimate perspective which Lissen compares to 'being backstage in Japan'. Japanese campers seem rather more reserved than I recall European campers from my childhood holidays. Though we encounter not a single foreign camper during the entire time we are in Hokkaido, no one approaches us or even acknowledges the existence of these foreigners in their midst. Still, it is not easy to blend in. The rules for rubbish disposal make the Brexit negotiations seem straightforward; not only that, but just to keep us on our toes they change from campsite to campsite (at one, we are encouraged to bring our refuse to reception, for instance). And, at virtually every site we arrive at the campsite staff seem utterly mystified by our arrival: 'What *could* these strange foreigners in a campervan possibly want at a campsite at 7 p.m.?'

At around ten o'clock that first night, just as we are all ready to clamber into our various cubbyholes, having feasted on convenience store sushi and spent a fraught hour trying to make up our respective bedding areas, the campsite police trundle up, complete with flashing red light on their toy-sized van. We all freeze, as if in the closing gambit of a game of Twister. What could they want? What rule have we transgressed? And what will be our punishment? It turns out the 'police' have chosen this late hour to come and check our passports.

We soon come to realise that Japanese campsites are more like overnight stops than destinations in their own right. Japanese campers bring all their belongings with them and set up shop like very neat Bedouins, with separate tents for cooking and sleeping, and mosquito net gazebos for dining. Everything they might conceivably require is brought along with them just in case. One morning I am woken by a neighbour cleaning his campervan with a power wash he'd packed specially. Funny what people choose to do on their holidays.

Sadistic GPS aside (and, I can tell you, within those three words is contained all the misery in the world), driving in Japan is a doddle. It helps that I proceed in blissful ignorance of the meaning of a large amount of the official roadside signage. In my defence, some of it is deeply perplexing. What *was* the sign with a centipede in a running race warning of? Or the one with the skiing potato? At one point we pass a sign depicting a mushroom playing golf. At least the Japanese drive on the correct side of the road and road signs are helpfully subtitled in English. Meanwhile, their petrol stations are the perfect embodiment of 'omotenashi', or good service: you feel like a Formula One driver making a pit stop as two or more men scurry out to tend to your vehicle, giving the windscreen a thorough wash, whether it needs it or not. And then there are the fabled Michi-no-eki – the unusually well-appointed roadside service areas with takeaway stalls and shops selling local crafts and produce. Paradoxically, though some have showers and are tourist destinations in their own right, none actually sold petrol. The Japanese are exceedingly polite motorists, but, boy, are they slow. They rarely exceed walking pace, which suits us fine. All the more time to take in the view.

We rise early the second morning and trundle on to Kushiro on the south-east coast where we have a great donburi lunch in the intriguingly named 'Fisherman's Wharf MOO', a kind of seafood mall on the harbourfront. Here, the highlight for Asger and Emil is one of those amusement arcade grabbing games which, instead of a cuddly toy or giant Toblerone, has live crabs as its prize. Nothing, though, compares to our lunch in Rausu.

We spend the next night at a campsite located on a cliff-top overlooking the harbour of Utoro, then cross the Shiretoko Pass, 738 metres above sea level, stopping at the highest point to do a yet more open-mouthed gaping over Hokkaido's most easterly peninsula, the Shiretoko National Park (a World Heritage Site). We have a rendezvous with a Rausu-based nature guide, whom we meet at the town's own especially amazing Michi-no-eki, filled with stalls selling local produce like sakebushi (katsuobushi made from salmon instead of bonito), and Bihoro Butasho Marumanma (a soy sauce made out of pork).

'Don't worry, we've never had a brown bear attack here, it's the black bears on the mainland that cause the problems.' Our guide, astrophysicist turned 'Stuff Naturalist' (according to his business card – I think it should read 'Staff'), Shinji Sato, is doing his best to reassure us as we discuss the plan for the day. 'The black bears tend to panic and attack humans but Hokkaido brown bears are much more shy.'

The idea is that we will go for a trek through the forests in search of a waterfall and see what wildlife appears. As well as having the highest density population of brown bears in Hokkaido – possibly in the world – Shiretoko is home to rare eagles such as the white-tailed sea eagle and Steller's sea eagle, plus fish owls and, off the coast, various whale species. Theoretically, this is one of the few places on earth where you can see bears and killer whales in the wild in the same day (your best chance is in June, apparently).

Emboldened by Shinji's reassurances about the friendly bears, I ask if, rather than actively seeking to *avoid* them, perhaps he might take us to see some. Shinji thinks for a moment, as if no one has ever asked this before, and pulls out his mobile phone.

A couple of hours later, following the waterfall trek and the aforementioned, staggeringly good lunch in Rausu – of freshly cooked king crab in a fisherman's hut by the sea (I do not say this lightly: it is one of the greatest meals of my life) – we are pulling on life jackets and crashing across white waves to the uninhabited tip of the peninsula in a sea urchin boat, basically a slender fibreglass bath tub with an outboard motor.

Sadly, after over an hour of bucking across the Okhotsk Sea, it seems as if we are out of luck. The unseasonal heat is keeping the bears in the woods during the day, says Shinji. The uni fisherman warns a storm is brewing. The sea is growing unrulier by the second. I finger my seasickness wristbands nervously as we pass two spectacular waterfalls which cascade right onto the beach. We are now deep into bear territory but, as we approach the Shiretoko Cape, at the very tip of the peninsula – 'The End of the Earth' according to Hokkaido's indigenous Ainu people – it is agreed we must turn back.

And then, suddenly, Lissen springs up, gesturing excitedly. There on the shore is a brown shadow. It is moving, *lumbering*. A bear! We draw closer. According to Shinji the bear is about three years old. This muscular furball is lazily turning over stones in search of insects. We stand in the boat just a few metres offshore watching it for some minutes until, finally, it lifts its head and slopes off into the undergrowth. Amazingly, we see another bear of a similar age as we hasten back to port, the sea now transitioning into *Perfect Storm* mode. At one point a bucket of sea water is dumped over my head but I don't care. It has been one of the Great Days, a day we will never forget, the day we saw wild bears.

What did I learn about Hokkaido during our five-day road trip? That everyone should come and see it if they get the chance. That the seafood gets better the further you get away from civilisation. That no one speaks English. That you should always make sure you have a full tank of petrol before you set off. And that the bears don't bite.

What did I learn during my time as captain of a campervan in Japan? Well, I will never again grow impatient when stuck behind one in traffic. I now realise that the poor fellow at the wheel will probably not have slept, eaten, or washed properly for days. Also, he will not have the slightest idea that there is a queue of traffic behind him. But what I really learned about camper-vanning is this: Don't do it. It's awful. You will end up constantly fighting with your family, repeating the same droning mantras: 'Don't leave the door open or bears will come in.' 'Don't leave the lights on, it will attract Jurassic insects.' 'Don't use all the water brushing your teeth or there'll be none left for the washing-up.' 'Turn the air conditioning off, or you'll run the battery down.'

I will never forget the feeling of relief we felt upon checking into the very lovely Vale Hotel at Niseko, with its mesmerising views of Mount Yotei, having finally dumped the wretched van back at the rental place. We were almost giddy with the luxury just of having some space in which to move. Proper beds! And a bath! Lissen and I looked at each other, and the penny dropped: I realise this is nothing to be proud of but it seems, in the final analysis, our family is only held together by room service and complimentary bath salts. If that's what it takes, we agreed, it would at least be no great hardship to never, ever make the mistake of renting a campervan again.

It says a great deal about the beauty of Hokkaido that our lust for the outdoors was not yet sated so, the next day in Niseko, we borrow some bikes and head out on a circumnavigation of Mount Yotei, the Fuji of the north. Aptly, today is Japan's newest national holiday, 'Mountain Day'. The view from the campervan had been panoramic, but nothing beats the silence of cycling for making you feel part of the landscape. A bike let's you creep up on the world. At one point a large snake crosses the road in the middle of us. We stop and watch it slither into the ridiculously lush undergrowth.

The late American-born film writer Donald Richie is perhaps the most celebrated expat chronicler of Japan. His 1971 travel memoir, *The Inland Sea*, is a kind of lament for the old Japan he feared was rapidly being lost to the tide of modernisation. At the beginning of his journey he writes:

> 'I know that ... right now, there are carpenters and stonecutters who take pride in their work, taxi drivers who polish their cars, salesmen who believe in the company ... And I know that such things have largely vanished elsewhere. And I wondered what depths of humanity the Japanese must contain that, even now, despite everything, they remain civil to each other, remain fond of each other.'

My family and I came to Japan because I wanted to show my children that pride in action, to present them with the evidence of that dedication and determination, but also of that civility and kindness which, like Richie, I too associate with the Japanese, and we found it all in abundance. He would, I hope, be pleasantly surprised that, for all the challenges this country faces – both self-inflicted, and acts of god – those 'depths of humanity' endure here in Japan.

While we were on Hokkaido, two major, epochal events were taking place back in Tokyo. In the first, ageing boy band SMAP, whom I had met on that first visit to Japan ten years earlier, announced they would be disbanding after twenty-five years in the spotlight. In the second, the Emperor gave his abdication speech, the first time an Emperor of Japan had done so since the Meji era.*

---

* Back in Tokyo I asked a Japanese friend which of these two stories had been the biggest. She paused: 'Definitely SMAP.'

In truth, it wasn't exactly an abdication. What he actually said was:

When the Emperor has ill health and his condition becomes serious, I am concerned that, as we have seen in the past, society comes to a standstill and people's lives are impacted in various ways ... placing a very heavy strain on those involved in the events, in particular, the family left behind. It occurs to me from time to time to wonder whether it is possible to prevent such a situation.

What the Emperor was doing was merely, ever so gently, *introducing* the notion that one day, he might *wonder* if, perhaps *possibly*, it could be *conceivable* for him to abdicate. It was the most Japanese thing ever.

There was something else that the Emperor touched upon in his speech which chimed more strongly with me than his tentative hints at retirement.

In my travels throughout the country ... I was made aware that wherever I went there were thousands of citizens who love their local community and with quiet dedication continue to support their community.

I am sure that I am guilty of fetishising Japan. I realise that I will always view this country from the rosy perspective of an outsider. Of course, I don't really know what it is like to actually live in Japan and I am aware of some of the darker aspects of Japanese culture: I am aware that there is crime and corruption, I know there is poverty and isolation, hardship, high levels of suicide and unemployment, growing economic inequality, and entrenched gender inequality, plus 'karoshi', the Japanese word for working yourself literally to death. And on this journey I also learned that the Japanese have been as careless as the rest of us with their natural resources: that they have poisoned their lakes, overfished their seas, saturated the land with pesticides and insecticides, and pumped their food full of additives. Furthermore, the forces of globalisation and 'progress', coupled with changing demographics, are endangering a precious one-thousand-year-old food culture. Many of the regional food traditions of Japan could be lost for ever within a generation due to lack of interest, impatience, changing tastes and ignorance.

All the same, whenever I think about Japan, that sense of community to which the Emperor referred, that 'quiet dedication', continues to impress me. The Japanese seem to have found, if not an antidote to the rampant individualism and the age of narcissism in which we now find ourselves, then at least they are striking a better balance between the individual and the collective, between the egotistical and the altruistic.

Ten years on from our first visit, I am only more impressed by the dedication of the food shokunin we met, even more heartened by the appreciation and understanding of the importance of quality food shown by the Japanese as a whole, and more confident than ever of the role Japan's traditional food plays at the heart of this unique, fascinating and rewarding culture.

Acknowledgements

While I have tried to adhere as much as possible to the chronological order in which the various encounters and experiences detailed in these pages occurred, I have sometimes shuffled or condensed time-lines, mostly to avoid unnecessary or dull exposition about who travelled where and when. The journey with my family from Okinawa to Hokkaido described in these pages took place over three visits to Japan during the course of winter, spring and summer 2016. Some of the other research for this book was gathered during solo visits in the previous year.

Now to the thanks:

Major 'this book would not have happened without' thanks go to Satoshi Gunji, Tetsuya Sugahara and Tamako Gunji of my Japanese publisher, Kadokawa. Tetsuya in particular, and Tamako most especially, gave me amazing support throughout the researching and editing of this book for which I am eternally grateful. Sorry we dragged you along to AKB48 that time, Tamako-san. That was a *really* weird show.

Thank you, too, to all the people we have met along the way, especially those who generously allowed me to interview them for this book.

Others not necessarily named to whom I am nevertheless grateful for their generosity, hospitality, time, wisdom and expertise are (in no particular order, not even alphabetical): Chieko Fujita, Kenjiro Suzuki, Takamune Yano, Takeshi Kadokami, Zaiyu Hasegawa and Noriko Yamaguchi, Melinda Joe, Hitoshi Hasegawa, Ryo Okada, Hiroko Suzuki, Tatsuya Onishi, Muneki Mizutani, Hiroshi Sakurai, Kenzo Oimatsu, Tad Shimotakehara, Toshihiro Ezoe, Atsushi

Sakaida, Nobuyuki Shiki, Hideki Ito, Juni Mamitsuka, Shintaro Sumiyoshi, Masatoshi Yasuda, Yoshihiro Narisawa, Remco Vrolijk, Yukiko Fujita and Minako Ando.

Often, there was a translator/interpreter present during my encounters with the people featured in this book. I rarely refer to their presence in the text, not to make myself seem brilliant and clever, but to streamline the narrative. So, again, thanks are overdue to: Maki Crabbe (Tokyo), Katsuko Kemanai (Hokkaido), Russell Goodall (Tokyo), Yoko Ikeda (Tokyo), Yoko Negita (Tokyo), Ruadhan Treacy and Sondey Olaseun (Matsue), Kazuyo Okudaira (Shikoku), Masumi Tsuha (Okinawa), Anthony Blair Guardia (Nagano).

I would also like to thank those of Japan's excellent regional tourist boards who gave us their support and guidance. First and foremost, Kylie Clarke and Hollie Mantle of the London office of the Japan National Tourist Organisation, but also Haruna Ishikawa (Okinawa); Chie Ariyoshi, Yukiko Tanaguchi, Tomoko Takae (Kyushu); Sayaka Yamane, Hideno Umebayasi, Yukio Yoshikawa (Matsue); and Mamoru Watanabe, Teddy Yamaishi (Nagano, Matsumoto).

Thanks also to Katsunobu Suzuki, my shochu go-between; to Yukiko Yagi and Keisuke Tsuchihashi at NHK; Akira Takayama, Rarecho and the team at FanWorks; and Eri Goto at the Asahi Shimbun.

Thank you to Dan Franklin, my publisher at Jonathan Cape, for his continued support over many years, and to my agents, Antony Topping at Greene & Heaton in London, George Lucas at Inkwell Management in New York and Miko Yamanouchi at the Uni Agency in Tokyo.

And, finally, thanks to Lissen, Emil and Asger. I will always be grateful for our time together in Japan. Sorry again about the campervan.

Gochiso sama deshita.

(What a feast it was.)

Index

penguin.co.uk/vintage